The Civil War and Reconstruction

Life in America

The Civil War and Reconstruction

Rodney P. Carlisle
GENERAL EDITOR

☑Checkmark Books®
An imprint of Infobase Publishing

Life in America: The Civil War and Reconstruction, 1860 to 1876
Copyright © 2010 Infobase Publishing

Checkmark Books
An Imprint of Infobase Publishing
132 West 31st Street
New York, NY 10001

Library of Congress Cataloging-in-Publication Data
Handbooks to life in America / Rodney P. Carlisle, general editor.
     v. cm.
   Includes bibliographical references and index.
   Contents: v. 1. The colonial and revolutionary era, beginnings to 1783—v. 2. The early national period and expansion, 1783 to 1859—v. 3. The Civil War and Reconstruction, 1860 to 1876—v. 4. The Gilded Age, 1870 to 1900—v. 5. Age of reform, 1890 to 1920—v. 6. The roaring twenties, 1920 to 1929—v. 7. The Great Depression and World War II, 1929 to 1949—v. 8. Postwar America, 1950 to 1969—v. 9. Contemporary America, 1970 to present.
   ISBN 978-0-8160-7785-4 (set : hc : alk. paper)—ISBN 978-0-8160-7174-6 (v. 1 : hc : alk. paper)—ISBN 978-0-8160-7175-3 (v. 2 : hc : alk. paper)—ISBN 978-0-8160-7176-0 (v. 3 : hc : alk. paper)—ISBN 978-0-8160-8245-2 (v. 3 : pbk : alk paper)—ISBN 978-0-8160-7177-7 (v. 4 : hc : alk. paper)—ISBN 978-0-8160-7178-4 (v. 5 : hc : alk. paper)—ISBN 978-0-8160-7179-1 (v. 6 : hc : alk. paper)—ISBN 978-0-8160-7180-7 (v. 7 : hc : alk. paper)—ISBN 978-0-8160-7181-4 (v. 8 : hc : alk. paper)—ISBN 978-0-8160-7182-1 (v. 9 : hc : alk. paper) 1. United States—Civilization—Juvenile literature. 2. United States—History—Juvenile literature. 3. National characteristics, American—Juvenile literature. I. Carlisle, Rodney P.
   E169.1.H2644 2008
   973—dc22
                              2008012630

Checkmark books are available at special discounts when purchased in bulk quantities for businesses, associations, institutions, or sales promotions.

Please call our Special Sales Department in New York at (212) 967-8800 or (800) 322-8755.

You can find Checkmark Books on the World Wide Web at
http://www.factsonfile.com

Printed in the United States of America

MP GB 10 9 8 7 6 5 4 3 2 1

This book is printed on acid-free paper.

Contents

The Civil War and Reconstruction

*"The world will little note nor
long remember what we say here."*
— Abraham Lincoln

THE FLAVOR OF daily life in previous eras is usually only vaguely conveyed by examining the documents of state and the politics of the era. What people ate, how they spent their time, what entertainment they enjoyed, and how they related to one another in family, church, and employment, constituted the actual life of people, rather than the distant affairs of state. While governance, diplomacy, war, and to an extent, the intellectual life of every era tends to be well-documented, the way people lived is sometimes difficult to tease out from the surviving paper records and literary productions of the past.

For this reason in recent decades, cultural and social historians have turned to other types of physical documentation, such as illustrations, surviving artifacts, tools, furnishings, utensils, and structures. Statistical information can shed light on other aspects of life. Through examination of these and other kinds of evidence, a wholly different set of questions can be asked and tentatively answered.

This series of handbooks looks at the questions of daily life from the perspective of social and cultural history, going well beyond the affairs of government to examine the fabric and texture of what people in the American past experienced in their homes and their families, in their workplaces and schools. Their places of worship, the ways they moved from place to place, the nature of law and order and military service all varied from period to period. As science and technology advanced, the American contributions to those fields became greater and contributed to a different feel of life.

Some of this story may be familiar, as historians have for generations commented on the disparity between rural and city life, on the impact of technologies such as the cotton gin, the railroad and the steamboat, and on life on the advancing frontier. However in recent decades, historians have turned to different sources.

In an approach called Nearby History, academic historians have increasingly worked with the hosts of professionals who operate local historical societies, with the keepers of historic homes, and with the custodians of local records to pull together a deeper understanding of local life. Housed in thousands of small and large museums and preserved homes across America, rich collections of furniture, utensils, farm implements, tools, and other artifacts tell a very different story than that found in the letters and journals of legislators, governors, presidents, and statesmen.

Another approach to the fabric of daily life first flourished in Europe, through which historians plowed through local customs and tax records, birth and death records, marriage records, and other numerical data, learning a great deal about the actual fabric of daily life through a statistical approach.

Aided by computer methods of storing and studying such data, historians have developed fresh discoveries about such basic questions as health, diet, life-expectancy, family patterns, and gender values in past eras. Combined with a fresh look at the relationship between men and women, and at the values of masculinity and femininity in past eras, recent social history has provided a whole new window on the past.

By dividing American history into nine periods, we have sought to provide views of this newly enriched understanding of the actual daily life of ordinary people. Some of the patterns developed in early eras persisted into later eras. And many physical traces of the past remain, in the form of buildings, seaports, roads and canals, artifacts, divisions of real estate, and later structures such as railroads, airports, dams, and superhighways.

LAYERS OF HISTORY

For these reasons, our own physical environment is made up of overlapping layers inherited from the past, sometimes deeply buried, and at other times, lightly papered over with the trappings of the present. Knowing more about the many layers from different periods of American history makes every trip through an American city or suburb or rural place a much richer experience, as the visitor sees not only the present, but the accumulated heritage of the past, silently providing echoes of history.

Thus in our modern era, as we move among the shadowy remnants of a distant past, we may be unconsciously receiving silent messages that tell us: this building is what a home should look like; this stone wall constitutes the definition of a piece of farmland; this street is where a town begins and ends. The sources of our present lie not only in the actions of politicians, generals, princes, and potentates, but in the patterns of life, child-rearing, education, religion, work and play, lived out by ordinary people.

VOLUME III: CIVIL WAR AND RECONSTRUCTION

The years from 1861 to 1877 were dominated by the crisis brought on by the secession of 11 southern states and the formation of the Confederate States of America, or the Confederacy. The bitter Civil War began with the firing on Fort Sumter on April 12, 1861, as the Confederacy sought to prevent the resupply of federal troops who held out on that fortress island in the harbor of Charleston, South Carolina. Almost exactly four years later, in April 1865, the armies of the Confederacy were shattered, much of the south had been devastated, and slavery as an institution in the United States had been destroyed forever.

Between the end of the Civil War and 1877, the northern-dominated Congress of the United States sought to ensure that the former Confederate states obeyed the spirit as well as the letter of the Thirteenth, Fourteenth, and Fifteenth Amendments to the Constitution that ended slavery and guaranteed the rights of citizens to the former slaves. By refusing to admit senators and representatives from southern states to Congress until they at least formally accepted the new constitutional amendments, and by requiring the stationing of troops in the south, radical Republicans hoped to achieve a social revolution that would recognize the former slaves' rights. However throughout the south, former Confederates and their supporters succeeded in establishing state governments that, while accepting the abolition of slavery, effectively denied the vote to former slaves. Furthermore without land reform that would distribute land to the freed slaves, little social progress could be achieved. Systems of labor resembling slavery, in the form of debt peonage, tenant farming, and sharecropping kept the majority of African Americans in the south in near-poverty.

While this political contest was played out, the United States at the same time underwent vast economic changes. Spurred on by the war, agriculture in the north had modernized with the widespread use of mechanical reapers and other equipment. Railroads expanded, tying together formerly isolated regions, allowing the transportation of products from one area to another. The completion of the transcontinental railroad, much heralded in 1869, was only one aspect of the vast railroad expansion of the era.

As new regions were reached by the rails, they were able to send their products to distant markets. Within a few years, the potential of this continental economy began to be realized, as great fortunes were made in meat packing, iron and steel manufacture, sugar refining, flour-milling, coffee-distribution, and petroleum refining. Although not used as an engine fuel until late in the 19th century, petroleum products were used for lighting, having replaced whale oil.

With the specialization of various regions in the production of wheat, corn, cattle, and other basic commodities, a national price and market system began to emerge that drove prices gradually downward, in a long-term decline that did not turn around until nearly 1900. As a consequence through the late 1860s into the 1890s, farmers found themselves squeezed between fixed prices on loans and mortgages and declining revenues from crops. As conditions worsened, farmers increasingly blamed those on the other side of the market from them: the bankers who held the mortgages, the railroads that charged as much as the market would bear for transporting goods, and the middle-men in the meat-packing and milling industries who processed their products for sale.

The disparity between wealth and poverty that had increased in the decades before the Civil War now accelerated. With the emergence of great fortunes in industry, railroads, shipping, and banking, and with the increasing numbers of urban workers who owned no property at all, the social fabric of the nation was clearly changing. Although reformers still hoped to address the problems of widespread poverty through education, public campaigns to clean up unsanitary conditions in the urban tenements, and the establishment of improved hospitals, a growing undercurrent of agricultural and labor discontent suggested that such approaches did not get to the root of the matter.

Labor unions and farm organizations that began in the late 1860s and early 1870s were the forerunners of later movements that would reshape American politics in the era of protest and radical movements of the 1870s through the 1890s. Some began to turn to government for reforms that would regulate railroad rates, while others supported inflationary schemes that would devalue the dollar and thus make it easier to pay fixed-dollar amounts on mortgages. Hints of these programs in the 1870s would suggest the nature of the ideological conflicts that would surface over the next decades.

FABRIC OF LIFE FOR AMERICANS

Thus the Civil War and Reconstruction decades saw several deep transformations in the daily fabric of life for Americans. Most familiar is the story of the war itself and the great changes that it wrought in the south, with the ending of slavery and the destruction of much of the wealth of the planter class. However, behind that development, the burgeoning industrial economy, led by the railroads, the iron and steel industry, and by the new national companies and combines that processed commodities into marketable products began a transformation that was just as profound for those in the north and west.

For a generation raised before the Civil War, it seemed that the new class disparity between worker and capitalist, most strongly evident in the large cities of the east, had fundamentally changed America. Searching for someone to blame for the difficulties they saw around them, some blamed the poor themselves, often focusing on immigrants. Others blamed the businessmen who had understood the transformations and had organized industries to take advantage of them.

Even as the gulf between the very rich and the very poor widened, a growing middle class of Americans looked askance at many of the developments. Salaried professionals, like members of the clergy, teachers, academics, journalists, government employees, and mid-level managers in expanding businesses saw the increasing power of the great wielders of capital as dangerous. They also felt threatened by the growing numbers of urban poor, by the rise of crimes against property, and by the graft of corrupt politicians. Many were attracted to civil service reform that would reduce the influence of political machines. Through replacing patronage with civil service testing, the clean government movements would allow those with appropriate educational qualifications to take positions in the expanding bureaucracies of local, state, and federal government. Yet the hold of political machines based on graft, corruption, bribery, and patronage was extremely difficult to loosen.

Technological improvements made life of the middle class more comfortable. Improvements in plumbing, house construction, and some household appliances allowed many in the middle and upper middle class to acquire somewhat more elegant housing, and several new popular architectural styles spread rapidly. Among those were the Second Empire style imported from France, with its Mansard roofs, and increasing amounts of "gingerbread" or jigsaw-cut trim decorating the Victorian houses of the era. Mills often turned out pre-cut wooden lace-work and spindle shapes that were shipped by rail to be incorporated in homes through the growing cities and towns.

Advances in science, technology, and understanding of the root causes of some diseases led to reforms. The expanding cities faced numerous crises, not the least of which was the vast accumulation of manure and the floods of urine from horse-drawn transport. Good government advocates pushed for better urban sanitation, with the construction of sewers, public water systems, and street-cleaning authorities. Spectacular fires, like the Great Chicago fire of 1871 led to improvements in fire departments and their equipment. By the 1870s there was some hope that the cities of the future could be cleaner and more healthy. Horse-drawn rail cars, cable cars, and steam-powered elevated trains showed that, when electric power and other power sources could be applied to urban transport, there would be a ready reception for those technologies.

The next decades would see proposed reforms converted into political action, beginning to give shape to the political movements that would flourish in the early 20th century.

RODNEY CARLISLE
GENERAL EDITOR

Chapter 1

Introduction

*"Our present political position has been
achieved in a manner unprecedented
in the history of nations."*
— Jefferson Davis

FROM 1860 TO 1876 the United States was in turmoil. A bloody civil war tore the country apart from 1861 to 1865, and in the war's aftermath the United States struggled to put itself back together as it dealt with a host of complicated social problems created by the demise of slavery in the south. By 1876 the nation was politically reconstructed, but the social system that condemned African Americans to a subordinate position in the region was quickly re-established with segregation replacing slavery. Meanwhile in the north, the war accelerated the process of industrialization and set the stage for the United States to emerge as a true industrial power on the world stage.

The political, economic, and social factors that led to the Civil War were complex, but in the end they were all tied to the fact that in 19th-century America one section of the country maintained the institution of slavery while the other did not. From the founding of the United States under the Constitution slavery was a major part of American life, and the great contradiction of the entire American existence. Thomas Jefferson, the founding father who authored the Declaration of Independence and also owned slaves, embodied this national turmoil. Speaking for enlightened southerners of his day, Jefferson famously declared that slavery was like a man holding a wolf by the ears. The man might not like it, but he did not dare let it go. As the abolitionist movement in the north began to emerge in the 1830s southern politicians and many white

1

southerners in general began defending slavery with greater vigor, and a succession of national events widened the gulf between America's slaveholding and non-slaveholding states. In 1848 the United States acquired a vast amount of western territory as the result of the Mexican War, and the question of whether or not slavery would be allowed there began to dominate political discourse at the national level. Two years later the slaveholding and non-slaveholding states reached a temporary compromise on the issue, but during the 1850s the national debate over slavery escalated. Radical politicians in the south fanned the flames of secession through the decade with blustering, emotional speeches designed to instill fear in their constituents. The "southern way of life" was under siege, they claimed, and white southerners as a whole should be ready to fight if necessary to maintain their station in society. The rhetoric grew stronger with the publication of *Uncle Tom's Cabin* in 1852, and in 1854 when pro-slavery and anti-slavery partisans went to war in what became known as Bleeding Kansas.

JOHN BROWN'S RAID ON HARPERS FERRY

As if to confirm everything that states' rights politicians had said during the 1850s, the fanatical abolitionist John Brown launched his famous raid on Harpers Ferry, Virginia, in 1859. Though unsuccessful, Brown's attempt to capture a federal arsenal and provoke a slave rebellion struck fear in the hearts of whites throughout the south.

Many in the north condemned the violence, but many others lauded Brown's efforts as the notion of a vast abolitionist conspiracy became believable in the minds of many southerners. For months after the raid radical southern politicians and the newspapers that supported them exploited the fears of the electorate by printing account after account of rumored slave atrocities that were supposedly taking place around the south. Whether threats to their safety were real or imagined, southern whites, especially those involved in state government, took them seriously. In 1860 the south fortified itself for whatever trials might lay in the future. State legislatures appropriated funds for arming and reorganization state militias, and throughout the region many communities began recruiting new volunteer Home Guard units.

Meanwhile in Washington, D.C., the nation was unraveling in part because the national Democratic Party was fracturing. During the spring of 1860 the slavery issue irreparably divided the Democrats, thus ensuring a Republican victory in the presidential election the following fall. The Democratic National Convention met in Charleston, South Carolina, in April and there northern Democrats passed resolutions endorsing the concept of popular sovereignty, with the people of a given territory or state deciding the issue, as a solution to the slavery debate. Democratic delegates from the south condemned popular sovereignty and any other form of compromise on the slavery issue, insisting on blanket federal protection of the institution in all states and territories.

Crittenden Compromise

Lincoln's election in 1860 was viewed by many white southerners as a sign that the federal government was about to take steps to end slavery, whether the south agreed with the proposition or not. The Republican Party was dedicated to stopping the spread of slavery into the territories, and many believed that it was only a matter of time until Lincoln and his supporters would threaten the institution where it already existed.

As secession and civil war loomed on the horizon in late 1860, U.S. Senator John J. Crittenden of Kentucky promoted a political compromise that he hoped would keep the nation whole. Called the "Crittenden Compromise," the proposal primarily dealt with concerns among the southern states that Republican Abraham Lincoln's election as president posed a serious threat to the institution of slavery. Crittenden introduced legislation calling for six new amendments to the U.S. Constitution, and several congressional resolutions designed to protect slavery in states where it already existed and in the territories.

Abraham Lincoln's election as president was interpreted as a serious threat to slavery.

Crittenden's plan included permanently reinstituting the so-called Missouri Compromise line and extending the protection of slavery south of that line all the way to the Pacific Coast; protecting slavery in the District of Columbia; strengthening fugitive slave laws; accepting popular sovereignty as the method through which questions related to slavery in the territories could be resolved; and in general restricting the power of the federal government to tamper with the institution of slavery. Crittenden introduced his proposal as a joint resolution on December 18, 1860. The south supported the plan, as did representatives from the border states, but it was met with disapproval by Lincoln and northern Republicans who were dedicated to stopping the expansion of slavery. After much debate the compromise was defeated in both the Senate and the House of Representatives.

Crittenden also introduced legislation calling for a national referendum on his proposal, but the Senate took no action on the bill. The Crittenden Compromise represented the final effort to reconcile the slaveholding and non-slaveholding states. A few months after it was voted down, the Civil War began with the firing on Fort Sumter on April 12, 1861.

The convention as a whole eventually voted to endorse popular sovereignty. In response the states of the lower south walked out on the proceedings. Eventually the two wings of the Democratic Party met separately to nominate candidates for president. Northern Democrats nominated Stephen Douglas of Illinois while the southern states' rights advocates chose the vice-president of the United States, Kentuckian John C. Breckinridge, as their candi-

Emancipation Proclamation

When the Civil War began, political leaders of the ruling Republican Party differed with regard to a precise policy concerning slavery. Radical elements within the party pushed for an immediate statement from the federal government abolishing the institution. Others, including Lincoln, initially preferred a more moderate course, but as the war progressed momentum for emancipation grew stronger. Not wanting to announce a major policy shift on slavery until federal armies had achieved a significant victory in the field, Lincoln delayed any announcement on the subject.

Finally in September 1862, after Union forces stopped Robert E. Lee's invasion of Maryland at Antietam, the president announced his intention to free the slaves using his war powers. Lincoln officially signed the Emancipation Proclamation on January 1, 1863. The order freed the slaves in the Confederate states but did not apply to the border states of Kentucky, Missouri, Maryland, and Delaware.

While in practical application the proclamation did not free any bondmen in areas under Confederate control, it had a great effect on the war effort.

It transformed the war into a moral struggle to end slavery in addition to preserving the Union, and made it less likely that England would ally itself with a Confederacy fighting to preserve the institution. The proclamation also clarified the status of those slaves who by the thousands flocked to the Union armies as they made their way through the south.

President Lincoln officially signed the Emancipation Proclamation on January 1, 1863.

date. Along with Republican nominee Abraham Lincoln, a fourth candidate rounded out the field in the general election. John Bell of Tennessee represented the Constitutional Union Party, an upstart organization that hoped to become an effective agent for compromise. Bell and his followers argued that southerners should fight for their rights within the Union, and did their best to side-step any inflammatory political discussions of slavery. This moderate strategy would garner significant support in some parts of the south, but the Constitutional Union Party was not destined to carry the day in a region still haunted by the ghost of John Brown. Lincoln emerged victorious, though he only garnered around 40 percent of the popular vote.

SECESSION AND THE WAR'S EARLY STAGES

After Lincoln's election southern states began calling secession conventions and, one by one, began leaving the Union. South Carolina was the first state to vote for secession (December 20, 1860) followed by Mississippi, Florida, Alabama, Georgia, Louisiana, and Texas. These states sent representatives to a meeting held in Montgomery, Alabama, where they formed the Confederate States of America. Meanwhile Lincoln called for 75,000 volunteers and began taking steps to protect federal installations in the south. In April 1861 the first shots of the Civil War were fired at Fort Sumter, South Carolina, prompting four other

slaveholding states, Virginia, Arkansas, Tennessee, and North Carolina to leave the Union and join the Confederacy. The Confederate capital was moved to Richmond, and Jefferson Davis, former secretary of war under Franklin Pierce and a U. S. Senator from Mississippi, became president of the Confederate government.

Once the war began in earnest both sides struggled to organize themselves militarily. The Federals enjoyed far more material resources

A gun mounted in the interior of Fort Sumter's thick masonry walls, where the Civil War began April 12, 1861.

for a military undertaking, but the Confederates held a strategic advantage in that rather than having to conquer the north, they could initially fight a defensive war. At the outset neither side was prepared for a prolonged struggle. In 1861 the U.S. Army numbered less than 20,000 men, many of whom were stationed in the west, while the Confederates had to create an army from scratch. At first both sides recruited volunteers, but as the war progressed it became apparent that reliable forces could only be maintained through conscription. Much to the chagrin of states' rights advocates in the south, the Confederate congress passed national conscription legislation in 1862 and the Federals followed suit not long afterwards, despite a significant amount of resistance.

The federal war strategy involved blockading southern ports, gaining control of the Mississippi River in the west, and capturing the Confederate capitol at Richmond, though this proved to be an easier strategy to devise than implement. While the blockade hurt the Confederacy, it was never completely effective, and it would take some time and struggle to clear the Mississippi and take the Confederate capital. Abraham Lincoln would appoint and dismiss a series of commanders before finally settling on Ulysses S. Grant as the man who could most effectively lead the federal effort. Meanwhile Confederate goals were a bit simpler.

The south did not have to invade and occupy the north in order to achieve independence. The Confederacy only had to wage war until public opinion in the north soured on the conflict. The southerners sought to protect strategically important points such as Richmond, the ports along the Mississippi River, and a number of major railroad centers, but otherwise felt they merely had to hang on and wait for the northerners to tire of fighting. Because it was home to the Confederate capital, Virginia was a focal point from the war's outset.

AN EPIC, BLOODY STRUGGLE

At the beginning of the war, Lincoln appointed General George McClellan commander of the Army of the Potomac and army chief of staff, but replaced him a year later for moving too slowly. Meanwhile Robert E. Lee was given command of Confederate forces in the region. A courtly aristocrat who graduated first in his class at West Point, Lee proved himself an excellent defensive tactician and eventually won his greatest victory at Fredericksburg, December 11–15, 1862.

Regardless of the strategies, tactics, or commanders, both sides soon found themselves in an epic, bloody struggle unlike anything that had been predicted. On April 6 and 7, 1862, over 24,000 Americans fell during the Battle of Shiloh in the western theater, more than had fallen in all previous American wars combined. Six months later around 5,000 men died and another 15,000 were wounded at the Battle of Antietam in what would be the bloodiest single day of the war. For the remainder of the war casualty counts remained high.

The war had a great effect on the national economy, and in many ways shaped the economic future of the country well into the 20th century. In the north, industrialization had already begun by the time the Confederates fired on Fort Sumter, but the conflict accelerated the process. Once southern Democrats resigned to join their states in the Confederacy, the Republican Party had firm control of the government and Republican lawmakers began promoting a decidedly pro-business agenda that favored northern manufacturers. At the same time many parts of the industrial economy began to expand due to increased wartime output. Coal production soared, as did railroad construction. In the agricultural sector, the loss of farm workers to the military led to greater mechanization. The war had the opposite effect on the economy of the south.

Tied to a single-crop cotton economy, the south was vulnerable to the northern blockade that cut off cotton exports to Europe and to northern markets. The Union navy also kept much-needed imported items away from southern ports. Particularly after the war's first year, those on the Confederate home front began to suffer as a result of massive inflation and shortages of food and other basic necessities. The Confederate armies in the field were also perpetually undersupplied. Most of the war's major battles and campaigns took place in the south, scarring the landscape and leading to a great deal of destruction in many cities and towns.

THE WAR'S LATER STAGES

July 1863 marked a major turning point in the Civil War, and the beginning of the end of the Confederacy. In the eastern theater Robert E. Lee, desperate to move the fighting out of war-torn Virginia and determined to take the offensive, launched another invasion of the north. Moving through Pennsylvania, Lee's Confederates eventually met a large Union army under the command of George Meade at a sleepy little crossroads town called Gettysburg. Advance units from both armies clashed on July 1, 1863, launching a three-day battle during which the Confederates suffered almost 28,000 casualties to around 23,000 for the Federals.

One of the pivotal points in the battle took place on July 3 when Lee ordered a division under the command of General George Pickett to charge the center of the Union lines, a position that proved impenetrable. The Confederate assault failed miserably, decimating the division and creating the legend of Pickett's Charge, a story that would be told, retold, and embellished in the south for generations. The next day found Lee's Confederates retreating back into Virginia, where they would never take the offensive again. Meanwhile in the western theater, Ulysses S. Grant was creating a reputation for himself that would eventually lead him to the White House. By mid-1863 one of the primary Union war goals was the capture of Vicksburg, Mississippi, the last major city on the Mississippi River still in Confederate hands.

In May Grant launched his campaign for the city against Confederate forces under the command of General John C. Pemberton. As the campaign progressed the Federals successfully fought several battles and captured Jackson, the state capital. Grant finally moved on Vicksburg but, because the city rested atop a large bluff, he found that its fortification could not be breached by direct assaults. Instead he decided to "outcamp" the Confederate army inside Vicksburg, settling in for a siege that lasted several weeks. On July 4 as Lee's army limped away from the Gettysburg battlefield, Pemberton surrendered the city.

Coupled with the defeat at Gettysburg, the fall of Vicksburg marked the beginning of the end of the Confederacy.

After Gettysburg and Vicksburg the fighting went on for more than a year. General William Tecumseh Sherman captured Atlanta in late 1864 and followed his success with his famous "march to the sea" through Georgia. Not long afterward the formidable Confederate Army of Tennessee was devastated at the battles of Franklin and Nashville.

Finally in early April 1865 the Confederate capital at Richmond fell, and days later Lee surrendered to Grant at Appomattox Courthouse, Virginia, on April 9, ending the conflict. Though he had led the United States during the war, Abraham Lincoln would not live to orchestrate the peace process. On the evening of April 14, 1865 actor John Wilkes Booth assassinated Lincoln at Ford's Theater in Washington, D.C.

RECONSTRUCTION

When the war ended Republican leaders differed in their opinions on what course of action the government should take to put the United States back together. Moderates leaned toward allowing the southern states back into the Union on relatively lenient terms, while radicals promoted a harsher policy. Lincoln favored a moderate course and before the war ended began implementing his own plan for Reconstruction in those states already under federal occupation.

He was concerned with restoring the Union as quickly as possible, and also hoped that by imposing a lenient peace on the south, he might be able to establish a southern wing of the Republican Party by appealing to former Whigs in the region. Lincoln's plan gave the vast majority of former Confederates a general amnesty if they would pledge a simple loyalty oath. Once 10 percent of the registered voters in a state had taken the oath, that state could begin organizing its state government and drawing up a new state constitution. While the general amnesty did not apply to some high-ranking officials, Lincoln was open to generous terms in granting pardons.

State governments created by this "10 percent plan" had to recognize federal authority, accept the end of slavery, and provide for the education of the African-American popu-

Robert E. Lee, in command of the Confederate forces, eventually won his greatest victory at the Battle of Fredericksburg.

A print of Appomattox Court House in Virginia where the Civil War came to an end. After the war, Republican leaders differed on what the government should do to reunite the United States.

lation. Lincoln did not insist on full suffrage for the former slaves, and was willing to recognize states that forbade African Americans from voting.

Radical Republicans, led by Charles Sumner of Massachusetts in the Senate, and Thaddeus Stevens of Pennsylvania in the House of Representatives, protested against Lincoln's lenient terms and argued that it was the duty of Congress to oversee the Reconstruction process. The Radicals introduced the Wade-Davis Bill in Congress, which would have temporarily placed the southern states under military rule and disqualified former Confederates from setting up the new state governments. Lincoln refused to sign the bill once it passed Congress, but before his assassination he was apparently willing to compromise with the radicals on some issues.

TURNING BACK THE CLOCK

After Lincoln's death the complexion of Reconstruction changed dramatically. Andrew Johnson ascended to the presidency firm in the belief that he should take charge of the process. Johnson's plan was similar to Lincoln's in that it offered the south lenient terms, and southern states quickly went to work putting together governments. The new president required the former Confederate states to officially revoke their secession ordinances, and ratify the Thirteenth Amendment ending slavery. Johnson's plan offered no political rights to the former slaves, and the southern states quickly began organizing state governments designed to turn back the clock.

The Gettysburg Address

U.S. President Abraham Lincoln delivered the Gettysburg Address at the dedication of the Soldiers' National Cemetery in Gettysburg, Pennsylvania, on Thursday, November 19, 1863, four and a half months after the Union armies defeated those of the Confederacy at the Battle of Gettysburg. Lincoln invoked the principles of human equality espoused by the Declaration of Independence and redefined the Civil War as a struggle for equality and a unified nation.

Four score and seven years ago our fathers brought forth on this continent, a new nation, conceived in Liberty, and dedicated to the proposition that all men are created equal.

Now we are engaged in a great civil war, testing whether that nation, or any nation so conceived and so dedicated, can long endure. We are met on a great battle-field of that war. We have come to dedicate a portion of that field, as a final resting place for those who here gave their lives that that nation might live. It is altogether fitting and proper that we should do this.

But, in a larger sense, we can not dedicate—we can not consecrate—we can not hallow—this ground. The brave men, living and dead, who struggled here, have consecrated it, far above our poor power to add or detract. The world will little note, nor long remember what we say here, but it can never forget what they did here. It is for us the living, rather, to be dedicated here to the unfinished work which they who fought here have thus far so nobly advanced. It is rather for us to be here dedicated to the great task remaining before us —that from these honored dead we take increased devotion to that cause for which they gave the last full measure of devotion—that we here highly resolve that these dead shall not have died in vain—that this nation, under God, shall have a new birth of freedom—and that government of the people, by the people, for the people, shall not perish from the earth.

White southerners elected provisional legislatures that included many former Confederates, and those bodies began passing laws restricting the activities of the freedmen. These "black codes" mirrored many of slave codes of the antebellum period. Former slaves were not allowed to serve on juries, testify in court against whites, or hold certain jobs. In some states freedmen were restricted to agricultural labor and forbidden to own land. The goal of the system was to keep the African-American population subordinate and recreate, more or less, the conditions of slavery without violating the Thirteenth Amendment.

Johnson's plan for Reconstruction was doomed once Congress reconvened. With little political capital and lacking the personality and popularity of Lincoln, the new president found himself with few friends in Washington. Upon their return, radical elements of the Republican Party quickly took control of the Reconstruction process, ignoring Johnson's wishes, and even trying unsuccessfully to have the president removed from office.

Congressional Reconstruction divided the states of the Confederacy into five military districts, each governed temporarily by a federal army officer. Former Confederates, most of whom favored the Democratic Party, were not allowed to participate in the setting up of new state governments and were

The Mississippi Plan

Named for the state in which it was created, the Mississippi Plan was a systematic campaign of violence, intimidation, and voter fraud that successfully reestablished the dominance of the Democratic Party and white supremacy in the south at the end of Reconstruction. As a result of the Civil War, African-American slaves in the south attained their freedom, and policies put in place during congressional Reconstruction gave adult African-American males the right to vote.

As a result the African-American vote coupled with a minority of the white vote in the states of the former Confederacy, led to the election of Republican governments in the south that included a number of African-American officeholders. Desperate to stem the tide of Republican ascendance, Mississippi's Democratic leaders organized White Men's Clubs and promoted racial violence as a means to drive Republican office holders out of the state and once again subordinate the state's African-American population. As the federal government lost interest in the Reconstruction process during the 1870s, the Mississippi Plan went into effect.

In 1874 and 1875 violence was widespread in the state, as armed bands of men roamed the countryside intimidating African-American and white Republicans. During elections some polling places became battlegrounds, and race riots broke out in a number of cities and towns. When the dust settled it was apparent that despite the chaos, the Mississippi Plan worked for the Democrats. Large segments of the Republican vote were neutralized, and in counties where Republicans had managed to cast significant numbers of votes, election returns were simply falsified. The Democratic Party regained control of the state and would maintain control for a century. Preoccupied with other issues and generally losing interest in the cause of civil rights for the former slaves, the federal government took little action to stop the violence. The Mississippi Plan became the blueprint used by Democrats in other southern states to gain control of their governments. By 1877 Reconstruction in the south was over.

The south was solidly Democratic, and a process had begun through which African Americans in the region would be stripped of their civil and political rights and segregated for almost a century into a "separate but equal" world of their own. It was a world that was clearly separate, but notably not equal.

not immediately given back their right to vote. As a result Republican governments formed in the southern states and the electorate initially included northerners who had recently moved into the south, native southern whites who had not participated in the rebellion, and the freedmen, who represented the largest voting block. Under this system most office holders in the southern states were white, but for the first time a significant number of African Americans also held office. Hiram Revels became the first African American to serve in the U.S. Senate, representing the state of Mississippi and ironically taking the seat last held before the war by Jefferson Davis.

The Republicans also pressed successfully for the ratification of the Fourteenth Amendment to the U.S. Constitution, which defined citizenship; and the Fifteenth Amendment, which protected voting rights. Despite these advances, Revels and other African-American officeholders would serve only a short time. By the early 1870s most former Confederates had regained their right to vote, and the white south began to stringently resist the Republican governments and any political system that promised equality for the newly freed slaves.

During Ulysses S. Grant's two scandal-plagued terms as president (1869–77), the Reconstruction process began to break down. As former Confederates began casting their votes for Democratic candidates in state and local elections, some joined violent organizations determined to keep Republicans, and especially the freedmen, away from the polls. The most prominent terror organization of the period was the Ku Klux Klan, which began in Tennessee in 1866. The Klan killed hundreds and injured hundreds more, drawing national attention and a congressional investigation. After passage of the Ku Klux Klan Acts in 1870 and 1871, the federal government sent federal enforcement officials and troops into the south to silence the Klan and protect the civil rights of the freedmen. This represented the high water mark for Republican Reconstruction in the region. Despite such efforts northern interest in the process began to wane, particularly after the Panic of 1873 took the public's focus off Reconstruction and placed it on the country's financial woes. Coupled with massive resistance from whites in the south, northern apathy ultimately doomed the Reconstruction process.

PRESIDENTIAL ELECTION OF 1876 AND COMPROMISE OF 1877

In the presidential election of 1876 the Republicans chose Rutherford B. Hayes as their candidate. Hayes was a Union war veteran who had served in the U.S. House of Representatives and as governor of Ohio. The Democrats chose Samuel Tilden, the New York governor who had gained notoriety by successfully fighting corruption in his state. Though neither candidate was remarkable, the contest proved to be one of the more unusual elections in the history of presidential politics. After a rough and tumble campaign, Tilden won the popular vote by a margin of around 300,000, and initially garnered 184 electoral votes to 165 for Hayes. However due to disputed election results from Louisiana, South Carolina, Florida, and Oregon, 20 additional electoral votes remained unpledged so that neither candidate gained a true majority.

There was no constitutional process to solve such a dilemma, but most observers agreed that Congress should be responsible for sorting things out. In response Congress created a special electoral commission to rule on which candidate should receive the disputed votes. The commission was comprised of five Supreme Court justices, five U.S. Senators, and five members of the U.S. House of Representatives. Of the 15, seven were Republicans, seven were Democrats and one was supposedly an independent, though he was sympathetic to the Republican cause. In the end the commission voted 8–7 along party lines to give the 20 disputed votes, and the presidency, to Hayes by the thin margin of 185–184.

What the general public did not know about the process was that before the commission voted, northern Republican and Democratic leaders from the south had struck a deal. Southern Democrats agreed not to dispute the commission's decision in exchange for a number of concessions from Hayes. Once they controlled the White House, the Republicans would order any remaining federal troops out of the south, appoint a southerner to Hayes' cabinet, give southern Democrats control of federal patronage in their states, and see that funding was made available for railroads and other internal improvement in the south. The bargain was known as the Compromise of 1877, and it marked the official end of the Reconstruction period.

Ben Wynne

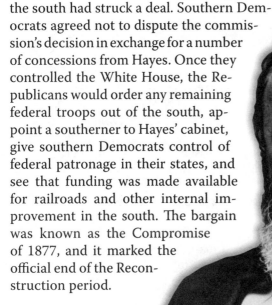

Rutherford B. Hayes was a Union war veteran who served in the U.S. House of Representatives and as governor of Ohio.

Further Readings

Ash, Stephem V. *When the Yankees Came; Conflict and Chaos in the Occupied South*. Chapel Hill: The University of North Carolina Press, 1999.

Barney, William L. *Battleground for the Union: The Era of the Civil War and Reconstruction, 1848–1877*. Englewood Cliffs, NJ: Prentice Hall, 1990.

Carter, Dan. *When the War was Over: The Failure of Self-Reconstruction in the South, 1865–1867*. Baton Rouge: Louisiana State University Press, 1985.

Davis, William C. *The Imperiled Union*. New York: Doubleday and Co., 1983.

Foner, Eric. *Reconstruction: America's Unfinished Revolution, 1863–1877*. New York: Harper & Row, 1988.

Franklin, John Hope. *Reconstruction after the Civil War*. Chicago, IL: University of Chicago Press, 1961.

Glatthaar, Joseph T. *Forged in Battle: The Civil War Alliance of Black Soldiers and White Officers*. Baton Rouge: Louisiana State University Press, 2000.

Goodwin, Doris Kearns. *Team of Rivals: The Political Genius of Abraham Lincoln*. New York: Simon & Schuster, 2005.

Heidler, David Stephen, ed. *Encyclopedia of the American Civil War: A Political, Social, and Military History*. New York: W.W. Norton and Co., 2002.

Paludan, Philip Shaw. *The Presidency of Abraham Lincoln*. Lawrence, KS: University Press of Kansas, 1994.

Simpson, Brooks D. *Let Us Have Peace: Ulysses S. Grant and the Politics of War and Reconstruction, 1861–1868*. Chapel Hill: The University of North Carolina Press, 1997.

Summers, Mark W. Railroads, *Reconstruction and the Gospel of Prosperity: Aid Under the Radical Republicans, 1865–1877*. Stoughton, WI: Books on Demand, 1984.

Trelease, Allen. *White Terror: The Ku Klux Klan Conspiracy and Southern Reconstruction*. Baton Rouge: Louisiana State University Press, 1995.

Ward, Geoffrey C., Ken Burns, and Ric Burns. *The Civil War: An Illustrated History*. New York: Alfred Knopf, 1990.

Chapter 2

Family and Daily Life

"Home is a place not only of strong affections,
but of entire unreserve; it is life's undress rehearsal,
its backroom, its dressing room..."
— Harriet Beecher Stowe

THE SOCIAL, POLITICAL, and economic changes within the United States during the Civil War and Reconstruction eras increased the diversity of American family and daily life. The social turmoil of the Civil War and Reconstruction disrupted family life and daily routine, especially in southern states that saw more of the destruction and social upheaval of war and its aftermath. The nation's physical expansion, with its concomitant westward migration, meant that more mid-19th century families had to adapt to frontier living and establish new lifestyles and routines. The nation's economic growth, technological innovation, and rising industrialization and urbanization altered traditional patterns of everyday family life. Home life became an increasingly private affair and the family, rather than the community, increasingly served as the foundation of mid-19th century American society. A person's family largely determined their role within the community and their day-to-day activities.

FAMILY STRUCTURE AND GENDER ROLES

Most mid-19th century Americans lived within a family unit. Marriage rates remained high by the mid-19th century, and most Americans lived as part of a family. Those that did remain single often lived with relatives or boarded with another family, rather than live alone. Birthrates had been declining during the antebellum period, so the average American family of the mid-19th century

15

Life for farm families was shaped by the area in which they lived. In the mid-Atlantic states, homes often had fireplaces at each end of the house, as in this Maryland farmhouse of the 1860s.

was smaller than the families of previous eras. It consisted of a father and a mother, and on average three children. City families tended to be smaller than rural families, where the need for farm labor often resulted in larger families. Extended families containing elderly grandparents, maiden aunts, or orphaned relatives were still quite common. Many families also housed a boarder, servant, or hired hand. Family life and daily routines would vary depending on social status, location, and occupation.

Marriage remained the primary goal behind the courtships of adolescents and young adults. Young women protected their virginity, as questions about their virtue would lead to an undesirable reputation as a loose woman of low moral character. Chaperoning was not yet a common feature of the dating routine. Premarital sex was still socially unacceptable, and the rate of premarital pregnancies remained low. Young men were expected to have sexual urges and occasionally give in to them by visiting prostitutes or women of ill repute, but many Americans believed that women had few sexual urges. Debates arose as to whether married women should enjoy sex, or if its sole purpose for the wife consisted of procreation.

When couples decided to marry, engagements were increasingly announced in newspapers, and engagement rings were becoming more common. Marriage ceremonies were also becoming increasingly elaborate. Divorce was still relatively uncommon, although it was becoming legally easier to acquire after the Civil War and the numbers of divorced couples were growing. Most women divorced their husbands for neglect, cruelty, desertion, or drunkenness, while most men divorced their wives for desertion, adultery, cruelty, or their inability to serve as obedient housewives.

After marriage most couples began planning for the arrival of children. Pregnant women continued their household chores throughout their pregnancies and were expected to stay out of the public view as much as possible. During the mid-19th century, the idea of separate spheres governed gender roles within the American family even as debates arose over the proper roles and vocations of women. Work life and home life were becoming increasingly separated as industrialization and urbanization increased in the newly developing market economy.

New working conditions meant that many men were absent from the home during the course of the workday. The social view of men as the breadwinners and women as guardians of the hearth, wives, mothers, and housekeepers had risen to prominence. This cultural belief in separate spheres was especially prevalent among the newly emerging middle class in the more industrialized and urbanized New England region, where a cult of domesticity had taken root. The public sphere of work, society, and politics was a rough, competitive arena in which men aggressively sought to do whatever it took to get ahead and support their family. The private, or domestic sphere became a sanctuary in which women fostered tranquility and raised the next generation of productive citizens and leaders. The American home became a retreat, a cozy haven that offered respite from this workaday world with its seeming immorality and temptations.

By the Civil War era, women began assuming the main responsibility for guiding and disciplining the family's children as men went off to work. Fathers became more and more absent from their children's daily lives and guidance. It became the mother's responsibility to raise good citizens of the republic. Women also became the main advisors in the course of their daughters' courtships, and asking the father's permission to marry became more of a formality in many 19th-century households. Although these growing roles gave 19th-century women more prestige within the home, they were still

A 19th-century child's doll. Many girls in poor families played with dolls made from rags, but wealthy families' children might play with toys made in factories.

largely considered inferior to men and expected to obey their husbands' wishes in a male-dominated society. Women who were dissatisfied with these roles were often blamed for their own unhappiness.

Although most women remained at home in mid-19th century America, there were greater social freedoms and economic opportunities opening for women in the growing number of cities. A number of educational reformers claimed that women were entitled to a full education in more than just the domestic arts. Employment opportunities for northern women also increased as a result of the outbreak of the Civil War, as many men enlisted or were conscripted (drafted) into the military.

Some women eagerly sought employment, while others were forced to work due to poverty or the loss of their husbands in the war. During the expansion of the federal government, such as the War Department, women served as secretaries and clerks. In addition to the traditional female careers such as schoolteachers, women worked in the growing numbers of industrial factories or as clerical workers for growing private businesses. The Civil War also fueled demand for the new female profession of nursing. A few women even worked in the military as cooks, laundresses, or in other supporting roles, with some even disguising themselves as men to fight.

The Abraham Lincoln family at home. Mary Todd Lincoln, Robert, and Thaddeus are depicted gathered around the table in this Currier & Ives print published c.1867.

THE DAILY ROUTINES OF FAMILY LIFE

Most Americans rose before sunrise to eat breakfast and prepare for their day. Women or servants generally prepared a hot and hearty breakfast, as many Americans believed it was an important start that helped fuel one through the upcoming day. Urban dwellers generally took their meals in the dining room, while rural families generally ate in the kitchen. Urban dwellers and more wealthy Americans spent more time and care on their grooming and dressing routines. Most Americans still followed the custom of bathing once a week, often on Saturday night, but others had begun the practice of daily bathing. Mid-19th century

The Cult of Domesticity and True Womanhood

Many middle class women's roles in 19th-century New England were shaped by the cultural beliefs in the cult of domesticity and the virtues that true womanhood was to possess. The four basic characteristics of the true woman were piety, submissiveness, purity, and domesticity. Women's magazines such as the popular *Godey's Lady's Book*, advice books, and other forms of popular culture advised women on proper rules and behavior and warned of the dire consequences for those women who did not follow them.

Men were expected to be bold actors in the public spheres of business and politics; their basic characteristics included rationality, independence, and strength. Women, on the other hand, were pure, religious, submissive, emotional, and delicate; their true place was in the home nurturing their husbands and children. Housework and child rearing were morally uplifting tasks that properly filled the bulk of a woman's day. The cult of domesticity also influenced views on female education. Women were believed to be emotional, not logical and reasonable. Those girls who attended school did so to learn to become good wives, mothers, and household managers, not thinkers or businessmen.

Many of the beliefs in gender roles were based on the scientific thoughts of the day. Many scientists stated that men and women had distinctive character traits rooted in biological differences. Women were physically and mentally inferior to men and were naturally suited to serve as helpmates and mothers. Menstruation was believed to leave women weak and invalid during its course. They were frail and delicate creatures that cheerfully and dutifully obeyed their husbands. Many believers also argued that women were naturally indifferent to sexual relations, instead experiencing a pure love not tainted by passion. Women's roles as mothers made it essential that they follow these cultural standards, since it was women that raised the next generation of society. Their examples and guidance would ensure the continuation of a moral and democratic republic.

Americans debated the supposed virtues or dangers of the frequency and types of baths practiced. Rural farmers performed early morning chores such as feeding the animals and milking the cows, before heading into the fields for a full day of work planting or harvesting, depending on the season.

The urban working class often walked to work to begin a 12 to 14 hour day from Monday through Saturday. Urban businessmen and professional men such as doctors and lawyers enjoyed a later start to the workday than their un-skilled counterparts. Those children who received a public education, more common in the north and among more wealthy families, usually helped with household or farm chores before walking to school. The children of poor and immigrant families in the cities often worked full days to help support their families, as a father's factory wages were not enough to survive. Many farm children only attended school part time or in the winter, after the fall harvest and before the spring planting, when their labor was needed at home.

DAILY HOUSEKEEPING

While some women went to work, most stayed at home and completed the daily housekeeping tasks. Even with the development of new technology and labor-saving devices, housework was still time consuming and difficult. Everyday, women prepared the midday and evening meals, washed dishes, emptied chamber pots (as most households did not have indoor plumbing), and cleaned. Weekly tasks included laundry, ironing, dusting, baking, and shopping. Water for bathing, cooking, and laundry often had to be hauled from public water pumps, wells, or rivers. Seasonal tasks included candle making and the canning of fruits and vegetables. Farm wives often helped their children with outside chores as well. Once a year during spring-clean-ing, women would beat the dust out of drapes, carpets, and furniture and give most household surfaces a good scrubbing.

Families tried to gather daily for the midday meal, known as dinner. Din-ner served as most families' principal meal. Urban workers, however, increas-ingly began eating luncheons at saloons or restaurants rather than returning home for dinner. Work continued in the afternoon for many men and women. Middle and upper class women often visited friends or entertained their own guests in formal parlors after dinner. Others attended lectures or meetings of the growing numbers of women's clubs or temperance and charity societies. Lower class and rural women carried on with their daily and weekly chores af-ter serving the midday meal and clearing the dishes. Some children returned to school in the afternoon, but many farm children came home to spend the afternoon helping out on the farm.

In the evening, families returned home from school, work, or entertaining to clean up and enjoy a light nighttime meal, known as supper. Most night-time meals consisted of cold foods. Many urban dwellers, however, were be-ginning to adapt the custom of eating their main meal in the evening. Family

A 19th-century country retreat. By 1860 some wealthy members of society were beginning to look for summer homes in cooler places along the coast of New England or in the interior of New York.

members then sat in their living room, kitchen, or porch and enjoyed a quiet respite from the day. At this time most servants or hired hands retired to their own rooms for the evening. Some people went for a stroll, and some men had men's club meetings to attend. The men usually smoked and read the day's newspaper. Women often used the time to sew and mend clothing or write letters to friends and relatives. Evening entertainments included reading, often done aloud, praying, and games. Families would then turn in to bed. Some people had begun adopting the daily habit of brushing their teeth before bed, and many people slept with the windows open because of the widespread belief in the health benefits of fresh air.

Weekends were increasingly becoming viewed as an opportunity for relaxation, entertainment, and a break from the everyday routine. Children played outdoors, with the activities changing with the seasons and weather. Parents often visited friends on Saturday evenings and rural families broke up the isolation and loneliness of frontier life with barn dances and other types of socials. However most workers still worked on Saturday while farmers often went to town to attend to business. Children were expected to help out around the house, with girls cooking and cleaning and boys working outdoors, chopping wood, tending to animals, or performing yard work. Families usually spent Sunday evenings quietly at home or visiting relatives.

Although the custom would begin to fade after the Civil War, many American families still observed the Sabbath (Sunday) as a day of rest. Mothers, daughters, and servants frequently prepared Sunday dinner the day before, and many servants or hired hands were given Sunday off. Religion was still central to American

A Diary from Dixie

Mary Boykin Chesnut was the daughter of a governor of South Carolina, and wife of a U.S. senator who became a military aide to Jefferson Davis during the Civil War. As was customary for women of the time, Mary Chesnut kept a journal that effectively chronicled the impact of the war on the daily life of a southern family. Below is an excerpt from her journal written in 1864 while in Columbia, South Carolina.

March 24. Yesterday, we went to the capitol ground to see our returned prisoners. We walked slowly up and down until Jeff Davis was called upon to speak. There I stood, almost touching the bayonets when he left me. I looked straight into the prisoners' faces, poor fellows. They cheered with all their might, and I wept for sympathy and enthusiasm. I am very deeply moved. These men were so forlorn, so dried up and shrunken, with such a strange look in some of their eyes; others so restless and wild looking; others, again, placidly vacant, as if they had been dead to the world for years. A poor woman was too much for me. She was searching for her son. He had been expected back. She said he was taken prisoner at Gettysburg. She kept going in and out among them with a basket of provisions she had brought for him to eat. It was too pitiful. She was utterly unconscious of the crowd. The anxious dread, expectation, hurry, and hope which led her on showed in her face.

A sister of Mrs. Lincoln is here. She brings the freshest scandals from Yankee-land. She says she rode with Lovejoy. A friend of hers commands a black regiment. Two Southern horrors—a black regiment and Lovejoy.

September 21. Went with Mrs. Rhett to hear Dr. Palmer. I did not know before how utterly hopeless was our situation. This man is so eloquent, it was hard to listen and not give way. Despair was his word, and martyrdom. He offered us nothing more in this world than the martyr's crown. He is not for slavery, he says; he is for freedom, and the freedom to govern our own country as we see fit. He is against foreign interference in our state matters. That is what Mr. Palmer went to war for, it appears. Every days shows that slavery is doomed the world over; for that he thanked God. He spoke of our agony, and then came the cry, "Help us O God! Vain is the help of man." And so we came away shaken to the depths.

The end has come. No doubt of the fact. Our army has moved as to uncover Macon and Augusta. We are going to be wiped off the face of the earth. What is there to prevent Sherman taking General Lee in the rear? We have but two armies, and Sherman is between them now.

September 24. These stories of our defeats in the valley fall like blows upon a dead body. Since Atlanta fell, I have felt as if all were dead within me forever. Captain Ogden, of General Chesnut's staff, dined here today. Had ever brigadier, with little or no brigade, so magnificent a staff? The reserves, as somebody said, have been secured only by robbing the cradle and the grave—the men too old, the boys too young.

family life and most families dressed in their Sunday best clothes and headed off to Sunday school and church. Church was a family activity. Mid-19th century America remained a predominantly religious society, and even those Americans who did not attend church regularly found time for prayer and Scripture reading. Religion continued to be a guiding factor of day-to-day life.

LIFE ON THE SOUTHERN PLANTATIONS

Daily life and family roles had developed their own patterns on the plantations of the antebellum south. Households consisted of the master and his family and a slave labor force that numbered anywhere from a handful to several hundred. The larger plantations also housed overseers or managers who were often related to the family. The master was responsible for the daily business of managing the crops and slave labor force, as well as the financial aspects of running the business of growing cash crops and of their often-extravagant lifestyles. Despite the chivalric ideal of the plantation mistress being placed on a pedestal and their reliance on slave labor for the performance of domestic chores, most plantation mistresses spent their days hard at work managing the household and caring for sick slaves. The larger planters dominated the economic, political, and social life of the south on the eve of the Civil War, but most white southerners were small planters or yeoman farmers. These families owned few slaves and often spent their days working alongside them in the fields.

At the outbreak of the Civil War there were approximately four million slaves in the United States, most of them in the south. Their family and daily lives were diverse, despite the restrictions imposed upon them by the institution of slavery. A slave's daily routine depended upon their location and status. Slaves on small farms often worked the fields all day and lived side by side with their masters. Slaves on larger plantations were divided among skilled laborers, house slaves, and field hands. Skilled

An 1863 Currier & Ives print titled "The Soldier's Memorial." Family life in the 1860s included mourning the loss of so many men in the Civil War.

The Daily Lives of Civil War Soldiers

The Civil War soldiers, both Union and Confederate, spent most of their day-to-day military lives in camp. Most companies and regiments were locally based, and their members had known one another for many years. They often had distinctive banners or nicknames to reinforce their local identity. The popularity of letter writing further tied the men to their local communities. The men often considered their companies or regiments as surrogate families. Enduring the hardships of war, such as the unsanitary camp conditions, rampant disease, poor diet, and constant dangers further forged the bonds between soldiers. Camp life tended to be monotonous, structured, and disciplined.

According to historian Daniel E. Sutherland, a typical day in a Civil War camp began with a bugle at dawn. Men would turn out for roll call, then wash, shave, and dress before a second bugle called them to breakfast. For those men not assigned to guard detail, daily camp chores included cleaning, chopping firewood, and hauling water. A noon meal and rest period would follow morning drilling and training exercises. Next the men would prepare for daily inspection by readying their uniforms, shoes, weapons, and tents. Inspections, plus roll call and parade made up the evening routine known as "retreat." Next came supper and a period of free time. The final roll call, known as "tattoo," was called shortly after dark. "Taps" was called around 10:30 P.M. to signal lights out and the end of a typical camp day.

An 1871 lithograph depicts camp life for Confederate soldiers during the Civil War. Daily life as a soldier could be monotonous, yet disciplined and structured.

laborers spent their days at a variety of occupations, such as blacksmithing and carpentry. Female house slaves spent their days cooking, cleaning, or caring for the children, while male house slaves served as butlers or coachmen. Field hands worked the fields all day under the watchful eyes of overseers. Prevailing southern ideology viewed African-American slaves as inferior and childlike people who relied on their owners for sustenance and protection.

Many southerners paternalistically viewed their slaves as part of a family, with the master fulfilling the role of father. A similar ideology guided relations between the federal government and Native Americans in the western United States. Owners expected that their slaves would be obedient, loyal, and content children. State and local laws known as slave codes regulated and restricted slaves' daily lives and behavior to keep them in their proper place and prevent uprisings. Slave marriages were not legally sanctioned, and slave families could be divided at their owners' will. Despite these circumstances, however, slave marriages were common and family ties remained strong as a bulwark against the degradation of slavery. The coming of the Civil War and emancipation would further strengthen the bonds of family at the same time that it ended the institution that had governed the daily lives of African Americans for generations.

DISRUPTIONS OF WAR AND RECONSTRUCTION

The outbreak of the fighting of the Civil War in 1861 drastically changed everyday family life in both the north and the south. Many men joined the military, often with the encouragement of the females in their lives. The Civil War had one of the highest participation rates of all wars in which the United States has been involved. The Civil War also had one of the highest rates of death and disability, as well.

The north, with its higher population, lost more men, but the southern losses had more social impact because with their smaller population they were less able to absorb the losses. The regimentation of daily camp life became the new experience for many men of fighting age, as revealed in their letters home. The close communication between soldiers and their families kept them tied to the communities they had left behind on the home front. Both men and women placed great importance on letter writing, diaries, and private journals during the course of the Civil War. Women's diaries and letters reveal both their new roles within the wartime family and the hardships and disruption to daily routine that the fighting caused. Many women were forced to take full responsibility for family homes and businesses when their husbands went off to war. Other women left home themselves to serve as nurses or in military support roles such as laundresses and cooks. Some women even fought disguised as men.

Many women served as civilian volunteers, adding activities such as rolling bandages and joining sewing circles and so-called "thimble brigades" to make uniforms, socks, and banners for the soldiers in their communities. Families

An 1868 illustration that appeared in Harper's Weekly *with the caption: "Man representing the Freedman's Bureau stands between armed groups of Euro-Americans and Afro-Americans."*

in both the north and south suffered from inflation and price increases, but the effects were much more pronounced in the south.

The Union's Anaconda Plan, which centered on a blockade of the Confederate coastline, increased the acute Confederate shortages of basic food and supplies. Much of the fighting occurred on southern soil, with some areas alternating between Union and Confederate control during the course of the war. Destitute refugees and escaped slaves followed the Union Army or gathered in the larger towns looking for food.

By 1863 acute food shortages led to the eruption of bread riots in cities like Richmond, Virginia and Mobile, Alabama. Laws allowed the Confederate government to seize food and livestock from family farms and plantations and pay for it with IOUs or inflated, worthless Confederate currency. Looting and stealing added to the chaos and deprivation. As a result southern women had to find creative substitutes to provide their families with food and clothing. They made coffee from acorns and bark, and boiled the dirt from beneath smokehouses to reclaim salt. In Florida, woven palmetto fronds became hats.

POSTWAR DAILY LIFE

The Civil War's impact on the daily life of families and communities lasted long after the fighting ended in 1865. Federal military forces still occupied the defeated Confederate states for much of the period. The Reconstruction era was filled with civil unrest and social turmoil. Widows and disabled veterans struggled economically. Those soldiers emotionally traumatized by war struggled to readapt to their civilian lives. Those who had deserted their military posts returned home to face the stigma placed upon them by their families and communities. Both northerners and southerners, whites and newly freed African-American slaves (freedmen) had to adapt to new political, economic, and social realities. Various tenancy systems, predominantly sharecropping, replaced slavery as the basis for the postwar agricultural labor force. The races became more segregated and racism and prejudice remained rampant.

Southern planters had to adjust to the new realities of the postwar south and its economic devastation. Many had lost their fortunes during the war. Many homes had been looted, confiscated, and destroyed. Those that remained could not be kept up as they had before the war due to economic distress and declining land values. Confederate veterans and widows lacked the federal pensions many Union veterans and widows received from the government to help them survive. Wealthy southern women had to perform more daily domestic chores as slave labor ended. Many younger southern women rejected the old antebellum plantation lifestyle in favor of keeping house. Some even entered the workforce in female occupations as teachers, librarians, and secretaries.

ADAPTING TO A NEW DAILY LIFE

Freedmen's lives were no longer governed by the strict regimentation of slavery, and they painfully adapted to their new daily lives. Religion and family life became even more important to the daily lives of African Americans during Reconstruction. Many freedmen searched to reunite families in the immediate aftermath of slavery. Others left the rural areas for urban life or left the south altogether, migrating north or west. Congress established the Bureau of Refugees, Freedmen, and Abandoned Lands (Freedmen's Bureau) in 1865 to aid former slaves in the transition to freedom.

The Freedmen's Bureau also helped establish public education for African Americans, forbidden under slavery, and schooling became a valued part of many African-American children's daily lives. New African-American churches were created and many African-American families, like their white counterparts, spent much time in church. Churches often served as the center of social life. The development of new African-American family life and daily routines were tinged with the fear of violent organizations such as the Ku Klux Klan (KKK) and the legal restrictions imposed by the passage of black codes and Jim Crow laws.

While the hardships of the Civil War and the turmoil of Reconstruction had disrupted family life from 1860 to 1876, family life remained a dominant feature of American society. The processes of agricultural growth, industrialization, urbanization, technological innovation, and immigration had all begun to impact society by the mid-19th century. These trends would continue to further change the family lives and daily routines of many Americans after Reconstruction ended in 1876.

Marcella Trevino

Further Readings

Censer, Jane Turner. *The Reconstruction of White Southern Womanhood, 1865–1895*. Baton Rouge: Louisiana State University Press, 2003.

Degler, Carl N. *At Odds: Women and the Family in America from the Revolution to the Present*. New York: Oxford University Press, 1980.

Dunaway, Wilma A. *The African-American Family in Slavery and Emancipation*. New York: Cambridge University Press, 2003.

Foner, Eric, and Joshua Brown. *Forever Free: The Story of Emancipation and Reconstruction*. New York: Knopf, 2005.

Gallman, J. Matthew. *The North Fights the Civil War: The Home Front*. Chicago, IL: I.R. Dee, 1994.

McPherson, James M. *Battle Cry of Freedom: The Civil War Era*. New York: Oxford University Press, 1988.

Mintz, Steven, and Susan Kellogg. *Domestic Revolutions: A Social History of American Family Life*. New York: Free Press, 1988.

Ryan, Mary P. *Mysteries of Sex: Tracing Women and Men Through American History*. Chapel Hill: University of North Carolina Press, 2006.

Silber, Nina. *Daughters of the Union: Northern Women Fight the Civil War*. Cambridge, MA: Harvard University Press, 2005.

Sutherland, Daniel E. *The Expansion of Everyday Life 1860–1876*. New York: Harper and Row, 1989.

Van Doren Stern, Philip, ed. *Soldier Life in the Union and Confederate Armies*. Bloomington: Indiana University Press, 1961.

Varhola, Michael J. *Everyday Life During the Civil War: A Guide for Writers, Students and Historians*. Cincinnati, OH: Writer's Digest Books, 1999.

Vinouskis, Maris A., ed. *Toward a Social History of the American Civil War: Exploratory Essays*. New York: Cambridge University Press, 1990.

Welter, Barbara. *Dimity Convictions: The American Woman in the 19th Century*. Athens: Ohio University Press, 1976.

Chapter 3

Material Culture

*"As a man is said to have a right to his
property, he may equally be said to
have a property in his rights."*
— James Madison

IN THE 1820s a group of Boston merchants leased some property just north of the city, along the great falls of the Merrimack River. By the 1830s this vacant plot of land became the cradle of the Industrial Revolution in America, the mighty factory town of Lowell. The rise of industrialism ushered in the modern consumer era, as factories began to crop up all over the eastern United States, producing thousands of different items for a hungry marketplace.

At the start of the Civil War the age-old relationship between people and material possessions had irrevocably changed. For generations, centuries even, common people had gone through life with limited amounts of personal goods. From clothing to furniture to kitchenware, items had either been made by hand at home, or purchased from regional artisans—often an expensive proposition. Cheap, durable, replaceable goods were simply not available. By the 1860s and 1870s, only the very poor and those living beyond the reach of the railroads on the distant frontier were blocked from participating in consumer culture. The growing middle and professional classes, on the other hand, were presented with an array of goods that their grandparents could never even have imagined.

Consumerism became tightly intertwined with social status. It formed a type of coded language: the type of house you lived in, the way you decorated it, the clothing that you wore, all were messages to the outside world about your income, education, and breeding. This created a symbiotic relationship between consumers and producers—consumers could only participate in this social language through purchasing, so producers had a vested interest in providing an endless stream of new and exciting ways to make your desired statement. They were helped along by a flood of books and periodicals dedicated to guiding the new middle class through the social and domestic minefields of the era.

Changes in material culture probably affected women more than men. A study of Victorian consumer culture shows that men were enthusiastic participants in the market economy, but their purchases tended to be for things like clothing and accessories, tickets to sporting events, fancy cigars, and other forms of immediate gratification. Women, who were increasingly identified by their roles as homemakers and mothers, were more drawn to durable goods for the home.

COURTSHIP AND ROMANCE

Commercialism wormed its way into every aspect of life by the 1870s. Courtship was an extremely tricky business by the mid-19th century. Rules of good social behavior, spelled out in dozens of etiquette books published during the period, made the process more of an obstacle course than a whirlwind of romance. Courting couples were permitted very little time alone together: most interactions took place under the watchful eyes of the lady's household in the parlor, the most public room in the house. Unless they had been acquainted since childhood, a couple could not even address each other by their first names without raising eyebrows.

The process of courtship created a minor industry for expressions of affection. In the early stages of a relationship, it was appropriate for a gentleman to bring his lady flowers or candy—perishable items were deemed to have no hidden meanings of obligation. As the romance progressed, a gentleman might deliver an elaborate greeting card, especially for Valentine's Day. A small commemorative book or photo album was also a common gift. A lady, on the other hand, was not supposed to give her gentleman a gift other than a modest card, or perhaps a small drawing or painting she had made herself.

The piano became an important part of the courtship ritual. Pianos, once the province of the wealthy, had become a valued status symbol for the middle-class by the 1860s. Mass production had reduced the price of a piano to the point where even an average family could afford one on an installment plan. In 1864 one female journalist decried the "piano mania," consigning young girls to "sit and exact dreadful screechings and wailings from some unhappy instrument for at least ten years of her natural life." All that practice could pay off when a suitor came calling. It was entirely appropriate for a gentleman to stand beside the piano while the lady played, patiently turning her sheet music for her. Sheet music publishers commissioned dozens of duets for couples to play, allowing them to sit close together on the piano bench as they played.

Lydia Pinkham

Lydia Pinkham was a New England woman who fell on hard times after the Civil War—her husband had gone bankrupt in real estate and money was tight. In 1875 she began to sell Lydia Pinkham's Vegetable Compound, an herbal medication she had cooked up to help deal with what were delicately called "female complaints."

Her compound was mix of unicorn root, life root, black cohosh, pleurisy root, and fenugreek. Some of these herbals, especially black cohosh, have since been scientifically proven to help relieve exactly the types of menstrual and menopausal symptoms they were advertised to treat. But Pinkham's formula included a "preservative"—the compound was about 20 percent alcohol. This wasn't quite as bad as other patent medicines of the time, which contained both alcohol and opiates, but it was enough to give it quite a kick. A bottle of Mrs Pinkham's concoction cost $1, or $5 for six bottles. It quickly became one of the most popular patent medicines of the era. By the 1880s the family was grossing $300,000 annually, and at it's height in the 1920s the company was bringing in $3.8 million a year. Pinkham's company used her formidable (if motherly) image and her signature in advertising long after her death in 1885. The following is the text from one of the ads:

- *Lydia E Pinkham's Vegetable Compound Is a Positive Cure for all those Painful Complaints and Weaknesses so common to our best female population.*
- *It will cure entirely the worst form of Female Complaints, all ovarian troubles, Inflammation and Ulceration, Falling and Displacements, and the consequent Spinal Weakness, and is particularly adapted to the Change of Life.*
- *It will dissolve and expel tumors from the uterus in an early stage of development. The tendency to cancerous humors there is checked very speedily by its use.*
- *It removes faintness, flatulency, destroys all craving for stimulants, and relieves weakness of the stomach. It cures Bloating, Headaches, Nervous Prostration, General Debility, Sleeplessness, Depression and Indigestion.*
- *That feeling of bearing down, causing pain, weight and backache, is always permanently cured by its use.*
- *It will at all times and under all circumstances act in harmony with the laws that govern the female system.*

The most popular pieces allowed the couple to touch hands as they played their parts—one of the few times physical contact was allowable.

ENGAGEMENT AND MARRIAGE

The point of courtship was, of course, to test the waters for an engagement and an eventual marriage. The engagement process began with a formal meeting or letter to the lady's father for permission to "pop the question" as the phrase went in the 1860s. If permission was given, the gentleman then had to face the issue of the ring. Engagement rings increased in importance after the Civil War, becoming a tangible sign of a couple's intent to marry. But a young man of limited means often had to deal with a harsh dilemma.

Generally a lady's parents wouldn't allow the wedding to go forward until they were sure their prospective son-in-law could support their daughter in some comfort. Purchasing a ring could put enough of a dent in his personal finances to set the wedding date back by months. Fortunately the ring did not have to be large and it did not have to be diamond. Some of the most popular rings featured semi-precious stones like amethysts and pearls in modest gold settings.

WEDDINGS AND DRESSES

Weddings were generally small ceremonies held at the bride's home. Special wedding dresses were reserved for families of some means. White dresses were symbolic of a bride's purity and virginity, and were popularized by Queen Victoria at her 1840 wedding to Prince Albert, but they were not particularly practical. It was more common for a bride to wear a nicely tailored

"Godey's Fashions for December 1861"—A fashion illustration from Godey's Ladies Book, featuring the newest styles in wedding gowns.

Horatio Alger (1832–99)

Horatio Alger was one of the most popular and prolific writers of the late 19th century, and his name has since become synonymous with people who overcome hardship to achieve great success.

Alger was the son of a Unitarian minister, born in Revere, Massachusetts in 1832. He entered Harvard around 1848 at the age of 16 and graduated four years later. Following a short stint teaching and writing and a 10-month tour of Europe, he decided to enter the ministry.

After graduating from Harvard Divinity School in 1864, Alger took a post as minister at the First Parish Unitarian Church in Brewster, Massachusetts. Two years later he abruptly resigned and returned to Boston. He had been accused of "practicing on [the boys of the church] at different times deeds that are too revolting to relate," although the exact nature of the charges were never clear. Alger's family convinced the church to keep the story quiet, and in return, Alger agreed never to return to the pulpit. By late 1866 he was living in New York City and working as a writer.

Alger didn't really write 130 different books; he wrote the same book in 130 different ways. The plot was always about the same: a young boy, just on the verge of puberty, with few resources and plenty of temptations, but rather than falling into a life of vice and crime, he works hard—and eventually attracts the notice of an older man who takes the boy under his wing and introduces him to a life of middle-class propriety and ease.

The idea that even the most downtrodden of society could work their way up in the world through diligence, clean living, and that catch-all American quality of "pluck" resonated with Victorian audiences, and Alger's works sold an estimated 20 million copies in the late 19th century. He never became wealthy from his works, with some biographers believing that he gave much of his money away to the impoverished young men who were the prototypes for his stories. He died at his sister's home in Massachusetts in July 1899 at the age of 67. Shortly after his death his sister destroyed most of his personal papers.

dress of blue, green, brown, or some other favorite shade, although red and black dresses were frowned upon—"Marry in black, you'll wish yourself back; marry in red, you'll wish yourself dead," went part of a common superstition. No matter what the color, most brides chose dresses they could wear on formal occasions for years afterward. She might wear a veil, and almost always carried a bouquet. During the ceremony, she would receive her wedding ring . . . invariably a plain gold band, perhaps with a loving inscription inside. Men usually did not wear a band.

An 1854 charcoal drawing of the home of Zadock Pratt, representative to U.S. Congress 1836–42, with fountains in the foreground, and the Catskill Mountains in the background.

Social and religious commentators were appalled by the commercialization of weddings that took hold after the Civil War, particularly when it came to gift giving. When a couple decided to marry, they would send out invitations, which obligated the recipient to provide a gift even if they couldn't attend the wedding. In an essay in *Godey's* magazine in the 1870s provocatively entitled "Wedding Bazaar," Reverend Henry Ward Beecher denounced the practice of giving and receiving elaborate wedding gifts, saying that it turned the sacred rite of marriage into little more than a crass marketplace, and he heaped scorn on the bride who "does not shrink from calculating" the value of her gifts.

While bridal gift-giving was a key way to display social status and taste, in the most practical sense, wedding gifts were supposed to start out their lives with the raw materials they needed to start their own home. Nor would it be correct to assume that brides were merely mercenary. The pretty and decorative gifts she might receive as she set off to her new life often became treasured objects that remained in a family for generations. Honeymoons were another commercialized aspect of the wedding ritual. By mid-century honeymoon trips were becoming more common, as improvements in transportation made it easier to get to popular destinations like Niagara Falls or the White Mountains of New Hampshire. It was seen as a necessary period of transition as the bride was introduced the conjugal side of married life, and prepared to move from her father's to her husband's house.

MAKING THE HOME

Once the excitement of the wedding was over, and the honeymoon and string of post-homecoming receptions were done, the newlyweds began the process of making their new home together. The dream of virtually every middle-class American was a home of their own. "The love of a decent home is implanted in the heart of a man earning only 30 or 40 dollars a week quite as strongly as it is in the heart of a millionaire," a New York man wrote in a letter to the editor published in 1869. But a man earning $2,000 a year could not easily afford a home in a nice neighborhood that cost anywhere between $10,000 and $80,000. For many young people starting out, transitional housing was needed.

In the past a couple might have to live with one or the other sets of parents, or take a room in a boardinghouse. But mid-century couples had a variety of housing options that had not been open a decade or so before. In large urban areas, there was the new innovation of the "French flat," what would later come to be called apartments. These units were several steps above the squalid tenements that housed the tens of thousands of immigrants that were arriving in America each year. The flats were at least a step better than boardinghouses, where a person might have a bedroom and perhaps a small sitting room, but shared all other common rooms and meals. An apartment allowed people to live much as they would in a private, free-standing home.

Outside the big cities, people with modest means who could obtain a small piece of land had a better chance of moving into a private home. Home construction had been made much simpler by the introduction of the balloon-frame house in 1833. Balloon-frame homes were an innovation of the industrial age, relying on milled boards and machine-made nails. Unlike the timber-frame construction or brick homes of the previous generations, balloon frame houses did not have to be square or unadorned. By the 1860s there were catalogs full of plans for fanciful homes with turrets, verandas, bay windows, and all types of trims and decorations. Plans could be purchased from any one of a number of mail-order catalogs. Most catalogs had line drawings of the exterior of their houses and a floor plan with measurements. "Shows plans and elevations of a six-room cottage, suitable for a working man of small means. Cost: $860," a common description reads. "Plans and perspective view of an attractive little Cottage of four rooms with bath-room and conveniences, laundry in cellar. It is suitable for anyone having a small family. Cost: $900," reads another. Once a set of plans had been selected, the prospective home-owner had to purchase materials and workmen to put it all together.

FILLING THE HOME

Once purchased (or built), the family had to decorate the home in an appropriate fashion. This usually fell to the wife. To aid her in the job, there was an almost limitless selection of guidebooks, all of them driving home the point that it was critically important to get all the details right.

Parlor furniture was often purchased as a set, usually consisting of a chair each for the gentleman and lady of the house, a small sofa, and a side chair.

The public rooms—the entryway, the parlor, and the dining room—tended to have the most elaborate decoration. The proper entryway, for example, had a decorative rack for coats, walking sticks, and umbrellas. One all-important piece was a card-receiver. The practice of calling on friends and acquaintances was one of the most important social rituals of the period; many families had a specific "at home" night when they would be there to receive visits from friends. If a person stopped by to visit and could not be received, they would leave their calling card in the decorative card-receiver.

About 3 by 2 inches in size and imprinted with the caller's name, even these humble cards had special meanings. A folded top-left corner meant the visitor had come by in person. A folded top-right corner was for congratulations for some other happy event. If the lower-left corner was folded, this meant a goodbye, and the lower-right was folded if the person was offering condolences. A set of 50 cards cost around $3.50 in 1868.

Ladies' chairs were armless, both to accommodate the voluminous skirts of the period and to encourage good posture; a lady was supposed to sit up straight with her back not touching the chair back, her hands folded demurely in her lap. Proper parlors also had a small table with a lamp either placed on it or hanging above it. Another popular piece was an étagère, a set of open shelves where the family could display their good taste in the form of books, small decorative objects, or other bric-a-brac. There was also the all-important piano, and perhaps a small fireplace or stove, designed more for beauty than warmth and light.

There was at least a minor backlash against the heavy, ponderous furniture rolling off factory assembly lines during the period. British architect Charles Eastlake believed that the furniture and drapery of the time did little more than trap dust and dirt and create an unhealthful environment. His *Hints on Household Taste in Furniture, Upholstery and Other Details* found wide readership in the United States.

Furniture makers eschewed one of his main premises—that pieces should once again be handmade by craftsmen who took pride in their work—but adopted his suggestions for pieces to be built along clean lines, with flat surfaces and low-relief, geometric designs. Eastlake-style furniture was attractive, but more important to hardworking housewives, it was easy to wipe clean and to dust.

Decorative cloth coverings, including window drapery, tablecloths, and lambrequins (a short ornamental drapery meant for the top of a window or doorway or the edge of a shelf) were another important element of a home's public spaces. The function of such covers was not primarily to hide the suggestive legs so offensive to delicate Victorian sensibilities, but to soften the visual impact of straight lines, and more practically, to protect expensive objects from stains and spills. They were also a way for a lady to show off her skills in needle arts, although as the period progressed, machine-made laces and mass-produced printed fabrics became more common.

Kitchens and bedrooms were private spaces where simplicity was key. Sanitation and health had become an obsession after the war, and some interior design experts preached the gospel of good air and soothing colors in private rooms. For example wallpaper in bedrooms was often discouraged, as it might harbor dust or bugs, and because complex patterns or bright colors might cause nervousness or irritability.

THE WAR ON DIRT

No matter what the room, the war on grime was never-ending; dusting, cleaning, polishing, and washing took up a good portion of the average housewife's day. By the 1870s women could turn to a new armory of weapons in her fight. One of the most popular was the carpet-sweeper. Hand-sweeping rugs, which was usually needed a minimum of twice a week, was deemed a form of torture by one female commentator of the era "prosecuted until every nerve is throbbing in fierce rebellion at the undue pressure to which it is subjected." A mechanical sweeper, with two brushes mounted on an axle to pick up and hold dirt and debris as it was pushed across a carpet, was considered a lifesaver.

Personal cleanliness was another battlefield entirely. A full bath meant pulling out a heavy portable tub, drawing water, and heating it on the stove—enough of a production that most people were not inclined to bother more than once a week at most. Daily washing took place in the bedroom, with the humble assistance of a washstand that contained a pitcher, a basin, a sponge, a towel, some soap, and a small carpet of oilcloth to protect the floor. Water closets, or indoor toilets, became more common after the war, at least in the cities, but the modern bathroom, with a hot and cold running water, a tub, and a toilet, did not become a standard feature until the turn of the century.

Ready-made clothing, especially for men, was becoming fashionable by the 1870s, but most women still did most of the sewing for themselves and their families. This take was made infinitely easier by what *Godey's* magazine termed "The Queen of Inventions" in 1860—the home sewing machine. At $50–$75 they were hardly cheap, but most women did enough sewing to make it a worthwhile purchase. *Godey's* suggested that a group of families pool their financial resources and share a machine, but most made do with buying on an installment plan. With a machine, a woman could make 10 stitches in the time it took to make one by hand; one estimate showed that it cut the time of sewing a man's shirt from over 14 hours down to just one and a quarter hours.

Laundry stubbornly resisted innovation during the period. Women who had a choice sent their laundry out, generally every other week. Those that could not afford the $2 charged by most laundresses for a full load had to do it themselves. An 1868 article described the process: clothing was first put in a tub of warm, soapy water and agitated with a plunger or scrubbed on a washboard. Then it was transferred to a second tub, covered with more water, and boiled for about 30 minutes. The second tub was drained, and the clothing was rinsed with water until all the soap was gone. Each piece was then wrung out by hand and hung up to dry.

Since it was better to separate out whites and delicates from colors and prints, the process often had to be repeated for several loads. It could easily take up an entire day, and the next day, almost every item needed to be ironed. Washing machines were introduced in the early 1880s, but did not meet with immediate acclaim, since they tended to rip clothes as they spun around the agitator. However hand-cranked clothes wringers were popular, saving women at least the labor of hand-wringing.

An 1870 lithograph about progress shows views of the New York & Brooklyn Suspension Bridge, sewing machines, and inset drawings of people sewing by hand and with sewing machines.

A late 19th-century pencil drawing of an African-American cabin in Spotsylvania, Virginia. Cooking in these cabins required stooping over a fireplace and maneuvering heavy iron pots and pans.

IN THE KITCHEN

The kitchen was another room that saw change in the mid-19th century. At one time the kitchen had been the hub of the household: the open hearth assured that it was the warmest and brightest room in the home. With the advent of the woodstove and different types of lighting, the kitchen had gradually become a separate space, the domain of women, where men rarely tread.

By the 1870s housewives worked on cast-iron stoves heated with either wood or coal. Unlike the open fireplace hearths of their grandmothers, where temperature could be controlled by distance from the fire, the "modern" cook had little ability to regulate the heat on a cast-iron stove, judging the temperature by approximate distance from the side-mounted firebox. The fine control offered by gas or electric stoves was another generation or two in the future. Cooking food without burning it took concentration and skill. But few women would have wanted to return to the old days of stooping over a fireplace and maneuvering heavy iron pots and pans. Whatever their drawbacks, the kitchen range allowed women to work standing up, and they were far easier to clean. Many models came with large water heaters that made laundry and bathing a little less of a chore.

Even heavy pots and pans were becoming a thing of the past. In the 1870s German immigrant brothers Frederick and William Niedringhaus patented a process of stamping kitchen items out of thin metal and coating them with an enamel mixed with pulverized granite. The resulting graniteware was lightweight, easy to clean, durable, and inexpensive.

IN THE NURSERY

Childhood as a separate phase of life was one of the social innovations of industrial America. As in most agrarian societies, the sheer amount of work on a farm meant that children were put to useful tasks as soon as they were walking, even if it was just rocking the cradle of a younger sibling or scaring crows out of the family cornfield. Rural children had time to play, but too much leisure was discouraged.

The shift in attitude came from the growth of the middle class, living in an environment where there were no fields to work or as many chores to be done. It also reflected the elevation of a woman's role as a mother to a near-sanctified state. A mother's duty was to nurture her children and guide the development of their moral characters; it was her highest calling, and for many, almost a full time job. The marketplace played on the natural anxiety of mothers in a time where child mortality was still high. While most doctors and social scientists encouraged mothers to breast-feed their babies, a competing body of literature extolled the virtues of bottle-feeding and the use of supplemental liquid foods. Liebig's Soluble Food, a concentrated milk powder that was supposed to have the same makeup as human breast milk, arrived on the market in 1868. Mellin's Food used aggressive marketing tactics including door-to-door sales and placements in magazines of advertorials, advertisements dressed up to look like legitimate articles.

Children had more toys in the post-war period than before, and more and more often, these toys were designed to reinforce gender roles. Little boys were given little toy guns or trains. Little girls might play with a miniature cook stove or make clothing for her dolls with small, functional sewing machines. Dolls themselves changed during the period, from adult figures to baby dolls, which had first become popular in France.

THE RITUALS OF MOURNING

Despite improvements in health and sanitation, death was still a frequent visitor to Victorian households. The Civil War alone cost hundreds of thousands of lives; periodic epidemics took thousands more; limited medical knowledge and a lack of effective medicines meant even commonplace injuries and illnesses could turn fatal. The rituals of mourning became increasingly complex after 1860, and an entire industry developed to help consumers commemorate the passing of those they loved.

The death of a close relation—a spouse, a child, a parent, or a sibling—set off an official period of full mourning lasting a full year and a day. Widows

Gettysburg cemetery. The mid-19th century took a toll on American lives. The Civil War cost hundreds of thousands of lives and limited medical knowledge meant illnesses could turn fatal.

were supposed to dress all in black, wear no jewelry, and not be seen in public without a black crepe veil. During a period of half-mourning that could last up to a second full year, women could slowly integrate jewelry and some color back into her wardrobe, with deep purples or grays considered appropriate half-mourning colors. Some women, following the lead set by Queen Victoria after the death of her beloved Prince Albert in 1861, made half-mourning a lifelong practice. Men might wear black armbands or mourning badges as visible symbols of grief. Calling cards and stationary was bordered in black.

Tangible reminders of the dead were highly valued. Post-mortem photography was popular, particularly of deceased children, often posed with their families or favorite toys or mementos. Their photographs had places of honor in the family album. Hair jewelry was also favored. Ladies' magazines frequently contained instructions on how to weave or braid human hair into mourning brooches, bracelets, and other commemorative objects, while other women preserved locks of hair in mourning lockets.

HEATHER K. MICHON

Further Readings

Bushman, Richard L. *The Refinement of America: Persons, Houses, Cities*. New York: Alfred A. Knopf, 1992.

Cunningham, Patricia A. and Susan Voso Lab. *Dress in American Culture*. Bowling Green, OH: Bowling Green State University Popular Press, 1993.

Floyd, Janet and Inga Bryden. *Domestic Space: Reading the Nineteenth-Century Interior*. New York: St. Martin's Press, 1999.

Glassie, Henry. *Material Culture*. Bloomington: Indiana University Press, 1999.

Massey, James C. and Shirley Maxwell. *House Styles in America*, 1996.

Schlereth, Thomas J. *Artifacts and the American Past*. Nashville, TN: American Association for State and Local History, 1980.

Schlereth, Thomas J. *Cultural History and Material Culture: Everyday Life, Landscapes, Museums*. Charlottesville: University Press of Virginia, 1992.

St. George, Robert Blair, ed. *Material Life in America, 1600–1860*. Boston, MA: Northeastern University Press, 1988.

Thompson, Eleanor. *The American Home: Material Culture, Domestic Space, and Family Life*. Hanover, NH: University Press of New England, 1998.

Weitzman, David. *Underfoot: An Everyday Guide to Exploring the American Past*. New York: Scribner, 1976.

Zakim, Michael. *Ready-Made Democracy: A History of Men's Dress in the American Republic, 1760–1860*. Chicago, IL: University of Chicago Press, 2003.

Chapter 4

Social Attitudes

*"The affirmative class monopolize the
homage of mankind. They originate and
execute all the great feats."*
— Ralph Waldo Emerson

THE ERA OF the Civil War and Reconstruction was a complex historical period most marked socially by the bitter sectional conflicts between north and south and the bitter racial conflicts between African Americans and whites. These conflicts had a social, economic, and political basis. Social attitudes played a key role in how north and south, Republican and Democrat, African American and white, would approach the difficult questions raised by the Civil War and its aftermath. Sectional, racial, and class stereotypes had a long history in America before the fighting began, and would continue to influence society long after the fighting had ceased.

In the beginning both sides experienced an initial surge of patriotism and a rush among men to volunteer for the Union and Confederate armies. Many young men sought the opportunity for adventure, glory, and victory in their beloved cause. Those who did not join the rush often found themselves the targets of scorn and derision, often by women, and many were shamed into volunteering. Thus even after both the Union and Confederacy passed conscription (draft) laws, many men volunteered anyway to avoid the social stigma attached to being drafted. The draft laws also fostered class resentments, as many draftees from poorer families bitterly complained about wealthy draftees who were able to buy substitutes to fight in their stead, echoing the phrase "a rich man's war but a poor man's fight." Charges of class discrimination were echoed in the draft riots that broke out on both sides, such as those in New York City in July 1863.

The necessities of war expanded women's socially-acceptable roles. Dorothea Dix, superintendent of the Union Army's corps of nurses, and Clara Barton, later founder of the American Red Cross, were instrumental in establishing female nurses in the United States. They had to overcome the resistant attitudes of many male doctors. Many women served as nurses during the Civil War, which helped overcome the old social belief that nurses were, more often than not, women of inferior moral character. It was in response to this widely held attitude that Dorothea Dix instituted a policy that Union nurses in her corps must be over 30 years of age and plain in appearance.

African-American women also worked as Union nurses, as well as in positions as cooks, laundresses, and other vital functions. As men went off to fight, it became socially acceptable for women to take charge of their families and family businesses or farms and plantations. The absence of men in military service also opened up temporary jobs in factories, government agencies, and schools. Women also aided the military in socially unacceptable ways, as bawdy houses (houses of prostitution) arose in many locations.

African Americans faced much harder discrimination in the military and in the workplace. At first neither the Union nor the Confederacy were willing to use African-American soldiers. Northerners and southerners alike rejected the ideas of emancipation and enlistment. Prejudice and racism were rampant on both sides. Both sides, however, used them in non-military service from the beginning. They dug ditches, drove cattle, butchered meat, and served as

Company E, 4th U.S. Colored Infantry at Fort Lincoln, defending Washington, D.C. At the beginning of the Civil War African-American soldiers were used in noncombat roles.

cooks, launderers, teamsters, boatmen, shoemakers, and a variety of other support positions. Many Union armies employed "contraband" slaves that escaped their southern plantations when Union forces were nearby. Abolitionist leaders, like former slave Frederick Douglass, had encouraged emancipation and the enlistment of African-American soldiers from the beginning. President Lincoln, however, feared alienating the border states.

Many northerners also feared that emancipation would bring a massive migration of African Americans to their region, which would result in job competition for white laborers. Support for emancipation gradually grew among the northern public as the Civil War continued. Eventually even many southerners began to see the military necessity of using African-American troops as desperation set in.

After President Lincoln issued the Emancipation Proclamation on January 1, 1863, the end of slavery officially became a Union war aim. African-American soldiers in the Union Army fought in segregated regiments under white commanders. No African-American soldiers in the Confederate Army would see military action. Whites on both sides believed that the African-American soldiers were cowards who would flee at the first shot fired rather than stand and fight.

They received lower pay and benefits and faced discrimination from white soldiers and civilians alike. The brave fighting of such African-American units as the 54th Massachusetts, however, would force many northern citizens to reevaluate their prejudices, if only temporarily. The participation of immigrant soldiers would have a similar effect on anti-immigrant feelings.

SECTIONAL ATTITUDES DURING THE CIVIL WAR

Northern and southern attitudes toward each other, already inflamed by pre-war rhetoric, would be further inflamed by wartime propaganda. Both sides employed a variety of forms of propaganda, both official and unofficial, to recruit soldiers and influence public opinion. Posters, pamphlets, poetry, newspaper articles, and speeches given at mass meetings encouraged the public to support the war effort, while sometimes disparaging the enemy. Special articles of clothing or ornaments marked one's political persuasion.

Bond selling and recruitment drives utilized appeals made on patriotism, but also often appealed to people based on their religion, gender, race, profession, or other identifying social characteristics. Men of certain ancestry or background often formed their own units. The Union League, created in 1862, distributed political literature and recruited troops to counter the demoralizing effect of early Confederate victories.

Pre-war and wartime propaganda helped ensure that each side treated the other with fear, suspicion, and hostility. Northern recruiters republished disparaging remarks about northern men and their unwillingness to fight that had appeared in the southern press as effective recruitment tools. Southern refugees

Finding the Last Ditch.

Northern propaganda: A Union soldier hurls Jefferson Davis (dressed as a woman) who drops a bag of "stolen gold" over the edge of a cliff.

fled in terror before an advancing Union Army that they believed would burn their homes and rape their women. Northern citizens pointed to atrocities committed at prison camps such as the notorious Andersonville, in Georgia, as examples of southern brutality. The Andersonville commandant, Captain Henry Wirz, would be the only Civil War soldier executed for war crimes. Those who did not disparage the enemy faced resentment, scorn, and social ostracism. For example, many northerners disparaged northern peace Democrats, known as Copperheads, for being cowardly southern sympathizers.

The deprivations of war fueled class antagonisms. While there was a wartime boom in the north, families on the southern home front were plagued by inflation and shortages of even basic necessities, such as food, clothing, and medicines. Families were forced to make do with whatever was available. For example, corn, peanuts, and acorns served as substitutes for coffee beans. Shortages in many areas of the south became acute by the later years of the war, increasing resentment toward both northerners and those wealthy southern whites that were profiting at the expense of others' misery.

Ships that ran the northern blockade of the Confederate coastline (Blockade Runners) smuggled high-priced luxuries for wealthy clients, rather than sorely needed food and medicines. Many southern planters refused to grow desperately needed food instead of cash crops. Wealthy Florida cattle barons chose Spanish gold in Cuba over loyalty to the Confederacy. Angry women led food riots in a number of southern cities, while deserters and draft dodgers roamed the countryside raiding farms and plantations. They sometimes posed as Confederate representatives as they seized food and goods.

The period of Reconstruction, from the end of the Civil War until 1876, would embroil the United States in many controversial social, as well as political issues. Questions arose even before war's end as to how the different sections, races, and classes would exist in the newly reunited United States.

Despite political advances, the nearly four million newly freed slaves would seek to rebuild their lives in an overwhelmingly hostile social atmosphere. Racism and prejudice would serve as limits to social and political change. Few people in either the north or the south viewed African-Americans as equals, regardless of how they had felt about slavery. Emancipation did not end the deep-seated and long-held suspicions each race held against the other. Thus the political and economic changes brought about by Reconstruction often resulted in social disorder.

Social fears and attitudes carried over into colored Reconstruction society. Southern whites feared that the now freed and armed slaves would rise up against their former masters and that the victorious Union would exact harsh revenge. They honored the myth of the lost cause of the Confederacy and approached Reconstruction with a mixture of apprehension and anger. Northerners approached Reconstruction with resentment at the losses they had suffered as a result of what they termed the southern rebellion. Radical Republicans and their northern supporters sought to punish the south and make southerners admit their guilt. They wanted to aid the freed slaves and expected their gratitude in return.

Other more conservative northerners felt it best to leave southerners to govern their own fate, rather than have it thrust upon them. Many northerners also felt that aiding the freedmen would result in a mass migration to

"Slavery Is Dead?" An illustration of a slave sold as a punishment for crime, before the Emancipation Proclamation, and an African American being whipped as punishment for crime in 1866.

The Myth of the Lost Cause

In the book *Ghosts of the Confederacy*, historian Gaines M. Foster argues that the myth of the lost cause arose out of the social tensions of the post-war south and provided a way for white southerners to understand and cope with the Confederacy's defeat. Foster also argues that it fostered sectional reconciliation and supported the region's new social order. Southern social organizations such as the United Confederate Veterans and the United Daughters of the Confederacy first built the myth through writings and memorial celebrations. They celebrated Confederate battlefield glory, viewing the soldiers as martyrs to a cause honorably doomed by lesser manpower and material resources. Confederate General Robert E. Lee became an almost god-like figure, while his Union counterparts such as Ulysses S. Grant and William Tecumseh Sherman became second-rate commanders who used butchery to win.

They painted the antebellum Old South as a paradise of moonlight and magnolias where contented, well-cared for slaves worked for their benevolent masters. The attachment to the Confederate past fostered by the myth of the lost cause included attachment to symbols of the Confederacy, such as the Confederate flag and the song "Dixie."

Critics have accused perpetuators of the myth of having ulterior racist motives. Angry, emotional debates over the display of Confederate symbols have continued in modern times. The myth of the lost cause helped shape both regional and national memories of the Civil War, and has been used to tie the Confederate past to contemporary political or social aims.

An 1865 lithograph idealizing the southern cause, titled "The Last Act of the Drama of Secession."

the north, with its concomitant job competition and amalgamation of the races. Most northern states had not yet granted African-American suffrage. Widespread racism continued to permeate American society during Reconstruction. Even those southerners who accepted emancipation did not accept African Americans in any way other than as a subservient and inferior laboring class. Confederate defeat may have ended slavery, but that did not make the new freedmen political or social equals. Most southern whites felt no need to treat the freedmen any differently as they had treated them under slavery.

They feared the "Negro Rule" that they felt would be the inevitable result if they lost their social and political dominance. They were openly hostile to the public schools that sprang up throughout the region, run mostly by northern school-teachers, designed to educate the freedmen.

They believed that the freedmen's natural barbarism and incompetence made them unfit for education and unable to fulfill the duties and responsibilities of citizenship. They also feared that Yankee teachers would instill their African-American pupils with a sense of equality that would threaten white supremacy. The Ku Klux Klan (KKK) and other southern secret societies used violence and intimidation to prevent them from exercising their newly won civil rights and to ensure that they remained in their proper social position. African Americans who dared vote Republican also faced economic repercussions, as many lost their jobs or were beaten or lynched.

Class, as well as race, was also prominent in the shaping of reconstruction society in the south. While the majority of Republicans in the north came from wealthy backgrounds, the bulk of the southern Republicans were poor, illiterate African Americans. Most of the southern Republican leaders, however, were white. Both northerners and southerners widely held the patronizing attitude that newly enfranchised African Americans needed white guidance, just as African-American soldiers had needed white leadership. Most of the African Americans who held office in the reconstruction governments were literate, and many had been free professionals even before the Civil War.

INCOMPETENT AND CORRUPT

These social attitudes had a direct impact on how white southerners viewed the politics of Reconstruction. They intimidated African-American voters and ridiculed those African Americans elected to public office in the Reconstruction southern state governments, reinforcing the myth that they were incompetent and corrupt. In exchange, the Union League sent members into the south to warn the freedmen that southern white Democrats were their worst enemies. The southern white Democrats expressed resentment and open hostility toward both the northern carpetbaggers who came south during the period, and the southern scalawags who supported them.

They bitterly resented what they saw as northern intrusion into their way of life. Even white southern Republicans faced social ostracism if they openly expressed their political views. Such ostracism often served both political and social functions, effectively intimidating many into changing their political views to maintain their social standing.

White southern Democrats used social control as one tool to help them regain control of their state governments as the U.S. military was removed, a process known as redemption. The newly freed slaves (freedmen) at first felt a mixture of joy and apprehension, promise and fear. They sought to break as far away from the restrictions of slavery as possible just as white

The Ku Klux Klan

The Ku Klux Klan (KKK), also known as the Invisible Empire, was the most famous of the secret societies that sprang up throughout the south during the aftermath of the Civil War. A group of Confederate veterans founded the KKK as a social club in Pulaski, Tennessee in 1866, but it quickly spread and took on a political and social role. They created a declaration of their purpose and beliefs at a secret convention in 1867 in Nashville, Tennessee. These were based on defending white supremacy against what they believed to be the innate inferiority of African Americans, the country, and the honor of white womanhood. The latter was fueled by the stereotype of the highly sexualized African-American male who routinely sought to rape white women. Local branches became known as klaverns and a Grand Wizard oversaw a series of local officials. Former Confederate General Nathan Bedford Forrest was the first Grand Wizard. Social control was one of their key objectives.

The Klan's most well known tactics included the use of violence and intimidation against African Americans, northern carpetbaggers, and their southern supporters. They often rode on horseback at night wearing long robes and pointed hoods that concealed their identities. They would use noise, the firing of guns, the burning of homes, beatings, and lynching to intimidate. They sought to prevent African Americans from exercising their new rights, such as voting, and to ensure that they maintained their place of social inferiority and deference to whites.

Some critics dismissed the KKK as nothing but lower class whites, but wealthy and powerful men were active participants. Intimidation and fear of social stigma meant that local law enforcement and the public did not challenge their activities. Their intimidation was instrumental in aiding the white southern Democrats gain redemption of their state governments. In the early 1870s Congress passed a series of Force Bills against illegal armed organizations, and hundreds of Klansmen were arrested. The group faded at that point, but did not completely die, and would periodically experience upsurges in membership and activity starting in the 1920s.

southerners were seeking to institute a system of labor and social relations as close to slavery as possible.

Many freedmen sought to test their newfound freedom by traveling and seeking to reunite families divided under slavery, while others continued to work on farms and plantations as they had before emancipation. Most importantly, they desired economic independence, primarily through land ownership, education, and equality before the law. They were initially reluctant to enter into labor contracts and were especially adverse to communal living arrangements or anything else that seemed to close to slavery. The promise of economic freedom, social equality, and political participation, however, would prove short-lived. Freedmen quickly realized that the dream of "forty acres and a mule" would remain just a dream for most.

The freedmen's disappointment did not extend to all areas of their social lives. The end of certain social restrictions that had been in place under harsh slave codes strengthened African-American social institutions such as marriage, family, and the church. Whites now legally recognized African-American marriages and families were no longer separated through sales. Many African Americans chose to separate from white churches and create their own religious institutions.

They took pride in the fact that many women and children no longer had to work and could stay home or attend school. Disappointments included the short-lived nature of their political participation, stagnant standards of living, and growing social segregation. The introduction of sharecropping and the revolving debt system kept many among the bottom rungs of the social and economic ladder along with poor white farmers. There were also tensions within the African-American community along class and color

A racist poster attacking Radical Republicans on the issue of African-American suffrage. Part of the title includes: "Support Congress & you support the Negro. Sustain the President & you protect the white man."

lines. For example, light-skinned African Americans, known as mulattoes, often enjoyed more favorable social conditions.

Northern apathy to the freedmen's plight as time wore on combined with racism and prejudice in both sections to effectively undermine the ability of Radical Republicans to maintain control of the southern state governments. Most Reconstruction achievements, such as the passage of the Thirteenth, Fourteenth, and Fifteenth amendments to the Constitution, had owed more to anti-southern sentiments in the immediate aftermath of the war than to a true northern commitment to the freedmen's social, political, and economic rights. As the chaos of Reconstruction dragged along, northerners became tired of what was termed the "southern question" and turned their attention to growing concerns with economic troubles and the numerous scandals of the Ulysses S. Grant administration. Many historians feel that northerners simply abandoned the freedmen, creating what Eric Foner termed "America's Unfinished Revolution." Thus these same historians mark Reconstruction as the forerunner of the political and social upheaval of the Civil Rights Movement of the 1950s and 1960s, or what some historians have termed America's "Second Reconstruction."

THE WEST AND NATIVE AMERICANS

As the Civil War and Reconstruction embroiled the country in military, political, and social struggles, Americans were also continuing the process of westward expansion that would flourish in the late 19th century. The Homestead Act of 1862, which offered western land to those willing to settle there, encouraged mass migration to the west in search of new opportunities. At war's end many newly freed slaves also went west in hopes of obtaining the dream of land ownership. Miners who hoped to exploit the bounty of the west's natural resources joined the ranchers, farmers, and cowboys. Social conditions often broke down in the newly settled west and the frontier towns were noted for their lawlessness, rowdiness, and social abandon. Many easterners viewed the west as a backwards, primitive region when compared to the culture and genteel life of the eastern cities. Westerners in turn resented what they believed was the eastern treatment of the region as a colony to be exploited. Farmers especially complained of oppression from the railroads and eastern politicians. The Patrons of Husbandry (Granger Movement) formed at the end of the Reconstruction era as a social and political outlet for isolated and disgruntled farmers.

Many westerners also resented and harassed immigrants who came west, such as the Chinese who came to California for gold and jobs building the Central Pacific Railroad. Their willingness to work long hours for low wages added to the westerners' resentment. The main cultural conflict along the frontier, however, would prove to be that with Native Americans. Both easterners and westerners struggled with what was termed the "Indian problem." Politicians, Native American advocates, and the public argued over the best policies to follow. The belief in white cultural superiority and the stereotypes of Native

Carpetbaggers and Scalawags

Southern Democrats ridiculed supporters of the Republican Party in the postwar south as carpetbaggers and scalawags. They resented what they felt to be an intrusion into their war torn region by northern opportunists looking to take advantage of them, and southern traitors who supported these outsiders. They felt these Republicans were corrupt and self-serving, and resented their control of southern state governments and their aid to the freedmen. They also resented the large debts the reconstruction governments incurred as they sought to improve the region's education and social services. Carpetbaggers and scalawags joined forces with African Americans in the south, most of which were supporters of the Republican Party.

Carpetbaggers, named for a popular 19th century luggage made from old carpets, were northerners who moved south after the Civil War. The carpetbag, or suitcase, was a way of identifying outsiders. Southerners who resented the Yankee intrusion used the term in a derogatory fashion. Carpetbaggers included Union soldiers who were stationed in the south and returned to live there at war's end, government representatives such as Freedmen's Bureau workers, and schoolteachers working in the newly established public schools and schools for African Americans.

They also included northern Republican politicians and northern businessmen flush with capital, who saw opportunities in the rebuilding south. Others were idealists who hoped to protect the freedmen's rights and build a new social order in the south. Carpetbaggers had a reputation as opportunists, exploiters, and con artists seeking their fortunes by taking advantage of a devastated region, but only some actually met this description.

Scalawag was an insulting term southerners used to describe southern whites who supported the Republican Party and the carpetbaggers who came down from the north. The term's supposed origin is from the Scottish Island of Scalloway, and was used to describe small or diseased cattle. Many scalawags had been hill country farmers who opposed secession or members of the deep south planter class who were in favor of southern industrialization in the prewar period. They made up approximately 20 percent of the white electorate and helped the Republicans gain control of southern state reconstruction governments.

Although southern Democrats disparaged them as traitors who dishonored their race and regional heritage, most scalawags were more committed to the pro-business policies of the Republican Party than they were to civil rights and suffrage for the freedmen. These charges of treason created an atmosphere of social pressure that made scalawags more likely to change or hide their position. The hostile southern reactions to carpetbaggers and scalawags tied in to the fact that these groups were trying to implement unpopular social and political changes on the newly defeated region.

Americans as either bloodthirsty savages scalping their enemy, or noble savages living in harmony with nature, continued to flourish and influenced eastern and western perceptions. The Plains Indians, with their tepees and feathered headdresses, became the classic stereotype of the Native Americans of the frontier.

Many Americans felt that the cultural gulf between them and the Native Americans would best be bridged by the policy of assimilation gaining favor during this era. The government began to replace the idea of maintaining a permanent Native-American frontier with reservations as demands for western land increased. Western wars between federal troops and Native Americans occurred even as the Civil War raged elsewhere.

Advocates of assimilation sent Native-American children to boarding schools where they were not allowed to speak their language or practice their religion. These western issues would become even more prominent in the late 19th century, when Reconstruction ended and Americans turned their attention away from its problems and conflicts.

MARCELLA TREVINO

Further Readings

Berkhofer, Jr., Robert F. *The White Man's Indian*. New York: Knopf, 1978.

Foner, Eric. *Reconstruction: America's Unfinished Revolution, 1863–1877*. New York: Harper and Row, 1988.

Foster, Gaines M. *Ghosts of the Confederacy: Defeat, the Lost Cause, and the Emergence of the New South, 1865 to 1913*. New York: Oxford University Press, 1987.

Fredrickson, George M. *The Black Image in the White Mind: The Debate on Afro-American Character and Destiny, 1817–1914*. New York: Harper and Row, 1971.

Gallagher, Gary W. and Alan T. Nolan, eds. *The Myth of the Lost Cause and Civil War History*. Bloomington: Indiana University Press, 2000.

Jordan, Winthrop D. *White Over Black: American Attitudes Toward the Negro, 1550–1812*. Chapel Hill: University of North Carolina Press, 1968.

Massey, Mary E. *Bonnet Brigades: American Women and the Civil War*. New York: Knopf, 1966.

McPherson, James M. *Ordeal By Fire: The Civil War and Reconstruction*. New York: McGraw-Hill, 1992.

Simmons, James C. *Star Spangled Eden: An Exploration of the American Character in the 19th Century*. New York: Carroll & Graf, 2000.

Woodward, C. Vann, ed. *Mary Chesnut's Civil War*, New Haven, CT: Yale University Press, 1981.

Chapter 5

Cities and Urban Life

*"Kindness is a virtue neither modern
nor urban. One almost unlearns it in a city. "*
— Phyllis McGinley

DURING THE EARLY 19th century cities, defined as areas with over 2,500 residents, became part of American culture. Rural life still dominated the American landscape, but not as much as it had. Even in 1850 New York State had 873,000 in cities, but over two million in rural areas. More intense urbanization occurred during the middle third of the century. Cities leading the way in this regard were New York City (Manhattan only at the century's end), Philadelphia, Boston, Washington, D.C., and Chicago. In the south New Orleans developed the most, followed by Charleston, South Carolina; Saint Louis, Missouri; and Savannah, Georgia. In the west San Francisco had survived the gold rush of the 1850s; by 1860 it had become the 15th largest U.S. city with 56,802 residents. Transportation and innovation transformed these urban landscapes, allowing increased commerce. The railroad's expansion spurred growth inland, for example in Memphis, Chicago, and Atlanta.

By 1860 two cities exceeded half a million inhabitants, and seven others contained over 100,000. By the census of 1870 a total of 14 cities exceeded 100,000 residents, and the United States was becoming transformed from a predominantly agrarian nation to an urban industrialized nation. The transformation was not easy as new migrants to cities ended up in squalid conditions in tenements. Already in 1861 over half of New York City's population, 400,000 people, lived in tenements.

By 1860 Chicago had become the nation's major rail center, through which crops and livestock were shipped to the east coast. By 1861 the title of "Porkopolis" shifted from Cincinnati to Chicago. Saint Louis doubled in size from 1850 to 1860, with 160,773 inhabitants, many who were German and Irish immigrants. Lincoln desired that the border states of Delaware, Maryland, Kentucky, and Missouri remain with the Union, due to their resources of livestock, mining, and their urban manufacturing and shipping centers, such as Baltimore, Louisville, and St. Louis. Tensions mounted, however, and on April 19, 1861, Confederate sympathizers attacked the Sixth Massachusetts Infantry as they marched through Baltimore; four soldiers and 22 civilians died.

As the Civil War began, the geography of Washington, D.C., was markedly different than today. The Washington Monument, the construction of which had begun in 1848, appeared as a stub just west of the Smithsonian Castle. The water of Tiber Creek and the Potomac River was only a few feet away. This meant that the White House faced the Washington Canal that fed the creek. Cattle grazed near the Treasury Building, only yards away from the White House. During the summer sewage dumped into the canal, and the slaughter of the cattle used to feed the army caused President Lincoln to spend much of his time at the Soldiers' Home, about four miles away. The dome of the Capitol Building was incomplete and flat. This would be completed in 1863 as a symbolic gesture by the Union government.

"A POOR MAN'S FIGHT"

On April 16, 1862 the Confederate Congress enacted the first conscription law in American history. This included mandatory reenlistment, a requirement that allowed the Confederacy to survive. As with the later draft of the Union, exemptions inspired resentment. Since plantation owners with 20 or more slaves were exempt, the non-slave-owners complained that this was "a rich man's war, but a poor man's fight." The law also allowed substitution. Southern urban lawyers became substitute brokers, advertising in local newspapers. In April 1862 David G. Farragut, a flag officer of the Union Navy, captured New Orleans, the Confederacy's major seaport and center of antebellum cotton trade. His army counterpart, Major General Benjamin Butler managed the occupation of the city. Butler's General Order number 28 of May 15, 1862 challenged the women of New Orleans who spit upon Union troops. Butler threatened to prosecute any offender as a prostitute.

The general went on to censor "The Bonnie Blue Flag," a southern song. He arrested the song's publisher, Armand Edward Blackmar, destroyed all existing copies, and threatened to fine anyone who sang or whistled the melody. When General John Pope invaded Virginia in July 1862, he notified southern civilians that he would not tolerate interference with his army: "If a soldier or legitimate follower of the army be fired upon from any house the house shall be razed to the ground."

A Chronology of American Cities

February 1861	Confederacy formed, Montgomery, Alabama, first capital
March 4, 1861	Lincoln inaugurated in Washington, D.C.
April 12, 1861	Fort Sumter, South Carolina attacked
May 1861	Confederate capital moves to Richmond, Virginia
April 16, 1862	First Confederate States of America Conscription Act; Congress abolishes slavery in District of Columbia
April 24, 1862	New Orleans captured by Union Naval Officer David G. Farragut
April 2, 1863	Richmond Bread Riot
July 1863	Battles of Gettysburg, Pennsylvania, and Vicksburg, Mississippi
July 13–17, 1863	New York City Draft Riots
June 1864	Siege of Richmond and Petersburg, Virginia, begin
July–August 1864	Atlanta captured by General Sherman
December 1864	Savannah captured by Sherman
April 1865	Lincoln assassinated in Washington, D.C.
April 16, 1866	Race riot in Norfolk
May 1, 1866	Race riot in Memphis
July 30, 1866	New Orleans Race Riot, killing over 30, injuring 200
March 4, 1868	Impeachment trial of Andrew Johnson begins in Washington, D.C.; declared not guilty on May 16
July 8, 1871	Tweed Ring of William Tweed (1823–78) is exposed in New York City
October 8, 1871	Chicago Fire leaves 100,000 homeless
November 9, 1872	Boston's worst fire destroys 65 downtown acres
April 13, 1873	Colfax Massacre in Colfax, Louisiana
May–October 1876	Philadelphia hosts the Centennial

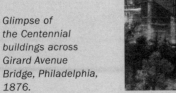

Glimpse of the Centennial buildings across Girard Avenue Bridge, Philadelphia, 1876.

THE DRAFT, TAXES, AND RIOTS

The year 1863 saw great tension. Fresh in the minds of New York residents was the battle of Antietam, in September 1862, in which more than 3,000 of the 23,000 casualties were deaths of soldiers, both Union and Confederate. President Lincoln had recently signed the Emancipation Proclamation, officially declaring all slaves free on January 1, 1863. On March 3, 1863 he signed the Enrollment Act, the nation's first military draft. On the heels of the news of the bloody battles at Vicksburg and Gettysburg, draft riots occurred in New York City and elsewhere in summer 1863. Part of the resentment derived from an exemption given to those who could hire a substitute or pay a fee of $300, several months' wages for some of the working class. One such substitute agent was John C. Briggs of Camden, New Jersey. Those seeking to avoid the draft could avoid public exposure by hiring him to negotiate personally with candidates for service.

The Union's naval blockade began by occupying strategic seaport cities: Port Royal, South Carolina (November 1861); Jacksonville, Florida (spring 1862); Savannah, Georgia (April 1862); Charleston, South Carolina (late 1863); Biloxi, Mississippi; and Norfolk, Virginia. This left Mobile, Alabama; Galveston, Texas; and Wilmington, North Carolina as ports that blockade runners entered.

Inflation in the Union during the Civil War ran about 80 percent, similar to the level experienced during both World Wars. The Union taxed liquor, tobac-

Boston in the mid-19th century. It became a major industrial center and increased its population by annexing various surrounding towns in eastern Massachusetts.

An 1860 wood engraving depicts a riot in Boston and the expulsion of African Americans and abolitionists from the Tremont Temple.

co, and yachts. Food was still used as payment in-kind for services and other products, as reflected by accounts books of a physician in Butler, Illinois.

The Confederacy fared far worse. Together with the blockade and runaway inflation, food and various dry goods became very scarce in the south. A severe shortage of coffee caused people to substitute, using boiled okra and other dried and ground food. In Raleigh, North Carolina, for instance, a pound of bacon cost $.33 in 1862; by 1865, it cost $7.50. During the same time a bushel of wheat rose from $3 to $50. By early 1863 the General Price Index for the eastern Confederacy was 762 percent of the prices at the beginning of the war. By the time of the surrender at Appomattox in April 1865, the index was 9,211 percent of 1861 prices.

By April 1863 the Confederate States of America had imposed taxes on salt, wine, tobacco, liquor, and cotton. In Richmond, as in southern cities, women and children faced starvation. Bacon rose from $.125 cents a pound in 1860 to $1.00 in 1863. Winter 1862–63 had been particularly harsh in Richmond. On March 19–20, 1863, the city received nine inches of snow. Subsequent melting made travel hazardous, both for farmers selling food and the urban residents buying it. Even President Jefferson Davis's proclamation for a national day of prayer and fasting on March 27 could not alleviate the crisis.

Bread riots had already erupted in Atlanta, Georgia (March 16, 1863); Salisbury, North Carolina (March 18); Raleigh, North Carolina; and Petersburg, Virginia. In Richmond, Virginia, on April 2, 1863, several hundred women rioted for bread. Their husbands were ironworkers at the Tredegar Iron Works, the south's largest foundry, whose wages lagged behind inflation. Rioters in Mobile,

Frederick Law Olmsted
(1822–1903)

One of the most influential people in the development of the American urban landscape was Frederick Law Olmsted. Born in Hartford, Connecticut in 1822, Olmsted grew up without a mother, who had died before he was four years of age. In 1837 he suffered sumac poisoning, which damaged his vision. He studied surveying, chemistry, and engineering. From 1855 to 1857 he was managing editor of *Putnam's Monthly Magazine*, a literary journal that printed essays by Herman Melville and Henry David Thoreau.

When the magazine ceased publication in 1857, Olmsted became the superintendent for planning of Central Park in New York City. With English-born architect Calvert Vaux (1824–95), Olmsted created Greensward, the entry chosen by New York for their park. In this plan they envisioned a day when the park would be surrounded by a large metropolitan city. Olmsted prophetically wrote "The time will come when New York will be built up." Appointed the architect-in-chief of Central Park in 1859, he supervised 4,000 construction workers.

In 1861 he was appointed to direct the U.S. Sanitary Commission, charged with providing medical care and sanitation for the Union troops. During the latter years of the Civil War he went west to California, where he managed the Mariposa Estate, a gold mining venture. He also developed a cemetery, at Mountain View in Oakland. He later developed the Oakwood Cemetery in Syracuse, New York (1874). He returned to New York in 1865, to serve as assistant editor to the newly founded magazine the *Nation*. He completed work on Central Park, and designed Prospect Park in Brooklyn (1866).

Olmsted influenced urban life in several locations and a variety of structures outside of Central Park. His creative ideas are present in the other urban parks he developed: Fort Greene Park (1868) in Brooklyn; South (now Kennedy) in Fall River, Massachusetts (1871); South Park (now Midway Plaisance) in Chicago (1871); and Morningside Park (1873) and Riverside Park (1875) in New York. Parkways designed included the Ocean Parkway in Brooklyn (1868); Humboldt and Lincoln, Buffalo, New York (1870); and Drexel Boulevard (later Martin Luther King) in Chicago (1871). Riverside Illinois was a residential community (1869). During this period he designed the campuses of Amherst College (1870–85), Yale University (1874), and Johns Hopkins University (1874–76).

He designed medical facilities, including Massachusetts General Hospital in Boston (1872), the Hartford Insane Retreat (1874) (today the Institute of Living), and the Buffalo State Hospital for the Insane (1875). He also designed the landscaping and terraces for the U.S. Capitol in 1874. In sum, Olmsted and his firm with Calvert Vaux completed 500 commissioned projects, including 100 public parks, 200 private estates, 50 residential communities, and 40 academic campuses.

Alabama carried signs reading "Bread or Blood." A Confederate soldier in North Carolina observed in February 1863 that meal cost $4 to $5 per bushel, flour was $50 to $60 per barrel, and bacon had climbed to $.75 a pound, all on his salary of $11 per month. By 1864, in Richmond, flour was $300 a barrel, and shoes cost over $100. Merchants closed their doors rather than accept Confederate paper money. Looting increased in the south, and barter became an increasingly used system for trade and commerce.

Cities also held medical facilities, used in the treatment of wounded soldiers. Louisa May Alcott served as a nurse at Union Hospital in Washington, D.C., during 1863, described in her book *Hospital Sketches* (1863). She later contracted typhoid fever from this experience. Poet Walt Whitman provided care at Armory Square Hospital, also in Washington, D.C.

An 1871 edition of a popular magazine with a feature on "New York City: improved project of a covered atmospheric elevated railway for city transit."

RECONSTRUCTION, GROWTH, INDUSTRIALIZATION, AND VIOLENCE

After the war Boston became a major industrial center, with increased usage of steam power. This influenced production of pianos, ships, candy, beer, iron, lithographs, and a thriving publishing industry. During this time Boston increased its population by annexing various surrounding towns. Its population of 141,000 in 1865 grew to 250,526 by 1870. During the 1870s Boston annexed West Roxbury, Charlestown, and Brighton, growing to 341,000 people by 1875.

In the west Chicago opened the Union Stock Yard in 1865. There were even regulations about driving animals through cities during daytime office hours. By 1868 this stockyard had space for 21,000 cattle and 75,000 hogs. Chicago meat packers began to dominate supplies due to the budding technology of refrigerated railroad cars. The G.H. Hammond Company shipped beef in ice-packed railroad cars in 1868. This was followed by Swift & Company's more efficient railcar.

The Bureau of Refugees, Freedmen, and Abandoned Lands, commonly known as the Freedmen's Bureau, assisted freed slaves, mostly from 1865 to 1869. In Washington, D.C. Josephine Griffing managed a vocational school for seamstresses. Howard University, a historically African-American university founded in 1867, was named for Union General Oliver O. Howard, commissioner of the Freedmen's Bureau. Originally founded as a university for people of all races, it also employed women as faculty and staff.

Washington, D.C., in the Eye of the Storm

In 1800 the U.S. capital was transferred from Philadelphia to the District of Columbia, and President John Adams moved into the yet unfinished White House. Its population of barely 14,000 grew to 75,000 by 1860, and 120,000 by war's end. In 1802 the city was incorporated as Washington, in honor of the nation's first president, George Washington. The city survived the Snow Riot of 1835 and the Pearl Riot of 1848, both caused by resentment toward the free African-American population. During the antebellum era, this 69 square mile city became the center of American political activity, and was surrounded by the slaveholding states of Maryland and Virginia. Construction of the Washington Monument, a 555-foot obelisk, began in 1848, discontinued due to lack of funds in 1854. However the Smithsonian Castle was completed in 1855. The dome to the U.S. Capitol was completed in 1863 as a symbol of Union solidarity.

During 1860 a statue of George Washington was placed at Washington Circle. That same year the city's first professional baseball team, the Washington Nationals, was organized. Washington, a center of war activity, converted many of its public buildings into barracks or hospitals during the Civil War. Preceding the national Emancipation Proclamation, the city had abolished slavery in 1862, resulting in the freedom of 3,100 slaves. Particularly contentious were the times immediately after the war's end, after the assassination of President Abraham Lincoln. Despite the popular vote to the contrary in December 1865, Congress passed a suffrage act in December 1866, granting all males aged 21 and older the right to vote. President Andrew Johnson vetoed the bill on January 5, 1867, but the Senate overrode this on January 7, 1867, and the House did the same on January 8. Further governmental changes occurred in 1871. Congress passed the Territorial Act, which created the District of Columbia by combining the cities of Georgetown, Washington, and the county of Washington.

In 1872 the city experienced a smallpox epidemic. In 1873 an economic panic swept the country, and the banks in Washington closed, unemployment increased, and the city became bankrupt. In 1874, with the city's debt at $19 million, Congress changed its governmental structure, terminating the Territorial Act and governing by three temporary commissioners appointed by the president. By 1876 the population had reached 140,000.

Reconstruction was often violent. There were race riots in Memphis in 1866. On July 30, 1866 a meeting of white supremacists in New Orleans triggered a police riot; 35 blacks and three whites were killed. The Ku Klux Klan practiced urban guerrilla warfare beginning in the 1870s.

IMPROVEMENTS IN TRANSPORTATION AND COMMUNICATION

Transportation during the 19th century was primarily by horse. In New York omnibuses had been introduced in 1826. Horse Railways (horse cars), were initiated in 1832. By the 1850s horse cars were dominant. Sanitation and public health was compromised as the waste left by horses released the tetanus bacteria. On July 3, 1868 the "els," or elevated steam rail began service in New York City. Railroads grew in the post-Civil War period. The New York Central Railroad built Grand Central Station in 1869. Railroad mileage in the United States had increased by ten fold to 30,000 miles in 1860. By its end, suburban neighborhoods evolved near the commuter rail stations of cities, such as New York City, Philadelphia, Boston, and Chicago.

Communication during the Civil War and Reconstruction era was primarily by the U.S. Postal Service, and by telegraph. In 1866 Western Union purchased two of its rival companies, American Telegraph and United States Telegraph. In urban areas, the intercity telegraph developed uses in journalism and commerce, these being the Associated Press and the Gold Indicator Company, respectively.

An 1866 Harper's Weekly *illustration of a riot in New Orleans over Reconstruction policies. City residents and police joined forces in the struggle.*

The Caledonian and Thistle clubs playing the Scottish national game of curling upon the frozen pond in Central Park, New York City, c.1860s.

Frederic Law Olmsted designed Central Park in 1858. By winter 1859 thousands skated on its lakes. By 1865 seven million people a year visited the park. Summertime offered concerts on Saturday afternoons. Olmsted and Vaux then designed Prospect Park in Brooklyn in 1866. In 1869 he designed Riverside, Illinois, a Chicago suburb south of Oak Park.

By 1870 Chicago had grown to house nearly 300,000 residents. Saint Louis at this time rivaled Chicago with a population of 310,874. Its East Bridge was completed in 1874, which connected Saint Louis to other midwestern cities. Also by 1870 William Marcy Tweed had become the most powerful political figure in New York City; he had built Tammany Hall, one of American's first political machines, and gained from extortion and real estate fraud. Readers of *Harper's Weekly* in 1871 saw cartoons by Thomas Nast depicting Tweed as an obese vulture to symbolize his corruption. Eventually in 1873, Tweed was indicted and jailed.

RIOTS, FIRES, AND ELECTIONS

Parades in 1870 and 1871 commemorated the Protestant victory in Ireland. In New York City on July 12, 1870, Orangemen, Irish Protestants, held one such parade; they were harassed by 200 Irish Catholics. Police intervened, but eight people were killed. The following year, New York's Police Commissioner James J. Kelso banned the parade, fearing more violence. Governor John T. Hoffman overruled him, and a parade occurred with a police escort of hundreds of officers and five National Guard regiments. In spite of this, 77 people were killed and 150 injured in the Orange Riots of 1871.

That year was a particularly dry year for northern Illinois, and especially Chicago, which had become the fourth largest city in the country. On October 8, 1871 a fire began that later consumed over three square miles of downtown Chicago and left 100,000 homeless. According to legend, the Great Chicago Fire had started when "Mrs. O'Leary's cow" kicked over a lantern. The situation was exacerbated when the water pumping station burned on October 9. By October 10 2,000 acres were burned and 18,000 buildings damaged. One consequence of the fire was that Chicago saw the construction of thousands of new buildings, many in newly-popular "Second Empire" style with high-rising and curved Mansard roofs.

Boston experienced its worst fire on November 9, 1872, which destroyed 65 acres of downtown. Damage exceeded $75 million. The fire killed 13 and left 1,000 out of work, as it burned 776 buildings. The situation was exacerbated by the Great Epizootic, a horse epidemic. In Philadelphia 2,250 horses succumbed to the epidemic in three weeks. Common until the 20th century, horses were used in transportation and to pull fire engines, and because of this illness, the fire department's services of Boston suffered. Only a few years earlier, Fire Chief John S. Damrell had requested tighter control of new construction and renovations, and the ability to enforce existing building codes, only to be denied by the city. Not only fires and riots took the lives of

An 1867 engraving shows the culture of urban life. A crowd of spectators buys tickets to a Charles Dickens reading at Steinway Hall, Boston, Massachusetts.

Exterior view of the popular Washington market in New York City in the mid-19th century. The food bazaar sold everything from cheeses and spices to rare delicacies like whale meat.

city residents, but disease took its toll as well. A smallpox epidemic infected many cities in 1872. For example, in Baltimore alone, smallpox took the lives of 2,000 residents between March 1872 and July 1873.

During early Reconstruction, from 1865 to 1873, railroad mileage in the United States doubled, and continued to increase during the next decade, connecting several cities. The pinnacle during the period was striking the Golden Spike in Promontory, Utah, on May 10, 1869, creating the first transcontinental railroad. The distance between the rails or "gauge" varied considerably from line to line, and railroad gauges were not brought to a standard until 1886.

Economic uncertainty also pervaded the society. In 1873 due to an economic panic, the banks in Washington, D.C. closed and unemployment increased. The West Coast's top resort, the Palace Hotel in San Francisco, opened in 1875 as the most luxurious hotel in America. Improvements in electric light bulbs during the mid-19th century allowed more flexibility in society. Alexander Graham Bell invented the telephone in 1876. In 1876 Philadelphia hosted the national Centennial Exposition and over 10 million people attended.

The Civil War and Reconstruction periods saw the dissolution of the United States into the Union and the Confederacy, with the slavery issue the underlying reason for the conflict. Following Lee's surrender to Grant in 1865 racial strife lingered, with riots in various cities. During this period cities grew, technology improved, and transportation allowed people to buy materials from far away areas. The landscape of America was changing and the domination by urban centers would soon become a reality.

RALPH HARTSOCK

Further Readings

Alcott, Louisa May. *Hospital Sketches*. Cambridge, MA: Belknap Press, 1960.

Bales, Richard F. *The Great Chicago Fire and the Myth of Mrs. O'Leary's Cow*. Jefferson, N.C.: McFarland, 2002.

Barth, Gunther. *City People: The Rise of Modern City Culture in Nineteenth-Century America*. New York: Oxford University Press, 1980.

Beveridge, Charles E., and Paul Rocheleau. *Frederick Law Olmsted: Designing the American Landscape*. New York: Universe Publishing, 1998.

Cimbala, Paul A., and Randall M. Miller, editors. *The Freedmen's Bureau and Reconstruction*. New York: Fordham University Press, 1999.

Goldfield, David, ed. *Encyclopedia of American Urban History*. Thousand Oaks, CA.: SAGE Publications, 2007.

Karamanski, Theodore J. *Rally 'Round the Flag: Chicago and the Civil War*. Chicago, IL: Nelson-Hall, 1993.

Kennedy, Lawrence W. *Planning the City upon a Hill: Boston Since 1630*. Amherst: University of Massachusetts Press, 1992.

Olmsted, Franklin Howard. *Creating Central Park, 1857–1861*. Baltimore, MD: Johns Hopkins University Press, 1982.

———. *The Years of Olmsted, Vaux & Company, 1865-1874*, edited by David Schuyler and Jane Turner Censer. Baltimore: Johns Hopkins University Press, 1992.

Passonneau, Joseph R. *Washington Through Two Centuries: A History in Maps and Images*. New York: Monacelli Press, 2004.

Schuyler, David. *The New Urban Landscape: The Redefinition of City in Nineteenth-Century America*. Baltimore, MD: Johns Hopkins University Press, 1986.

Simpson, Jeffrey. *Art of the Olmsted Landscape: His Works in New York City*. New York: New York City Landmarks Preservation Commission, 1981.

Volo, Dorothy Deneen, and James M. Volo. *Daily Life in Civil War America*. Westport, CT: Greenwood, 1998.

White, Dana F. *The Urbanists, 1865–1915*. New York: Greenwood, 1989.

Chapter 6

Rural Life

". . . You're thinking of leaving the homestead,
Don't be in a hurry to go.
The city has many attractions,
But think of the vices and sins . . ."
— Lyrics from the song "Don't Leave the Farm, Boys," 1871

IN 1860, THE year that Abraham Lincoln was elected president and one year before the Civil War started, America was still a rural nation. The proportion of the population that lived in the countryside or in very small towns and villages comprised 80 percent of the total. Despite large numbers of immigrants coming into the cities, the vast majority of Americans lived away from urban areas. They were engaged in agriculture as well as small-scale manufacturing, mining, logging, and fishing. In the 1870 census, five years after the conclusion of the Civil War, the population of rural America decreased to 74 percent, a still sizable majority.

There were other demographic changes in this time. These involved more than the proportion of urban to rural and reflected the significant results of the Civil War. This change was the new status of a large segment of the population from slave to free. The 1860 census had counted a total population of 31,183,744 Americans, of whom 3,950,528 were slaves. Ten years and thousands of battlefield casualties later, all of these slaves were free, although almost all who had been engaged in agricultural work before the war would be earning their living in the same way for many years after.

The division between north and south was the basis of the Civil War and also helps to delineate not only two different political and economic viewpoints, but also a difference in how land was cultivated and the texture of rural life.

A print shows the dwelling, grounds, and outbuildings, with tourists in the foreground, at George Washington's home at Mount Vernon in 1861.

There were other differences that existed, however, each of these shaping the nature of rural life with some very distinct differences even within the "north" or the "south." For example, within the north, there were very significant differences in perspective between the New England-New York region and the mid-Atlantic region of Pennsylvania and New Jersey.

What we now think of as the midwest was then considered the west. Even more rural than their eastern counterparts, people living in Wisconsin, Michigan, Minnesota, Indiana, or Illinois lived in a region where self-reliance and isolation from urban centers was even more pronounced. The manner in which they earned their livings only emphasized these differences. In the south, agriculture, politics, and society were different, based not only on the differences in climate and products created, but also the basic fact that in the south much of the labor had been performed by slaves. Even within the south, there were major differences in the terrain, climate, and the crops raised.

New England, New York, and upper Pennsylvania were predominantly haying and dairying regions, although Connecticut was known for the size and quality of its tobacco crops. Wheat was grown in the upper midwest; corn was the staple product in the lower midwest and upper southern states. Tobacco as well as corn was grown in great quantities in southern Maryland, and in Virginia, Kentucky, and Missouri. Another product of this region was human labor. Slave labor in this region was not as cost-effective as it was further south. Slaves became a commodity as they were sold to plantations in the deep south. This

Sherman's March

The song was based on a lively Irish tune that was probably familiar to many rural Americans from local dances or celebrations where local musicians played. The words, however, were new:

So we made a thoroughfare
For Freedom and her train,
Sixty miles in latitude,
Three hundred to the main.
Treason fled before us for resistance was in vain,
While we were marching through Georgia.

Union General William T. Sherman's devastating march through Georgia, from Atlanta to Savannah, was particularly brutal on rural southern residents and was etched in their memories. The letters and reports of what happened provide an excellent idea of what southern agriculture was like, with lists of the types of animals taken and slaughtered, the harvested food taken, and the houses and farm outbuildings destroyed.

A participant in that campaign of destruction wrote, "We [. . .] rioted and feasted on the country [. . .] found a rich and overflowing country filled with cattle hogs sheep & fowls, corn sweet potatoes & syrup." Sherman's soldiers on the march were not merely destroying farms, but laying waste to a rural society and economy.

A large part of the Confederacy's strength had been its predominantly rural nature, both in fact and in perception. Southerners believed that since they lived in the country, knew how to shoot and ride, and lived outside a great deal of the time, they would make better soldiers. Of more substance was the agricultural base of the south, which produced food for the use of the armies. In addition the rural economy that was based in large part on cotton sent around the world for use in making cloth would be a source of income from European manufacturers. Because the south's industrial base was limited, if one wanted to disrupt society and ruin the economy, the war had to be waged on the rural population and their capacities to support the Confederacy.

Sherman's march was not the only one. In western Virginia, the Shenandoah Valley had provided food for the Confederate Army since the beginning of the war. In 1864 General Grant ordered General Philip Sheridan to go into the Shenandoah Valley with his army and to completely destroy its stocks of food so that "a crow flying over would have to carry its own provender." Sheridan succeeded in his mission. The precedent set by Sheridan influenced the decision to employ similar tactics in Georgia. The immediate capacity of the rural south to support the war was destroyed, creating much bitterness and changing the landscape, the population, and the nature of life in the south.

human trafficking became a source of income in this region as well as helping to make labor-intensive agriculture possible. Slave labor was the main means of growing cotton from South Carolina to Texas, and growing rice in Georgia, South Carolina, and Louisiana. Additionally sugar was raised in Florida and Louisiana, relying heavily upon slavery.

Rural Americans by 1860 lived in a different world than previous generations. A fairly extensive and effective transportation network was based first on canals, and then increasingly on railroads. In 1860 there were almost 31,000 miles of railroad tracks across the nation, almost 10 times more than had existed in 1840. The expanded and increasingly dependable network allowed farmers to raise crops for market, allowing them to become a commercial entity and not just subsistence farmers. There has always been an element of rural life that was not agricultural, and this grew in size and importance from the beginning of the century to the time that the Civil War started. Many farmers along the New England coast also were fisherman. Mining, lumber, and small manufacturing facilities were opening up. Usually these were means of supplementing an agriculturally-based income, but they did grow in importance.

THE CIVIL WAR AND RURAL AMERICANS

The Civil War brought changes to all rural Americans, although the extent and precise nature of those changes varied by region.

In the north the war generally brought prosperity; there were substantial profits to be made selling to the government. Farmers sold their produce and livestock. Horses and mules were always needed by the army for transportation or for mounted combat. In addition to live animals, the Army seemed to have an unlimited demand for leather items as part of military equipment. Supplying hides as well as the tanning industry became a considerable source of income. Throughout the war there was a huge demand for beef and pork. Cincinnati, Ohio, which had been a huge pork slaughtering and packing center before the war, became even more important in answering the need to feed armies in the field.

After the increased opportunities to make money, the most significant effect in the northern states was the beginning of a labor shortage. During the war over two million men entered the Union Army; 40 percent of all men between 18 and 35 were serving at one time or another. Women and older children began to assume the tasks of operating farms. Some of the problems caused by the labor shortage were minimized by the increased use of machinery. Further, because railroad networks were becoming common in the north, transporting produce and livestock was easier than it would have been in the past. Despite the difficulties that arose because so many men were absent, agricultural production increased. Annual exports of wheat in the United States had been 8,000,000 bushels a year 1856–60. That amount grew to 27 million bushels a year from 1861–65.

In addition to creating the need for women to work on the farms in greater capacities than before, there were opportunities for income that had not existed before, directly resulting from the war. Many rural women, especially the wives and widows of soldiers, had preference in sewing clothing for the Army. Material cut according to pattern for coats, pants, and shirts would be sent to be sewn together and then sent back to the arsenal. This kind of supplementary work had been done for a several years before the war, but for a four-year period would become an important source of income for many rural women.

There were other changes in the north that affected northern rural America. One of the most important of these was the passage of the Homestead Act, which was supposed to solve the problem of making land available to Americans.

In the south there were also changes, but these were more adverse and of such severity that they would be felt for generations, and still affect the south today. First like the northern rural regions, the war created some severe manpower shortages. In fact this situation was worse than in the north. One estimate claims that 80 percent of the white Confederate male population was away at war. There were exemptions for men heading farms that had a large slave population in order to effectively manage the resources, as well as to discourage a recurrence of the slave rebellions of the 1820s and 1830s. As time went on and the Union armies advanced through the south, a growing problem was the number of slaves

By the 1860s, many prosperous farmers lived in comfortable farmhouses like this one fronting on the Delaware River at Church Landing, New Jersey.

The Homestead Act of 1862

One of the great ironies of American history in the 19th century was the difficulty and expense of obtaining land, even though there were thousands of square miles of open, unclaimed land. It was a problem that had existed ever since the early days of the republic.

Early programs had allowed farmers to acquire land, but they had to buy it in lots of at least 640 acres and had to pay $2 an acre. The combination of minimum purchase size and cash payment (when farmers had no ready cash available) was more than many farmers could afford. To remedy the situation, in the years leading up to the Civil War, Congress made adjustments by decreasing the minimum size of the lot to be purchased and the price per acre.

In May 1862 Congress passed the Homestead Act. The act, which went into effect on January 1, 1863, allowed a man or woman (who was an American citizen or had declared the intent to become one) to take title to 160 acres for a $10 fee. The act disqualified former Confederates, but this part of the act was repealed in 1866.

Improvements had to be made on the land, including building a house, and the farmer had to have lived on it for five years, and then title would pass to the individual. If the applicant were a soldier, he only had to occupy the land for three years. Optionally, the farmer could simply pay $1.25 an acre to take the title. The Homestead Act was significant in that it made it possible for individuals to own land at a very minimal cost.

It was not a happy ending for all involved, however. Improving the land and being able to live off it were not easy. Life in the west where these grants were given was difficult. Even with no cost other than the application, the labor used to improve the land did not always succeed. The land was not always good and the climate was often harsh. Even a lot the size of 160 acres under these circumstances would not be enough to maintain a family. At the same time, it was physically impossible to work a larger area of land, although there was an attempt to counteract the problem by doubling grant sizes. The difficulty is underlined by the fact that nearly all of those taking advantage of the grants were farmers. It was not a matter of amateurs making mistakes. The impetus given to migration by the act did a great deal to begin populating the west. Approximately 400,000 families would eventually settle in western territories, encouraged by the Homestead Act.

The Homestead Act was not the only government legislation that affected rural Americans. During the Civil War the government instituted the Department of Agriculture, which would over the years provide assistance in raising the effectiveness of farms. Additionally the Morrill Land Grant College Act was passed in the same year as the Homestead Act. The Land Grant Act gave each state 30,000 acres of federal land to be sold or otherwise used with the proceeds going to support at least one agricultural college in the state.

An officer returns to his family at the end of the Civil War. Millions who had served would return to their homes in rural America, with great differences between rural north and south.

that simply left the plantations, decreasing the available workforce. Despite the numbers of plantations, their productivity, and effect on the south's economy, most southern farms were small and had very few slaves, or none at all. In those cases the farms were run by the wives and children left behind. Unlike the north, there was very little machinery in the south as the crops raised there were so different, so mechanization did not mitigate the manpower shortage.

Southerners were encouraged to switch their planting from cotton to food in order to better sustain the war effort. But even this did not guarantee an income as the Confederate currency became inflated to the point that it became worthless, reducing the rural economy almost completely to a system of bartering.

The difficult situation of farms left behind would become more acute as the war progressed. While most northern farms, except some in Pennsylvania, Maryland, or Kentucky, were quite safely removed from the war, the rural south was often a battleground. Worse, as the war progressed, it was the target of destructive raids by Union commanders such as Sheridan, Grierson, and Sherman. The effect of hearing that their homes were being destroyed, their livestock driven off, and their crops destroyed, caused many rural southerners to leave the army as the war drew to a close.

Upon their return southern soldiers found that in many cases, their farms with equipment, livestock, and therefore, their livelihoods, had been destroyed. Further, in those cases in which plantations had been dependent on slaves, the owners who resumed agriculture found themselves dealing with a free population that demanded payment for their labor instead of a passive labor force. The transition to free labor with all of its political and social implications would be a major part of history in the south after the war, in the Reconstruction period.

Throughout the Civil War the country continued to expand westward, pushed by the continued influx of immigrants. The scale of immigration was so great that by 1880, the census would indicate that between one third and one half of the rural population in the upper midwest of Minnesota, Wisconsin, Iowa, Kansas, and Illinois were foreign immigrants. In this region, the increased white population created tensions with Native Americans, which would affect rural Americans in this region in the upper Midwest in 1862, and in Texas and the southwest in the years following the Civil War.

With the close of the war, the millions of men who had served would return to their homes; but depending on whether they were from the north or the former Confederacy, they would be returning to two very different versions of rural America.

RECONSTRUCTION

There is a painting by the great American painter Winslow Homer of a man cutting hay with a scythe. We do not see his face, but he is mowing and in a pile behind him is a stack of clothing he has temporarily discarded. Among the items is his Union blue sack coat. Homer portrayed a farmer who had gone to war and was now finally safe working his farm again. In a way, the picture gives a view of life in northern rural America in the immediate aftermath of the war.

For those who returned to their homes in the southern states, however, it was very different. What they encountered was Reconstruction; between that and the direct effects of the Civil War, the rural south was changed completely. What historians refer to as Reconstruction was the program of military occupation and civil rule that would ensure that the aims of the Civil War were enforced and that southern institutions on all levels were changed before states would be allowed to rejoin the Union. As Congress took over the process of Reconstruction, the former Confederate states would not have their representatives and senators seated in Congress until they ratified the Thirteenth, Fourteenth, and Fifteenth Amendments to the Constitution freeing slaves and guaranteeing the right to vote regardless of previous condition of slavery. Furthermore the states had to repudiate the war debt and prohibit former Confederate officials from serving in office.

The 11 states of the Confederacy nominally conformed to these requirements, and over the decade following the Civil War, their representatives were readmitted to Congress and federal troops were withdrawn. Very

Immigrants and Native Americans, 1862 and Beyond

Until the time of the Civil War relations between white settlers and Native Americans had been an important issue. In rural America, settlers living by themselves or in small settlements had to come to terms with Native Americans. For the most part, it had been an unhappy story, with the original settlers driven out or killed. By the Civil War, the threat of warfare between the new arrivals and Native Americans east of the Mississippi no longer existed. In the lands west of that river, however, farmers and settlers were confronting new difficulties with Native Americans living on the land where whites wanted to settle.

In Minnesota and the Dakota Territory, tensions built up between the new immigrants and members of the Dakota Tribe. In August 1862 fighting finally broke out after five Native Americans killed four whites in Minnesota. The next day another band of Native Americans attacked another group of settlers, killing several of them and destroying several buildings. On the next day the Minnesota militia was sent to suppress the uprising and was severely beaten. The reaction was quick and dramatic: there are photographs that survive showing the settlers sitting near their wagons, seemingly in a state of exhaustion as they briefly stopped on their way attempting to leave their communities and reach safety.

The fighting continued into the fall when federal troops, under the command of General John Pope (who had been defeated earlier in the year at the Second Battle of Manassas), fought the final battle in October. Between 300 and 800 settlers were killed. The number of Native Americans killed in this brief war is unknown. Eventually, with peace restored to western Minnesota and the Dakota Territory, the rural population returned and resumed their lives.

The fighting of 1862 was followed six years later by an unusual war between the U.S. government and the Dakota Indians. Known as Red Cloud's War, it was fought to keep settlers with interest in mining from taking over Dakota land, in what the United States designated as the Wyoming and Montana territories. The war was unusual because the Native Americans actually won, and got treaty concessions from the government guaranteeing the integrity of the Native-American territory. In the end, the treaty was not honored and the lands held sacred to the Dakotas were exploited by gold mining interests.

To the south, in Texas, friction between ranchers and farmers in Texas and Comanches following the Civil War slowed settlement. U.S. troops under the command of General Philip Sheridan, who had destroyed the farms of the Shenandoah Valley in 1864, campaigned 1868–75 before finally subduing the Comanches, opening the way for further settlement.

An illustration of the arrival of freedmen and their families in Baltimore, Maryland, 1865. Paying newly-freed African Americans was a new concept and finding a willing work force was difficult.

rapidly, however, former Confederates and supporters in the Democratic party seized power, through either legitimate elections or through the use of terror tactics and outright coups. By 1877 every state of the former Confederacy was dominated by a regime that regularly disfranchised African-American voters and denied the former slaves other civil rights.

The most obvious change to the rural south was that slavery no longer existed. The cotton plantations that had been the economic backbone of the south now had to find a new labor source. Actually they used the same labor source as before the war, but had to establish new rules for how it was done. Paying newly-freed African-Americans was a new concept, and finding a willing work force could sometimes be difficult under the new conditions. There had been the hope on the part of some planters that they could hire white field hands. This idea did not work out almost from the beginning, as the whites would not work for what they considered substandard wages. Further, as African Americans began to work in the fields, many of the whites would not work with them.

The African Americans, despite their new freedom, were at a disadvantage politically and economically. They were free, but they still had to eat. With only limited skills and limited capital, and for the most part, denied access to landholding, their range of options was very narrow. What eventually happened was an economic system that ensured that planters could have their land worked cheaply, while limiting the mobility of African Americans. A variety of systems of labor that approached the nature of slavery were adopted, including tenant farming, arrest for vagrancy and then hiring out the newly arrested workers to pay off fines, and various systems of debt peonage. One system was called sharecropping. Sharecropping came into existence very soon after the end of the war, and by the mid-1870s was already well-established. Under the terms an individual would work for a landowner. He would pay in the crops he raised a certain percent (a "share"). The percent varied due to circumstances. In many instances the land owner would allow the sharecropper to live on the land, requiring a certain percent as rent for living quarters. If the landowner supplied the seeds and equipment (often referred to as "furnish"), it would require a certain percent.

If the land owner provided other goods, much like the company store of mines and factories, the purchase would require payment when the crop was finally harvested. Finally all of these listed items were in addition to the basic rent for working the land that the sharecropper paid the landowner. The landowner also determined what the crop would be, usually cotton in the deep south.

Politically, the south had reverted back to the old control it had known in the years before the war. All of the states of the old Confederacy succeeded in negating the results of Reconstruction where the north had attempted to guarantee economic and political rights to African Americans. There was no slavery, but the keeping of people in debt to ensure their continued cheap labor on the land, assisted by the intervention of the Ku Klux Klan to keep order among the workers by terrorizing them, ensured that rural life for most African Americans would be at subsistence level, at best.

DAILY LIFE AND WORK

While the years 1860 to 1876 were marked by extraordinary changes, there was still a great deal of continuity with what had gone on before and many changes were the logical result of trends from before the beginning of the Civil War.

Mechanization had existed in one form or another since the 1790s when the cotton gin was invented. The appearance of the reaper in the 1830s and its constant improvement, as well as the introduction of other machinery meant that they were all in place in 1860. What was a key element in their dramatically increased importance was the lack of men to work on farms coupled with the need for more produce. By 1864 farmers in the north purchased 70,000 reapers and mowers, more than twice that bought two years before in an attempt to keep up with increased demand, while having a diminished workforce.

Another example of a trend that continued and grew dramatically was the use of science and practical instruction and literature. Scientific farming and the study of agricultural literature had been an important part of rural life dating back to the 18th century. The practice continued as books on almost every aspect of agriculture continued to be published in increasing numbers. To reinforce this self-study, the U.S. government began efforts that would lead to agricultural colleges in every state, endowed by public land given by the federal Government. Rural populations had always earned their livelihood primarily, but not exclusively, by farming, but non-agricultural pursuits grew during the years during and after the War. Depending on the season and opportunities; mining, logging, iron smelting, and light manufacture were all conducted. Completed goods such as wagons, barrels, carriages, leather goods (such as saddles and harnesses), and shoes were all produced by rural Americans.

There were some changes due to technological or other factors. Making butter and cheese had been an important industry in New England and especially New York. Urban populations began demanding more milk, so dairying expanded at the same time and changed to supplying milk rather than a milk product. Refrigeration had not yet been adopted on a large scale, but as it did, it sustained the demand for cold milk. The importance of sheep farming for wool in New England was generally falling out of favor for commercial reasons, and the number of sheep diminished while the population of beef and milk cattle grew.

Another change was the increased use of canning, which provided a new market for farmers. In Maine, for example, farmers grew sweet corn for a much larger market because it could be canned. The same situation applied to blueberries, also from Maine, or cranberries from Massachusetts. In another development, farmers began to build and use large greenhouses to grow food crops.

Social life in rural areas continued with many of the same patterns established before the war. Even though secular fraternal and political organizations would come into being, the church was very important. The centrality of the church was well-established, but new congregations populated by immigrants also combined a spiritual and social function. That was also true in the south after the Civil War. There, churches in rural communities became the centers for relief of destitute families or returning crippled soldiers.

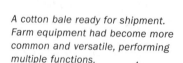

A cotton bale ready for shipment. Farm equipment had become more common and versatile, performing multiple functions.

One significant way in which life continued as it had before were the economic difficulties experienced by farmers and the rest of the rural population. Although the years of the Civil War were good for northern farmers, financial difficulties in the 1870s only showed how vulnerable farmers were and underlined

Rural Reconstruction: A sketch of workers rebuilding the railroad bridge over the Rappahannock River in the 1860s. Rural life benefited from improvements in transportation technology.

some of their longstanding concerns such as the availability of credit and the volatility of markets.

With increased production, prices of commodities such as cotton, wheat, and corn went into a long-term decline. As a consequence farmers were faced with a price-and-credit squeeze. Land and houses bought at 1865 prices required regular fixed mortgage payments based on the original price. Yet revenues from crops began to fall as prices dropped. As agriculture and transportation modernized, farmers were caught in a long-term economic squeeze that would continue until the end of the century. These problems affected the north and west. The effects were even more dire in the south, which had its rural base destroyed and would not recover for many years.

CHANGES IN RURAL LIFE

The 1880 census, taken four years after the nation's 1876 centennial celebrations, showed a nation that was still mostly rural (72 percent). The total population now numbered 49,371,340 and the status of the nation's 6,518,372 African Americans was dramatically different; they were now free. Freedom did not guarantee a better living and the promise of "forty acres and a mule," implying real ownership, did not come true. The African-American population was still rural and still bound to the land in a subsistence mode that technically was not slavery, but in reality was not far removed. The sharecropping system that came into being after the Civil War would persist for generations. From political and social perspectives at the end of this period, in 1876 African Americans were reaching the point where the newly-won recognition of their rights was already beginning to fade, and they were systematically disenfranchised, segregated, and relegated to an exploited position at the bottom of the economic scale.

In 1876, as the celebrations commemorated the 100th anniversary of the Declaration of Independence, many trends were in place that would continue to affect rural life and profoundly change it.

One of these was the increasing appearance and implementation of technology. Farm equipment had become more common and versatile; it could perform multiple functions such as harvesting and threshing, or harvesting and binding. In places such as New England, which had seen the heavy increase of machinery to make up for the loss of manpower during the war, the trend would accelerate.

Transportation technology grew and become more capable and complex, along with the increased amount of railroad mileage. A direct effect of the war had been the construction, maintenance, and operation of railroads. The lesson learned in operating railroads would translate directly into the intercontinental railroad system that would recruit, transport, and settle immigrants all along the railroad lines, a trend that would accelerate in the years following 1876. Railroads had been given land grants along the right of way by the government, which were then parceled out to farmers who would become the railroad's customers for transporting their produce to centers such as Kansas City and Chicago.

STURDY YEOMAN FARMERS

The nature of rural life changed in part because the war had made opportunities for making money by supplying goods for the government to use in the war. One historian has commented on how farmers in 1876 had retained the characteristics of the sturdy yeoman farmers that Thomas Jefferson had seen as the model for America. At the same time, they had become more commercially-minded, and had gained a financial presence along the model of Jefferson's rival, Alexander Hamilton.

In simpler terms, the war had brought the opportunity to make money by commerce which, combined with the increasing manufacturing capability of the nation, made it possible to buy goods and affect the way people lived in ways that would not have been imagined a generation before. Money, which had always been scarce for farmers who often had to live on credit between harvests, was more plentiful, but farmers were still at the mercy of the elements and market forces that they could barely understand, much less control. With the long-term decline in commodity prices, the benefits of improved transportation and technology only seemed to worsen their situation in some regards, as increased crops further depressed prices.

Farmers and other rural Americans began to develop a political consciousness in this period that would grow into the Populist movement of the 1880s and 1890s. Their protests tended to focus on the money and banking system and on the railroads, both of which seemed to benefit from their own distress. Rural

Americans began to organize. In 1867 the National Grange, a fraternal order based on agriculture, was formed. By the mid-1870s the organization's membership numbered nearly a million, especially in the northeast and midwestern rural areas. It combined social aspects with a political and economic program that sought to protect the rights and well-being of farmers from "middle men" who bought goods from farmers and sold them and the railroads, which were seen as a monopoly that hurt the farmer's well-being.

ROBERT N. STACY

Further Readings

Ambrose, Stephen E. *Nothing Like It in the World: The Men Who Built the Transcontinental Railroad, 1863–1869*. New York: Simon & Schuster, 2000.

Barron, Hal S. *Mixed Harvest: The Second Great Transformation in the Rural North, 1870–1930*. Chapel Hill: University of North Carolina Press, 1997.

Campbell, Jacqueline Glass. *When Sherman Marched North from the Sea: Resistance on the Confederate Home Front*. Chapel Hill: University of North Carolina Press, 2003.

Cashin, Joan, ed. *The War Was You and Me: Civilians in the American Civil War*. Princeton, NJ: Princeton University Press, 2002.

Cross, Coy F. *Go West, Young Man!: Horace Greeley's Vision for America*. Albuquerque: University of New Mexico Press, 1995.

Danbom, David B. *Born in the Country: A History of Rural America*. Baltimore, MD: Johns Hopkins University Press, 2006.

Fitzgerald, Michael W. *Splendid Failure: Postwar Reconstruction in the American South*. Chicago, IL: Ivan R. Dee, 2007.

Foner, Eric. *Forever Free: The Story of Emancipation and Reconstruction*. NY: Knopf, 2005.

Gates, Paul Wallace. *Agriculture and the Civil War*. New York: Knopf, 1965.

Hayter, Earl W. *The Troubled Farmer, 1850–1900; Rural Adjustment to Industrialism*. Dekalb, IL: Northern Illinois University Press, 1968.

Hurt, R. Douglas. *American Agriculture: A Brief History*. Ames: Iowa State University, 1994.

McMurry, Sally Ann. *Transforming Rural Life: Dairying Families and Agricultural Change, 1820–1885*. Baltimore, MD: Johns Hopkins University Press, 1995.

Patchan, Scott C. *Shenandoah Summer: The 1864 Valley Campaign*. Lincoln: University of Nebraska Press, 2007.

Russell, Howard S. *A Long, Deep Furrow: Three Centuries of Farming in New England*. Hanover, NH: University Press of New England, 1976.

Sutherland, Daniel E. *The Expansion of Everyday Life, 1860–1876*, New York: Harper & Row, 1989.

Chapter 7

Religion

*"We see God face to face every hour,
and know the savor of Nature."*
— Ralph Waldo Emerson

BY THE TIME of the Civil War, the Evangelical churches and denominations became more mainstream and less emotional in worship style. The decade before the war marked the end of Protestant dominance in America. The largest Evangelical fellowships were the Methodists, Baptists, and Presbyterians. After the war, Catholicism, due to the large influx of immigrants from southern and eastern Europe, would surpass the three largest Protestant groups and forever change the landscape of American life. A symbol of coming change was sophistication in rural areas and towns of the church buildings. Gone were the days when rural and village churches consisted of dilapidated buildings, or edifices previously used for other purposes. The churches across both the north and the south took on the dignified look of those in New England. The south, long a hedonistic frontier for much of the first half the century, became enamored with revivals and camp meetings during the Second Great Awakening. Evangelical religion and conservative orthodoxy surged throughout the region. Worship in the early part of the century was not reverent, organized, or worshipful. Noise, walking out during the service, and distractions abounded, making it very difficult for pastors to be heard, but by mid-century the free style worship predominated, and hymnbooks and other changes improved the tenor of the services.

Rural churches did not demand polished expository or exegetical sermons, because the members often lacked education to appreciate what the educat-

A drawing shows Union soldiers standing guard and sitting near St. Peter's Church in Virginia, with guns leaning against the wall and arranged as tripods during the American Civil War.

ed cleric had to say. In that context deep theological discourses did not find favor. The Methodist ministers maintained the itinerant system of traveling parsons, which helped alleviate the tedium of rural life for both the preachers and the parishioners. The Baptists, mostly farmer-preachers, adopted a rotation or "once-a-month" system in which a pastor would make rounds between established churches on a monthly cycle. The Baptist system made for shallow content in sermonizing, because it made preaching a series of sermons nearly impossible. By the 1850s a growing dissatisfaction grew over the system, and churches began to seek a more stable pastoral ministry. The Presbyterians, the descendent church of the original Puritans, was the more intellectual and educated of the three denominations, but did not succeed in the rural south. Their ministry settled in the cities and towns, although new pastors would serve in the outlying areas on a temporary basis. Most educated pastors preferred the cities and towns because of the intellectual and cultural opportunities they afforded, but a great many pastors preferred the rural churches because they afforded a great deal more time to study.

With a better-educated clergy, the content of sermons did improve, and the era's preachers expounded in a flowery oratory that gained in popularity among the clergy. However some parishioners did not approve. Church members often complained that the pastor was a bidder of the crowd, rather than a breaker of the bread of life. Many pastors treated the gospel ministry as a secular profession rather than a divine calling. Nevertheless a shortage of pastors remained throughout the period leading up to the war.

United States Christian Commission

The United States Christian Commission (USCC), organized in the autumn of 1861 at Philadelphia for the pastoral care of Union soldiers, elected George H. Stuart, a Presbyterian layman as president. Official enlistment required membership in an Evangelical church and the endorsement of a clergyman. Armed with a memo book, instructions, reading material, and other supplies, the delegates labored for an average of 38 days. The delegates did not interfere with military authorities, and received threats of dismissal for either personal or private misbehavior. They reported to an agent in charge of a geographical area, traveled to the assigned unit, and worked until relieved by another delegate.

As the war dragged on and the size of the armies grew, the Christian commission increased in size to keep pace with demand. Branch commissions served as the public relations and fund-raising arm of the Christian Commission. Though the branch commissions maintained their autonomy, they labored under the authority of the national group and within its organizational structure. In addition the women's auxiliary or Ladies' Commissions raised funds for the war effort, but their support came in more direct ways such as preparing clothes, food, and gifts for distribution by the delegates. According to the final report of the Christian Commission in issued in 1866, the ladies' commissions numbered 266, located in 17 states of the Union, and raised over $200,000 in funds.

The tasks of delegates were two-fold: to aid the chaplains in their direct pastoral and Evangelical work, and to perform acts of mercy in Christ's name. Delegates acted as nurses, social workers, librarians, postmen, worship leaders, lay-ministers, and directors of burial details. By the end of hostilities more than 5,000 delegates—all of them unpaid volunteers—provided selfless service in the Union armies camps. By the war's end, the commission's leaders had spent over $6 million, including over $2 million in cash and over $3 million in supplies, raised from a myriad of sources.

In units without chaplains, the delegates served as quasi-military pastors. In units served by chaplains, the commission kept the military clerics supplied in tracts and Bibles. The delegates succeeded in distributing millions of Bibles, hymnals, and tracts. In addition they preached over 58,000 sermons, led 77,000 prayer meetings, and wrote over 92,000 letters on behalf of the soldiers.

Worship evolved into an organized pattern, but a free worship style dominated the Methodist and Baptist churches. An official order of worship often did not exist; therefore preaching, rather than liturgy, dominated the service. Further-

General Oliver Otis Howard
1830–1909

Born in Leeds, Maine, the son of farmers, Howard received his higher education at West Point. After a stint in the regular army he returned to West Point in 1857 to teach mathematics, where he experienced the Evangelical religious conversion that earned him the sobriquet "the Christian Soldier." Almost immediately after his conversion, Howard began taking on the responsibilities common to Evangelicals—teaching Sabbath schools, delivering devotionals to his men and leading in prayers, and studying Hebrew under the tutelage of a local Episcopal rector. For a short time he toyed with the idea of entering the gospel ministry, but his wife Lizzie opposed the idea. Despite his sincere piety in his diary he noted his tendency toward inordinate pride, a fault he battled all his life, and often, without success. He opposed alcohol usage, profanity, and gambling, which caused some profane Union generals to dislike him and consider him effete.

Howard began the war as a first lieutenant, and ended the conflict as a brigadier general. Tragically, in the spring of 1862, Howard lost his lower right arm at Fair Oaks, for which a grateful nation awarded the aging general a belated Medal of Honor in 1893. As commander of the Federal XI Corps, on May 2, 1863, at Chancellorsville he suffered a humiliating defeat at the hands of Thomas Jonathan "Stonewall" Jackson. Jackson was a rival for whom Howard had the greatest admiration because of the Confederate commander's legendary piety.

At the war's end, President Andrew Johnson appointed Howard to leadership of the newly chartered Bureau of Refugees, Freedmen, and Abandoned Lands, known as the Freedmen's Bureau, to govern "all subjects relating to refugees and freedmen from rebel states." In addition Howard helped establish the university in the nation's capital that bears his name—which though predominately an African-American institution, was integrated at its founding.

Howard labored to raise funds for the establishment of a new institution of higher education in the mountains of East Tennessee, Lincoln Memorial University in Harrogate, Tennessee, which received its charter in 1897. He maintained exceptional humanitarian concern for the newly-freed slaves and others in need of educational opportunity. Though he retired from the army in 1894, he served with the Army and Navy Christian Commission during the Spanish-American War and continued to write about various subjects. He remained active until his death of an apparent heart attack on October, 26, 1909, at his home in Vermont.

more pastors and congregants prayed aloud without writing their petitions, and the emotional singing was performed with great zeal. The liturgical churches, however, maintained the formality of their ancestors. However the churches in antebellum America had greater problems than division over worship style.

THE CHURCHES AND THE COMING OF THE WAR

Slavery had long troubled the conscience of the nation. The framers and founders permitted the ownership of human chattel in the organizing document of the republic, despite the statement in the Declaration of Independence "that all men are created equal and endowed by their Creator with certain unalienable rights: among these are life, liberty, and the pursuit of happiness."

The practice of slavery seemed to fly in the face of the nation's highest ideals. Though from the beginning groups such as the Quakers protested the practice, many Americans did not give it a thought. It was not until after 1830 that the issue became inflammatory and dangerously controversial.

The south, sensitive to the northern clergy and abolitionists calling them "sinners" for owning slaves, began to resort in further justification of the practice on biblical grounds. Slavery always existed, they argued; the Hebrews suffered through it and they too owned slaves. Christ never mentioned the institution at all, and the apostle Paul actually told a slave to return to his master, which was the entire theme of the book of Philemon. Paul told slaves to obey their masters, as it was the Lord's will.

If southerners were heathens, how does one explain slavery in the Bible, in history, and as practiced by the founders of the Republic? These and other religious arguments were offered by both preachers and secular leaders in defense of slavery.

The north declared that just because slavery existed it does not mean that scripture condones, justifies, or commands the practice. In the Bible, references to slavery, especially in the Epistles, had to do with one's sins and being punished for them. In addition, it is against human nature for one to be a slave or to be satisfied with slavery as a lifelong condition. Abolitionists thundered against fornication with slaves, whippings, and the infamous auction block, which was notorious for dividing parents from their children. The northern anti-slavery activists argued that the south defended

19th-century church pews. The churches in antebellum America had greater problems than division over worship style.

the letter of the law, and not the spirit of divine law. The Presbyterians divided between north and south over other issues in 1837, but slavery was no doubt in the background. The Methodist divided over the issue in 1844, and the Baptists did so in 1845. Politicians became fearful. If the churches could not stay united over a political issue, how could the Republic stand? If those who preached brotherhood, forgiveness, and forbearance could not unite for peace and unity, the nation would surely divide. It is not surprising that both secular and church historians view the war as reflecting a theological crisis. Both sides claimed that God was on their side, and that the side that won received God's blessing and the side that lost received judgment. The war did severe damage to religion in the nation, because when the guns went silent, the victors gloated and grew complacent, and the losers refused to accept the outcome as anything more than chastisement to purify them and prepare them for greater days ahead.

CLERICS AND THE SECTIONAL ANTAGONISM

The northern and southern pastors used inflammatory rhetoric to demonize their opponents, and an example of the language from the northern pulpit comes from Theodore Parker. In 1848, 13 years before the cannons roared and the year the Mexican War ended, and only four years after the division of the Methodists and three years after the Baptist schism, Parker thundered from his pulpit:

Who fought the Revolution? Why the North, furnishing the money and the men . . . Who pays the national taxes? The North, for the slaves pay but a trifle . . . Who writes the books—the histories, poems, philosophies, works of science, even the sermons and commentaries on the Bible? Still the North. Who builds the churches, founds the Bible societies, missionary societies, the thousand-and-one institutions for making men better and better off? Why the North.

Then Parker refers to the south as the dominant, but negative force on the nation:

Well says the calculator, but who has the offices of the nation? The South. Who has filled the presidential chair forty-eight years of the last sixty? The South . . . .Who made the Mexican War? The South . . . But what is the South most noted for abroad? For her three million slaves; and the North for her wealth, freedom and education!

During the war Parker, Henry Ward Beecher, and other northern clergyman continued with such language. The south defended its peculiar institution and viewed itself as the New Israel. Some of the region's most notable clerics defended slavery, secession, and war. James Henry Thornwell of South Carolina, a scant two short years after Parker's diatribe, preached in direct opposition to his northern counterpart, by accusing those opponents of the

General "Stonewall" Jackson
(1824–63)

Born in poverty and orphaned, young Tom Jackson won an appointment to the U.S. Military Academy at West Point, New York, in 1842. Though a poor student, he pored over his books and literally memorized huge portions of his textbooks, and graduated from the academy in 1846 ranked 17th in a class of 59 cadets.

After graduation he served with distinction in the Mexican War and won appointment as an instructor at the Virginia Military Institute (VMI), where he stayed until the outbreak of hostilities in the spring of 1861. When Virginia voted to secede, he cast his lot with the new Confederate States of America and received a commission as major in the Army. At the Battle of First Manassas in early 1861 he earned the nickname "Stonewall" when fellow Confederate General Barnard E. Bee spotted him on the field and exclaimed, "Look, men! There stands Jackson like a stone wall! Rally behind the Virginians!"

The sobriquet fit him well. Jackson began his religious pilgrimage during the Mexican War with a study of Catholicism, received baptism as an Episcopalian, and finally settled on the stern Calvinism as practiced by Presbyterians. He embraced Christianity thoroughly, and practiced a devout Evangelical faith for the remainder of his life.

His religious practice seemed fanatical to his secular contemporaries, but none doubted his sincerity. While at VMI he started a Sunday school class for the slaves and gave the task his utmost effort. Others had failed, but soon Jackson had over 100 students. They adored Jackson, and he loved them in return.

Because his faith informed every aspect of his life, Jackson frequently evoked the name of Providence in his reports. The following report is a fitting example of his faith—even in military affairs: "For these great and signal victories our sincere and humble thanks are due to Almighty God. We should in all things acknowledge Him who reigns in heaven and rules among the armies of men [. . .]. We can but express the grateful conviction of our mind that God was with us and gave us the victory, and unto His holy name be the praise."

Severely wounded by Confederates when they mistook him for the enemy at Chancellorsville on May 2, 1863, Jackson lost his left arm and he contracted pneumonia within a week. After learning that he would not live the remainder of the day, Jackson stoically replied, "It is the Lord's day. My wish is fulfilled. I have always wanted to die on Sunday." At 3:15 in the afternoon of May 10 at Guiney Station, the mighty Stonewall uttered his last words, "Let us cross over the river, and rest under the shade of the trees."

region's peculiar institution of indulging in Leftist radicalism. On May 26, 1850, he asserted:

Truth must triumph. God will vindicate the appointments of His Providence— and if your institutions are indeed consistent with righteousness and truth, we can calmly afford to bide our time ... The parties in this conflict are not merely abolitionists, and slaveholders—they are atheists, socialists, communists, red republicans, jacobins, on the one side, and friends of order and regulated freedom on the other. In one word, the world is a battleground—Christianity and Atheism the combatants; and the progress of humanity is at stake.

After reading the rhetoric of two of the nation's most eloquent preachers, it is not surprising that war came a little more than a decade later. Shortly before his death in 1850, John C. Calhoun of South Carolina, frail, ill, and unable to read his final speech on the Senate floor, (Senator James M. Mason of Virginia read it for him), Calhoun warned how the fracturing of religious ties would eventually destroy the Union:

"The cords that bind the states together are not only many, but various in character. Some are spiritual or ecclesiastical; some political; others social . . . The strongest of those of a spiritual and ecclesiastical nature, consisted in the unity of the great religious denominations, all of which embraced the whole Union . . . but as powerful as they were, they have not been able to resist the explosive effect of slavery agitation. The first of these cords which snapped under its explosive force was that of the powerful Methodist Episcopal Church . . . The next cord that snapped was that of the Baptists—one of the largest and most respectable denominations. That of the Presbyterians has not entirely snapped, but some of its strands have given way . . . If the agitation goes on, the same force, acting with increased intensity, as has been shown, will finally snap every cord, when nothing will be left to hold the States together except force."

John C. Calhoun feared that the fracturing of religious denominations would destroy the country.

Calhoun was not the only Senator who on the eve of his death foresaw the trouble ahead. Henry Clay of Kentucky, the "Great Compromiser" in an interview with the *Presbyterian Herald* shared the same fear: "I tell you this sundering of the religious ties which have hitherto bound our people together, I consider the greatest source of danger to our country. If our religious men cannot live together in peace, what

John William Jones (1836–1909)
Evangelist of the Lost Cause

Born at Louisa Court House, Virginia, Jones underwent an Evangelical conversion experience at a camp-meeting in his youth and resolved to enter the Baptist ministry. He entered the University of Virginia at Charlottesville where he labored in the Young Men's Christian Association and taught Sunday school. After graduating in 1859 he entered the new Southern Baptist Theological Seminary in Greenville, South Carolina, where he graduated in 1860 and received ordination. His calling was to serve as a missionary to China, but the war intervened. He decided to return to Virginia where he became pastor of a church in Louisa County, and married in December 1860. With the outbreak of hostilities, he joined the Thirteenth Virginia Regiment as a private, and served as a private until accepting a chaplain's position the following year. The Southern Baptist Home Mission Board appointed him missionary chaplain in the Confederate Army corps of General A.P. Hill, an assignment he held until the end of the war.

While serving with Hill's corps in the Army of Northern Virginia, he worked with Generals Robert E. Lee and Stonewall Jackson in ministering to the needs of the soldiers, and was instrumental in forming the Chaplains' Association. During the war he wrote columns for the Virginia Baptist newspaper and the *Religious Herald*, in which he reported the number of conversions, baptisms, revivals, and religious needs of the Army. While encamped near Fredericksburg, Jones organized revival meetings, preached, and baptized soldiers. After the war he resumed his pastoral ministry at the Baptist Church in Lexington, Virginia, while simultaneously serving as chaplain at Washington University where Robert E. Lee presided as president.

Jones continued to serve in various pastorates and chaplaincies until his death in 1909, but he is remembered most for his writing and chronicling of the war years. His most famous literary work was *Christ in the Camp; or Religion in Lee's Army* (1887) in which he portrayed the gray-clad troops that were as zealous for Christ as Cromwell's Roundheads. He also published *Personal Reminiscences, Anecdotes, and Letters of General Robert E. Lee* (1874) and *School History of the United States* (1874), in which he wanted to demonstrate the role of the south in the history of the nation. During 1875–87 Jones edited the 14 volumes of the Southern Historical Society Papers. After the death of Jefferson Davis he edited a book of tributes (approved by the Davis family) *The Davis Memorial Volume* (1890).

During the postwar years Jones traveled extensively and spoke at Confederate reunions, memorial days, and historical remembrances. He died in Columbus, Georgia, in 1909 at the home of his son—active until his last days as a spokesman for the muscular Christianity of the Confederate faith and the Lost Cause.

can be expected of us politicians, very few of whom profess to be governed by the great principles of love? If all the Churches divide on the subject of slavery, there will be nothing left to bind our people together but trade and commerce."

Ironically the fulfillment Calhoun and Clay's worse fears occurred on December, 20, 1860 when the South Carolina legislature gathered at the First Baptist Church of Columbia and declared "the union now subsisting between

A Brief Chronology of American Religious Works, 1860–77

1860 Free Methodist Church established in Pekin, New York, a body advocating the abolition of slavery, abolition of pew rentals, opposition to secret societies, and more freedom in worship.

1861 The Women's Missionary Union established; Julia Ward Howe pens the "Battle Hymn of the Republic."

1862 Union army begins appointing Jewish chaplains; first of the Evangelical revivals in Robert E. Lee's Confederate Army of Northern Virginia.

1863 The revivals continue in the Army of Northern Virginia and begin winter at Dalton, Georgia, in Confederate general Joseph E. Johnston's Army of Tennessee.

1864 The Confederate revivals continue at Dalton through the winter. The last outbreak of revival for the Confederates in Virginia in the spring.

1865 Congress decrees "In God We Trust" on certain gold and silver coins; African-American Bishop Daniel Payne established Charleston, South Carolina's first African Methodist Episcopal Church.

1867 The National Organization for the Promotion of Christian Holiness organizes.

1872 Supreme Court hears the first case concerning a church controversy in *Watson v. Jones*; Sam Jones, (1847–1906), called "the Moody of the South," begins his career as a circuit rider for the Methodist Episcopal Church South in the North Georgia Conference.

1873 Evangelist Dwight Lyman Moody (1837–99) and musician Ira D. Sankey (1840–1908) begin a crusade in Great Britain that wins them international fame. They return to the United States in 1875.

1874 Women's Christian Temperance Union organized.

1875 Rabbi Isaac Meyer founds the Hebrew Union College in Cincinnati.

1877 Adas Israel, a disaffected Jewish group in Washington, D.C., becomes the first Orthodox Jewish group in America.

South Carolina and other States, under the name of the 'United States of America', is hereby dissolved."

The *Cleveland Daily Plain Dealer* editorialized after the secession of South Carolina: "For years the Union has in fact, been dissolving. Political parties first divided. The union Whig party was the first rent asunder. Then the churches North and South divided. Then our Bible, Tract, and Missionary Societies, and finally the social relations to an alarming extent . . . The Secession of South Carolina yesterday, was the culmination of events which had been progressing for years."

Southern Presbyterians actually credited the churches with the final break, calling the secession of South Carolina an "uprising" of Southern Christians: "Much as is due to many of our sagacious and gifted politicians, they could effect nothing until the religious union of the North and South was dissolved, not until they received the moral support and cooperation of Southern Christians."

WARTIME MINISTRY

The north reveled in the opportunity to mobilize its churches for the conflict. Church attendance increased, benevolent societies proliferated, and religious zeal intensified. Churchmen marveled at the unity in their fellowships for the war effort. The northern clergyman viewed the war as a purifying experience and hoped that the nation would become holier and ennobled after the conflict. The cementing of the Union, the death of sectionalism, and eventually the eradication of slavery must result. Julia Ward Howe's "Battle Hymn of the Republic," a poem full of Christian religious imagery and typology reflects religion of the north. Temporary setbacks on the fields of Manassas and Chancellorsville were the Lord's way of humbling a wayward and materialistic people for greater things to come. The war fostered patriotism in which the church and state cooperated to bring about victory.

One such organization so effectively used by the Union was the United States Sanitary Commission led by leaders of theologically liberal denominations. Organized in June 1861 and led by Henry W. Bellows, a Unitarian minister in New York City, it viewed its chief mission as overseeing medical care of the soldiers.

A Gothic Revival style church is an example of the new architecture being built in the mid-19th century.

The St. Michael's Church steeple in Charleston, South Carolina, served as a target point for Union artillery bombardment.

Another group was the United States Christian Commission, viewing its work as Evangelistic and pastoral in nature.

In the south clergy supported secession and the war effort through preaching morale-boosting sermons, but asserting that patriotism was not enough. The Confederacy must obey the Lord in all things to win. The churches of the less populated south lost many members due to the war. The hopes of the Confederacy lay in their armies, and the best place to work for the Lord was among the soldiers, for they would be amenable to the Evangelistic and comforting message of Christ. Southern Baptists released pastors to serve among the troops, who like the Methodists, sent missionaries and Evangelists to minister to the soldiers. Presbyterians and Methodists also provided chaplains and missionaries to the regiments. The Lutherans, Disciples, Catholics, and Episcopalians, though much smaller in number, also strived to gain adherents.

The most effective ministry in the southern armies was the tract ministry. Tracts were small publications with short sermons or devotionals that soldiers could read in a short time period. The Baptist Sunday School and Colportage Board of the Southern Baptist Convention led in the denominational printing of tracts, but by far the largest was the non-denominational Evangelical Tract Society of Petersburg, an organization that distributed millions of pages of devotional and Evangelistic material. Military-religious newspapers abounded across the Confederate armies.

The Methodist Episcopal Church South Soldiers Tract Association published *The Army and Navy Herald* and the *Soldiers Paper*; the Evangelical Tract Society produced the *Army and Navy Messenger;* Atlanta Baptists printed the *Soldiers Friend;* and the Presbyterians Committee on Publications in the Confederate states distributed *The Soldiers Visitor.* As to the local churches, most northern edifices were untouched by the war, but southern churches did not escape their use at the hands of the Yankees. Some churches in the Confederacy suffered destruction, but many were used by the Union troops as hospitals, and federal soldiers actually built houses of worship in the Confederacy for their own use.

THE WAR AS A THEOLOGICAL CRISIS

During the war theology and the vilification of the other side as out of the will of Providence and biblical teaching dominated the minds of the people and the soldiers.

When the north achieved victory, the region viewed the war's outcome as a victory for humanity and union. Lincoln did not rejoice as strongly—at least along theological lines. He fully understood the great tragedy the war produced. Lincoln viewed the national guilt as shared between the two sides.

On Saturday, March 4, 1865, in his Second Inaugural Address, Lincoln couched the religious dilemma for the nation as follows:

"Both read the same Bible and pray to the same God, and each invokes His aid against the other. It may seem strange that any men should dare to ask a just God's assistance in wringing their bread from the sweat of other men's faces, but let us judge not, that we be not judged. The prayers of both could not be answered. That of neither has been answered fully. The Almighty has His own purposes. 'Woe unto the world because of offenses; for it must needs be that offenses come, but woe to that man by whom the offense cometh.' If we shall suppose that American slavery is one of those offenses which, in the providence of God, must needs come, but which, having continued through His appointed time, He now wills to remove, and that He gives to both North and South this terrible war as the woe due to those by whom the offense came, shall we discern therein any departure from those divine attributes which the believers in a living God always ascribe to Him? Fondly do we hope, fervently do we pray, that this mighty scourge of war may speedily pass away. Yet, if God wills that it continue until all the wealth piled by the bondsman's two hundred and fifty years of unrequited toil shall be sunk, and until every drop of blood drawn with the lash shall be paid by another drawn with the sword, as was said three thousand years ago, so still it must be said 'the judgments of the Lord are true and righteous altogether.'"

In the south clergymen lamented the Confederacy's fall, but accepted it as the will of God. Most southerners reasoned their great sin had not been slavery per se, (although more than a few did not grieve over its destruction) but in not allowing slaves to legally marry, failing or refusing to teach them to read so they could understand the Bible, and treating slaves inhumanely by dividing parents from children.

They believed God would produce in the south a people better than before the conflict began. Due to the widespread revivals in the army during the war, religion remained individual and personal, rather than social. Therefore the racial attitudes that preceded the war remained for nearly a century after the guns fell silent.

The war's end also found itself shrouded in Christian imagery. Robert E. Lee surrendered his once invincible and legendary Army of Northern Virginia on Palm Sunday, and the following week, on Good Friday, John Wilkes Booth assassinated Abraham Lincoln. The death of Lincoln on such an occasion made him a Christ-figure to many, and especially to the former slaves who adored their fallen liberator and mourned his passing.

THE LEGACY OF THE WAR IN AMERICAN RELIGION

The greatest beneficiaries of the war were the newly-emancipated slaves, who took advantage of the opportunity to leave the slave balconies of their former master's churches and form their own assemblies. New African-American denominations formed and used their own worship styles. Moses Weir, a former slave, organized the Synod of Colored Cumberland Presbyterians, and in 1870 the Colored Methodist Episcopal Church (now Christian Methodist Episcopal Church) organized to minister to African Americans of Methodist persuasion. After Reconstruction African-American Baptists united to form their own convention. The exodus of former slaves from the three largest denominations in the south—Methodist, Baptist, and Presbyterian—depleted the membership rolls of the mostly white denominations.

Northern philanthropists sent large numbers of missionaries into the south in an effort to teach African Americans the blessings of freedom and education. Humanitarian groups worked toward the social and economic uplift of the former slaves based on their religious zeal. The Congregational Church's American Missionary Association (AMA) in 1868 sent 532 missionaries and teachers to the former Confederate states to minister to African Americans and educate them. Albert Raboteau, in his *African-American Religion*, tells the story of Harriet Ware, a white northern teacher in Port Royal, Virginia, who remarked on the religious devotion freedmen applied to education. At a funeral during the war, she later wrote, "as we drew near to the grave, we heard the children singing their A, B, C through and through again as they stood waiting round the grave [. . .]. Each child had his school-book or picture book [. . .].in his hand—another proof that they consider their lessons some sort of religious exercises." Raboteau concluded that "the desire to read the Bible for themselves—the Bible the slaveholders had so long misrepresented to them—motivated a good many slaves to seek education."

African-American denominational colleges sprang up all through the post-war era. Shaw University (Baptist) in Raleigh opened in 1865; Morehouse College (Baptist) in Atlanta in 1867; Morgan (now Morgan State), originally a Methodist institution in Baltimore, opened in 1867; and Fisk University in Nashville, founded by the American Missionary Association (AMA), opened in 1866. In addition the AMA founded Talladega College in Alabama in 1867, and Hampton Institute in Hampton, Virginia in 1868. Presbyterians established Knoxville College in 1875.

The mid-19th century marked the end of Protestant dominance in the United States. The influx of Irish, and eastern and southern Europeans who were mostly Catholic soon outnumbered Protestants in the large cities of the north. The challenges of Darwinism, modern philosophies, and liberal theology served to undermine the Evangelical consensus of the previous generations. All of these changes, including the dashed hopes of the south that divine providence should have sided with the Confederates, caused much religious angst in the region.

JAMES S. BAUGESS

Further Readings

Aamodt, Terrie Dopp. *Righteous Armies, Holy Cause: Apocalyptic Imagery and the Civil War*. Macon, GA: Mercer University Press, 2002.

Armstrong, Warren B. *For Courageous Fighting and Confident Dying: Union Chaplains in the Civil War*. Lawrence, KS: University Press of Kansas, 1998.

Beringer, Richard E., Herman Hattaway, Archer Jones, and William Jr. Still, *Why the South Lost the Civil War*. Athens, GA: University of Georgia Press, 1986.

Chesebrough, David B. *God Ordained This War: Sermons on the Sectional Crisis, 1830–1865*. Columbia: University of South Carolina Press, 1991.

Crowther, Edward R. *Southern Evangelicals and the Coming of the Civil War*. Lewiston, New York, The Edwin Mellen Press, 2000.

Gaustad, Edwin Scott, and Philip F. Barlow. *New Historical Atlas of Religion in America*. New York: Oxford University Press, 2001.

Goen, C.C. *Broken Churches, Broken Nation: Denominational Schisms and the Coming of the Civil War*. Macon, GA: Mercer University Press, 1985.

Holifield, E. Brooks. *Theology in America: Christian Thought form the Age of the Puritans to the Civil War*. New Haven, CT: Yale University Press, 2003.

Miller, Randall M, Harry S. Stout, Charles Reagan Wilson, eds. *Religion and the American Civil War*. New York: Oxford University Press, 1998.

Noll, Mark A. *America's God: From Jonathan Edwards to Abraham Lincoln*. New York: Oxford University Press, 2002.

———. *The Civil War as a Theological Crisis*. Chapel Hill: University of North Carolina Press, 2006.

Raboteau, Albert J. *African-America Religion*. New York: Oxford University Press, 1999.

Wilson, Charles Reagan. *Baptized in Blood: The Religion of the Lost Cause, 1865–1920*. Athens: The University of Georgia Press, 1980.

Shattuck, Gardiner H. *A Shield and Hiding Place: The Religious Life of Civil War Armies*. Macon, GA: Mercer University Press, 1987.

Chapter 8

Education

*"Education is considered the peculiar business
of women; perhaps for that very reason it is
one of the worst-paid businesses in the world"*
— Katharine Pearson Woods

EDUCATION IN THE early national period may best be noted for the lack of federal involvement. The founding fathers supported education generally. However education is not specifically addressed within the Constitution, and outside the debate over the establishment of a national university, education fell outside the interest of the federal government. As late as 1859 President Buchanan vetoed the first Morrill Act on the grounds that federal involvement in education was unconstitutional. This viewpoint would begin to change during the Civil War with the passage of the Morrill Act of 1862 and would evaporate further with the founding of the Freedmen's Bureau and passing of additional legislation in support of land-grant colleges.

Elementary education, which had primarily concentrated on the "three Rs" prior to the Civil War, began to explore ways to enrich the elementary curriculum and to examine the preparation of elementary school teachers. The concept of the kindergarten, first introduced in Germany, was introduced and gradually included in the elementary program. The kindergarten movement was also crucial to the study of how children learned and reformed in the elementary school curriculum. The study of the learning habits of children led to the discovery that learning could take place with the use of creative activities that did not rely on books and formal lessons. The "father" of the kindergarten and an early leader in the child study movement was German

Wilberforce University in Xenia, Ohio, a mid-19th century college for African Americans still operating in the 21st century.

Friedrich Froebel (1782–1852). Froebel's methods emphasized a wide variety of individual and group activities depending on the age of the child. Froebel's methods tended to be rather mystic and depended on self-discovery to educate even young children. There soon developed in the United States a split between conservative and liberal views regarding the use of Froebel's theories. However the notion of the kindergarten was accepted very quickly—proof lies in the incorporation of a separate kindergarten department by the National Education Association in 1884. The movement toward child study accelerated once psychologists began the formal study of the growth and development of children through experiments, questionnaires, and mental tests. All of these new methods allowed both psychologists and educators to get a better picture of how children mature and what influences their development. The results impacted upon elementary school education, as drawing and other handwork was incorporated into the curriculum. Educationalist Felix Adler (1851–1933), who was educated in Germany, was a leading proponent of handwork believing that the discovery of truth required both experimentation and observation.

The need to better educate teachers led to considerable growth in the number of normal schools operating throughout the country. The primary goal of normal schools was to better prepare more teachers for the rural school districts. In 1860 there were 12 state normal schools, as well as a number of other normal classes or departments attached to other educational institutions. The number of state normal schools grew to 22 in 1865 and continued to grow at an estimated rate of 25 new normal schools every decade for the next 50 years. However the growth in the number of normal schools could not keep pace with the population growth or the increase in attendance caused by passing of compulsory attendance laws in many states. In addition many of the normal schools were sadly lacking in facilities or trained staff. At the close of the 19th century many rural schoolteachers were still being certified to teach with little or no professional training.

The end of the Civil War and Reconstruction combined with the Industrial Revolution had a profound impact on the number and curriculum of high schools. The rising middle class used their power and influence to insure that the high school was a common school. Near the end of the century enrollment records of high schools grew and the curriculum was revised to include vocational education. Later, depending on the location of the high school, vocational programs expanded to include agriculture. Secondary education had three general purposes: to prepare students for life, college, and teaching. The growth in the number of high schools led to the movement to establish standards.

The end of Reconstruction allowed the southern states to concentrate on building state systems of education—something that had been largely missing from these states prior to the Civil War. In addition to efforts to

Charles William Eliot (1834–1926)

Charles William Eliot was a leader in educational reform who was president of Harvard for 40 years (1869–1909) and the editor of the 50-volume *Harvard Classics*. He was born in Boston and graduated from Harvard in 1853. He returned to Harvard in 1858 as a professor of mathematics and chemistry. As support for educational reform grew in the 19th century, many turned to European educational practices to inform American educational reform. Eliot left the United States in 1867 to travel to Europe in order to study European educational systems. Upon his return from Europe he published an account in the *Atlantic Monthly* in 1869 that caught the attention of the directors of Harvard who were searching for a new university president.

Eliot asserted early in his Harvard presidency that the collegiate curriculum needed to be "broadened, deepened, and invigorated." To that end he argued for the inclusion of the sciences in a liberal education and eliminated, except for English Composition, required courses from the curriculum of Harvard. Under Eliot Harvard revised and increased entrance standards. Eliot was a member of the 1892 national committee on secondary education that called for rise in the standards of secondary schools. As part of that report the committee recommended that the seventh grade curriculum be revised to include the study of mathematics and foreign languages. In addition to the *Harvard Classics*, Eliot published in 1898 a collection of his essays entitled *Educational Reform: Essays and Addresses* and *University Administration* that was published after his retirement in 1908.

"Rudimental Instruction of the Freedmen"

Freedmen's education began prior to the issuance of the Emancipation Proclamation and the end of the Civil War. As Union forces pushed into the Confederate states they were confronted with a growing number of former slaves and the responsibility of meeting their needs.

Among those needs was an effort to educate the former slaves, something that had previously been denied to them. Northern churches, such as the Methodist Church, formed the American Missionary Association to aid freedman. Early efforts at providing an education for the freedmen included a small school established at Fort Monroe in 1861 by Mary S. Peake. This school is considered the forerunner to the Hampton Institute. Many of the educators who went south to aid in the education of the freedmen were drawn from the abolitionist movement and supporters of the Underground Railroad. The educators were often treated with contempt by southern whites that viewed them as the enemies.

The Union army soon took formal steps to protect and educate the freedmen. Colonel John Eaton was appointed by General Grant in 1862 to act as the commissioner of the freedmen in the state of Arkansas. General Banks issued a directive in 1864 for the military district of New Orleans that outlined a "rudimental instruction of the freedman." The directive established a board of education with the power to tax and requisition in support of the directive. The federal government established the Bureau for Refugees, Freedmen, and Abandoned Lands—known simply as the Freedmen's Bureau—which had overall responsibility to protect the interests of freedmen. General O.O. Howard was appointed as the head of the new bureau. The bureau established a superintendent of freedmen's schools with an educational supervisor assigned to each state. The end of the Freedman's Bureau in 1870 transferred the responsibility of educating millions of African Americans to individual states. While southerners often accused the bureau of promoting a radical form of Reconstruction, the bureau distributed millions of dollars and built dozens of schoolhouses before its end.

Man reading a newspaper with headline, "Presidential Proclamation, Slavery," which refers to the January 1863 Emancipation Proclamation.

educate freedmen, northern philanthropic efforts were directed toward aiding education in the south in general. The Peabody Education Board, headed by Barnas Sears, allocated $2 million in support of education of "the entire population" of the south. The board hoped to stimulate educational development and reform by providing substantial funds to schools that would serve as models. John Slater established another philanthropic trust in 1882 for the education of freedmen and their descendants. Education for African-American teachers was a particular goal of the Slater Fund. Through the remainder of the 19th century the south experienced little progress in terms of education; and what progress was made was largely concentrated in urban areas. Progress was hampered by a lack of funds and the need to maintain separate facilities for the two races.

EDUCATIONAL REFORM

The establishment of new colleges and universities claimed the majority of educational energies during the early national period of 1783–1860. The first colleges and universities established in the United States offered a classical education based on the liberal arts. The opening of the Erie Canal in 1825 and the Industrial Revolution increased the calls for a practical education that focused on agriculture and engineering. The development of agricultural and engineering schools began during the Civil War with the passage of the Morrill Act of 1862 and the establishment of land-grant colleges. As the 19th century progressed the profession of education began to develop principles that addressed various aspects of teaching such as methods, curriculum, educational psychology, comparative education, philosophy, and history of education. The late 19th century witnessed the rise of special education. One of the hopes of educationalists was that education would become more scientific. As the century came to a close districts were beginning to combine primary and secondary schools into one system, as schools worked to expand their curriculum.

An idealized view of childhood from Currier & Ives. In reality, child labor was the norm and school was attended only for short periods.

Early in the history of American colleges it was not unusual for a young man to enter college as young as 14-years-old since admission was based on an examination, and not on completion of high school. As the number of high schools increased, colleges removed the entrance exami-

One of several military training colleges in the United States, the Citadel in South Carolina, prepared many of the generation of officers who served in the Confederate Army.

nation requirement in favor of a high school diploma. In addition professional colleges began to require a college degree, or the minimum of two years of college before admission to the professional course of study. The impact of this shift was that the average age of college graduates increased from 18 to 22 years of age, with individuals entering a profession such as medicine averaging between 25 and 27 years old.

Since many felt these ages were too old to be just entering professional life, a discussion began on how to reduce the time necessary to complete college. Charles William Eliot, president of Harvard University, was the best-known advocate of the elective system for college curriculum. Eliot believed all studies were of equal value and that an elective curriculum was more adaptable to the needs of its students. Under Eliot the only required course at Harvard was English composition.

In addition Eliot proposed reducing the college course to three years. Eliot believed that records indicated that the best-prepared students already graduated in three years, and reducing the course to three years would have the brightest students completing the course in an average of two years and two months. Eliot's elective system and shortening the college course never won wide acceptance.

The increasing desire to improve teaching methods spurred the discussion regarding how to increase a pupil's interest. Educationalist John Dewey placed great emphasis on increasing a pupil's interest because he asserted that it would lead to increased effort by the student. For Dewey and his philosophy of education the purpose of education was human growth and the means to this end was the teaching of thinking through experiences and simple problem solving. Critics questioned whether Dewey's emphasis on problems with

Land-Grant Colleges and Universities

Land-grant colleges and universities came into existence through the Morrill Act of 1862, signed by President Abraham Lincoln. The bill supported the development of new public universities by granting federal land to states to be sold to provide endowments for the establishment of universities. The amount of federal land holdings put up for sale was based on the size of the congressional delegation for the state. The bill called for the establishment of "at least one college where the leading object shall be, without excluding other scientific and classical studies and including military tactics, to teach such branches of learning as related to agriculture and the mechanic arts [. . .] in order to promote the liberal and practical education of the industrial classes in the several pursuits and professions in life."

The act was an outgrowth of an educational movement that believed that education should support useful ends and emphasize the emerging sciences of agriculture and engineering. Senator Justin S. Morrill of Vermont had sponsored bills during the 1850s calling for federally sponsored agricultural or industrial colleges. Morrill's bill passed Congress in 1859, only to be vetoed by President James Buchanan. Buchanan viewed federal involvement in education as unconstitutional. While well intentioned, the land sales did not provide a sufficient endowment for the new universities, and the states did not come forward with their own funds. The first two universities to function as land-grant schools were Michigan Agricultural College (now known as Michigan State University) and the Agricultural College of Pennsylvania (now known as Pennsylvania State University).

Despite the poor funding there were 24 land-grant schools by 1873. Two federal acts placed the land-grant schools on better financial footing. In 1887 the Hatch Act provided for federally funded agricultural experiment stations at the schools. The Morrill Act of 1890, in addition to allowing states to establish separate but equal land-grant colleges for African Americans, provided federal funding for general educational programs. Today there are 106 land-grant colleges and universities operating in the United States.

immediate results could promote the sciences, but Dewey countered that his philosophy stressed the "real business of living."

The founding fathers believed in the necessity of an educated populace to maintain a functioning republic. However there was a great reluctance to legislate compulsory school attendance requirements. Child labor, whether part of a family business such as agriculture, or in growing factories was the norm. The result is that many children did not attend schools at all or only for short periods of time. The demand for basic literacy led to an emphasis on the "three Rs" and primary education. The first compulsory attendance law in the United States was passed in Massachusetts in 1852 requiring total attendance of 12 weeks per academic year, with six of those weeks being continuous weeks for children between the ages of eight and 14 years.

Schoolbooks 1860–76

The adoption of schoolbooks in the 19th century was particularly important since classroom instruction relied heavily on memorization and recitation within the classroom. In addition this heavy reliance was strengthened by the fact that teachers exhibited a wide range of training and quality. In 1860 there were only 12 public normal schools (four of those existed in Massachusetts) and six private normal schools training future teachers. The move toward improving teacher quality finally gained momentum as the 19th century progressed. In general the books were designed for the first eight years of schooling, since attending high school was not the norm for the majority of Americans. In fact eight years became the established norm only later in the century.

Schoolbooks, no matter the subject matter, were compiled from other sources typically without citing the source in an effort to offer information and norms of behavior to children. Authors such as Noah Webster claimed that the purpose of 19th-century American public schools was to train citizens in character and proper American principles. Authors, except for William Holmes McGuffey (Ohio) typically were either born or educated in New England and tended to be either teachers or clergymen. McGuffey, growing up in the sparsely populated west, became a teacher at 13 and later an ordained Presbyterian minister before authoring his widely popular readers. Popular authors and their subject matter included Noah Webster on spelling, William Holmes McGuffey on reading, S. Augustus Mitchell on geography, and Charles Davis on arithmetic. Southern educators frequently complained about the lack of schoolbooks authored by southerners and how slavery was presented in the northern books. The establishment of the Confederacy did not address the shortage of southern presses and authors and the reliance on northern books continued in the south throughout Reconstruction.

Proper Education of Wayward Youths

In 1866 Archbishop Martin J. Spalding convened a national council of the Catholic clergy in Baltimore. This national council issued a Pastoral Letter of 1866 that touched on many of the social and ecclesiastical issues of the day, including the proper education of wayward youths.

Connected with this subject of education is the establishment of protectories and industrial schools for the correction or proper training of youth, which has of late years attracted universal attention. It is a melancholy fact, and a very humiliating avowal for us to make, that a very large proportion of the idle and vicious youth of our principal cities are the children of Catholic parents. Whether from poverty or neglect, the ignorance in which so many parents are involved as to the true nature of education, and of their duties as Christian parents, or the associations which our youth so easily form with those who encourage them to disregard parental admonition; certain it is that a large number of Catholic parents either appear to have no idea of the sanctity of the Christian family and of the responsibility imposed on them of providing for the moral training of their offspring, or fulfill this duty in a very imperfect manner.

Day after day these unhappy children are caught in the commission of petty crimes, which render them amenable to the public authorities; and day after day are thy transferred by hundreds from the sectarian reformatories in which they have been placed by the courts to distant localities, where they are brought up in ignorance of, and most commonly in hostility to, the religion in which they had been baptized. The only remedy of this great and daily augmenting evil is to provide Catholic protectories or industrial schools to which such children may be sent; and where, under the only influence that is known to have really reached the roots of vice, the youthful culprit may cease to do evil and learn to do good.

However irregular attendance remained the norm since enforcement of the law was nonexistent. Massachusetts would pass its second compulsory law dealing with habitual truants in 1862, five years before another state would pass a similar law. After the Civil War the number of states passing compulsory attendance laws increased, until 32 states had passed a compulsory attendance law by 1900.

Interest in whether or not Americans were literate led the United States government to ask as part of the 1840 census whether each person had the ability to read or write. The fact that half a million white Americans admitted that they were unable to read or write created quite a sensation on the editorial pages of newspapers across the country. In 1840 the U.S. Census Bureau defined literacy as the ability to read and write a little in any language.

The movement toward progressive education, the combining of primary and secondary education into one school district, and the desire for scientific education had a profound impact on curriculum developments as the 20th century progressed. Eighteenth-century spelling books had a tendency to concentrate on the spelling of the longest words and words infrequently used in everyday writing and conversation.

The American Library Association was founded in 1876 and it quickly adopted programs regarding books for schools. Charles Francis Adams, Jr., grandson and great-grandson of former presidents and head of the Quincy, Massachusetts school board, offered a paper in 1876 in which he proposed joining together the school and town libraries to create "a people's college." The importance of school libraries is reflected in studies conducted both by the National Education Association and the American Library Association on how to best address the issue of bookless schools. The 19th century witnessed the growth of public library systems with the Boston Public Library being the best example of the development.

ABBE ALLEN DEBOLT

Further Readings

Butts, R. Freeman and Lawrence A. Cremin. *A History of Education in American Culture*. New York: Holt, Rinehart and Winston, 1953.

Carlton, Chambliss, J.J., ed. *Enlightenment and Social Progress: Education in the Nineteenth Century*. Minneapolis, MN: Burgess Publishing Company, 1971.

Cremin, Lawrence A. *The Transformation of the School, Progressivism in American Education, 1876–1957*. New York: Alfred A. Knopf, 1961.

Cubberley, Ellwood P. *Public Education in the United States*. Cambridge, MA: The Riverside Press, 1962.

Fletcher, Shelia. *Feminists and Bureaucrats*. Cambridge, MA: Cambridge University Press, 1980.

Good, Harry G. and James D. Teller. *A History of American Education*. New York: The Macmillan Company, 1973.

Harlan, Louis R. *The Wizard of Tuskegee, 1901–1915*. New York: Oxford University Press, 1983.

Kett, Joseph F. *The Pursuit of Knowledge Under Difficulties*. Stanford, CA: Stanford University Press, 1994.

Meyer, Adolphe E. *An Educational History of the American People*. New York: McGraw Hill Book Company, 1967.

Washington, Booker T. *Up From Slavery*. New York: Oxford University Press, 2000.

Chapter 9

Science and Technology

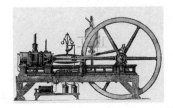

"Is it not a feat sublime?
Intellect hath conquered time."
— Motto of the trade journal the *Telegrapher*

THE CIVIL WAR has often been called the first industrial-age war, although it has been argued that the Crimean War or the wars of German unification could also claim that distinction. Certainly the American Civil War was the first war in which science and technology were systematically marshaled in the service of the military effort. Many historians have argued that the greater industrialization of the north was one of the most important factors in the Union victory over the Confederacy, counterbalancing the stronger leadership enjoyed by the Confederate armies.

The era of Reconstruction only exacerbated the strong north-south divide in terms of industrial strength. What little industry the Confederacy had managed to develop lay in ruins, and those southerners who might have rebuilt it were largely impoverished and disenfranchised as a result of their having participated in the rebellion. In contrast the north enjoyed further economic growth which allowed for technological developments, which would lay the foundations of the Gilded Age. The Civil War was notable for the way in which technology was systematically applied to the problems of warfare. In particular the railroad and the telegraph were put to work to support the armies in the fields.

In 1861 both the railroad and the telegraph were established technologies that had substantially transformed American culture. Because the telegraph was necessary for signaling trains to avoid head-on collisions, and because

Hanover Junction Railroad Station, Pennsylvania in 1863. The advantage enjoyed by the north in railroad strength was an important contributor to the Union's ultimate victory.

railroad right-of-ways provided an easily accessible place for telegraph wires to be strung, the two technologies had become intertwined over the previous decade. In the new industrial war machine, in which success upon the battlefield became increasingly dependent upon a lengthy logistical supply chain, both telegraphs and railroads were essential to military success.

The advantage enjoyed by the north in railroad strength was an important contributor to the Union's ultimate victory, in spite of often having inferior military leadership. In 1860 there were 25,000 miles of track in the north, compared to a mere 10,000 in the states that would secede from the Union. While most of the north's track was tightly interconnected, that of the south was often disjointed, limiting the ability to move goods and soldiers from one location to another. Even more important, every single factory for manufacturing locomotives was located in the industrial heartland of the north. When the southern states walked out, they cut themselves off from their source of rolling stock. As existing locomotives wore out or destroyed in military action, the south was forced to seek replacements from England. However the Union naval blockade of Confederate ports made it difficult for those few locomotives that were brought across the Atlantic to get to their purchasers. Both sides were often hampered by senior officers who failed to comprehend the potential of the railroad and used it in petty ways. Some used railroads selfishly, as personal conveniences, not knowing or caring that by doing so they were holding up

Celluloid: A New Material for an Industrial Society

Although plastic is generally considered an invention of the 20th century, in fact the first popular plastic was invented during the Civil War. Celluloid has since come to be associated primarily with cinematographic film, but when it first appeared on the market, it generated all the excitement of any novelty. Celluloid had its roots in collodion, a nitrocellulose solution used in the production of photographic plates. John Wesley Hyatt, a printer based in Albany, New York, had discovered that spilled collodion dried up hard and stiff, and saw in it a possibility to create a substitute for ivory in billiard balls. After the Civil War, a sudden explosion of interest in billiards and its oft-maligned stepchild, pool, had created enormous pressures on the populations of both African and Asian elephants. Only a few tusks had the perfect clear grain suitable for making billiard balls, and only a fraction of each tusk could actually be used. In one of the earliest examples of environmental awareness, billiards fanciers grew concerned that the elephant could be driven to extinction, ending the supply of ivory altogether.

However dried collodion proved unsatisfactory as an ivory substitute, largely because of its tendency to crack as it dried. Not to be discouraged, Hyatt substituted camphor as a solvent for nitrocellulose and in 1869 produced a hard, durable substance that could be molded into a variety of shapes. Celluloid thus promised to substitute not only for ivory, but for a wide variety of natural substances that were rapidly pricing themselves out of the reach of the burgeoning middle class, including rubber, whalebone, and tortoiseshell.

Within a few years industry was churning out a vast variety of objects made from celluloid, generally colored in ways that imitated various natural objects such as: ivory buttons, tortoiseshell combs, and marble soap dishes.

However celluloid was not entirely without its problems, for it retained much of the fierce flammability of the nitrocellulose from which it was made. A celluloid manufacturing plant on Ferry Street in Newark, New Jersey, burst into flames. In a mere two hours the fire leveled the entire four-story building. This unmistakable public demonstration of the volatile nature of this new substance soon bred tales of ordinary domestic situations turned into horrors because of the flammability of celluloid. A woman sat down by the fire only to have the celluloid buttons on her dress burst into flame, forcing her to choose between her modesty and her life. A gentleman accidentally brushed his cigar against a celluloid shirt cuff and ended up setting off a blaze that consumed an entire house. Although most of these scare stories were pure urban legend, there was just enough truth behind them to counterbalance the rapidly growing fashion for celluloid.

vital troops and supplies on their way to key battlefields. Others, not understanding the speed offered by the railroad, would refuse to allow troops to be sent until sufficient rolling stock was available to send all of them at once.

The north resolved the problem by placing all railroads under government authority in 1862. Two colonels, Daniel C. McCallum and Herman Haupt, were placed in overall control of Union railroads. Even generals were not permitted to gainsay their directives for the use of railroad assets. As a result northern railroads were used efficiently, to the point that they were one of the most effective parts of the northern war effort.

In contrast Confederate railroads remained a patchwork of conflicting authorities, largely because the Confederate states, having left the Union over issues of states' rights, were loath to turn around and impose harsh central authority upon their own countrymen. Many lines remained in private hands, and their owners placed the profitability of their companies above the overall war efforts. Even those railroads that were in government hands were not necessarily under the control of the central government in Richmond. State governments often handled their railroads in ways that primarily benefited their own states, much as many state volunteers resisted being sent to fight in other states.

WAR'S NEW NERVOUS SYSTEM

The telegraph also had a critical role to play in the new battlefield of the industrial war, creating the first modern system of command, control, com-

A photograph from the siege of Petersburg, June 1864–April 1865, shows a U.S. military telegraph battery wagon, stationed to maintain communication with the Army of the Potomac headquarters.

An 1867 wood engraving illustrates a Pony Express rider passing men stringing telegraph wires. In the Civil War the telegraph had created a modern system of command, control, and intelligence.

munication, and intelligence. For the first time in history it became possible for commanders to control troops not in their immediate vicinity, and for the national command authority in the capital to affect operational control over forces in the field. These factors were important in the Civil War due to the sheer breadth of the country over which the war was fought. Resources had to be marshaled to the areas that needed them most, not merely to the fighting that happened closest to the producers. While the railroad permitted the rapid deployment of troops to the battlefield, it was only as useful as the commanders' ability to know where those troops were needed.

Telegraph equipment was still too cumbersome to bring out into the field of battle and allow communication with individual units. So long as the telegraph was dependent upon wet-cell batteries that could drip and spill, it would remain in a central headquarters tent, providing only the broadest levels of command and control. But even that much could turn the tide of battle, particularly when two or more armies were brought to bear from different directions and needed to be coordinated in order to attack at the same time.

Because America's telegraph offices had been in the hands of private business before the outbreak of war, secession left these vital assets scattered on both sides of the split nation. The Union government moved quickly to nationalize all telegraphic assets wherever Union armies were operating, to prevent use by Confederate agents, or frivolous use. In addition, the Union established the Military Telegraph, which was operated by the Quartermaster Corps, normally in charge of supplies and other aspects of the logistical train.

To Stop a Train with the Wind

Even as late as the end of the 1860s the speed at which trains could travel was limited by the difficulty of bringing them to a halt. When the engineer signaled "down brakes" with the train's whistle, brakemen would scramble from car to car, turning wheels on each end that would press brake shoes against the wheels. As a result, stopping a train was a clumsy, jerky affair, dangerous for the brakemen who often fell from their perches or were crushed between the cars as they worked. Many times accidents occurred in spite of the engineer having plenty of warning, simply because the brakemen could not work rapidly enough.

An enterprising young man by the name of George Westinghouse decided there had to be a more effective way to stop a train. His first idea was to use the same steam that powered the train to stop it. However his attempts to run steam lines the length of a train fell victim to the simple fact that there was no way to keep the steam hot in such long hoses. It soon cooled, condensed, and lost its ability to function as a power source.

While struggling with the problem, he happened to read an account of the engineering difficulties encountered by a team boring a tunnel through the Alps. In particular he was fascinated by the account of a mechanical drill powered by compressed air. If air could power a drill, it could also apply to the brake shoes on a train. Since compressed air would not chill and lose its ability to do work as it traveled away from the locomotive as steam lines did, it would be possible for the engineer to stop the train from the cab of the locomotive, without needing a small army of brakemen scrambling atop the cars.

However convincing the railroad industry of the worth of his invention proved far more difficult than the process of inventing it. Cornelius Vanderbilt, greatest of the railroad barons, dismissed him out of hand with the mocking comment that one could not stop a train with the wind. Only the Panhandle Railroad was willing to allow a demonstration, under the stipulation that the installation of the air brake was to be at Westinghouse's expense, and that he would pay for any damage done to the locomotive or its cars.

When he tested the air brake for Panhandle executives, he had intended to simply perform a series of controlled stops. Instead they had barely gotten started when Westinghouse was horrified to see a man and a horse cart on a crossing in front of him. He applied the brakes so rapidly some of the executives were flung from their seats. However that indignity was quickly forgiven when the executives realized it was in the cause of saving human life.

Even after his air brake had proved its worth Westinghouse continued to improve it. He created a triple valve that allowed the air brake to automatically apply should air pressure be lost. Furthermore he invested the profits from his air brake into other technological efforts, making the Westinghouse company a leader in innovation.

When General Albert Myer suggested that the Military Telegraph be transferred to the Signal Corps, which handled communications on the battlefield (typically bugle calls, with some use of flags and semaphores), he was dismissed from his position. However shortly after the war his recommendation was carried out, and he was returned to his former position.

The telegraph was not entirely without its problems. Because the telegraph made it possible for higher-level commanders to keep in constant close contact with relatively low-level units, it became possible to micromanage to the point of destroying the initiative of junior officers. Fortunately Abraham Lincoln was not the sort of man to try to run every aspect of the war from the White House, but he often found that communication lines ran both ways. More than a few generals in the field used the telegraph as an opportunity to offer more detailed communications than the traditional dispatch, messages often including personal complaints and various efforts to jockey for favor.

FEEDING A HUNGRY ARMY

Even technological advances seemingly remote from the fighting front of the torn nation made important contributions to the ultimate success of the north and the restoration of the Union. The Civil War was one of the first wars in which the "tail" of logistical support behind the "teeth" of fighting men ran all the way back to the civilian populace, although the notion of a home front had yet to be formally articulated. One of the foremost ways in which Union social mobilization was critical was in the production and preservation of food. The spread of Cyrus McCormick's mechanical reaper through the wheat lands of the north in the previous decade was largely driven by a lack of skilled scythe men to harvest the yield. Where there was a surplus of labor, the mechanical reaper was met with hostility, even vandalism. Once the war began and men were desperately needed in uniform, the efficiency provided by the reaper gave northern agriculture a key edge over that of the south.

However increased food production meant little if it spoiled before it could be delivered to the forces on the fighting front. In previous wars soldiers had relied primarily on the old traditional standbys of hardtack and salt beef. Hardtack was a heavy biscuit so hard it could break teeth, therefore it was generally soaked immediately prior to being eaten. Its denseness permitted its storage for extended periods of time without spoiling, although weevils and other vermin could infest it. Salt beef was generally packed in casks for storage and transportation, but after several years it could become hard enough to carve like the wood of the cask, assuming that it too did not become infested by vermin. It generally had to be boiled for several hours to make it minimally edible.

Although these old standbys still made their appearances in significant quantities on the manifests of the Quartermaster Corps (with some casks of salt beef supposedly left over from the Mexican-American War or even the War of 1812), new alternatives for food preservation were beginning to make an appearance.

This preserved sutler's wagon at the Civil War Museum in Harrisburg, Pennsylvania, was typical of those from which soldiers purchased food, alcohol, and tobacco.

In particular canning in canisters of tinplate with soldered lids became a major method of storing such items as pork and beans, meat stews, and various kinds of vegetables. However most canned goods were to be found in the hands of sutlers, private supply merchants who followed the armies in the fields and sold their wares at a profit to those soldiers and particularly officers who had the money to afford them. After the war canned goods expanded exponentially in availability, becoming a common item in civilian pantries. As the railroads made transportation of bulk goods cheaper and easier, it became possible to transport such goods as fruits and even Pacific salmon to the cities of the east coast.

WITH LIGHT AS HIS PAINTBRUSH

The Civil War was also notable as the first war extensively documented through photography. By 1861 photography had advanced to the point that an image could be captured within less than a minute, rather than the tens of minutes that had been required for some of the earliest photographic processes. As a result, although it was not yet possible to capture actual action shots, it became feasible to take photographs of units at parade rest, or of a battlefield shortly after the heat of a battle had passed.

By far the most famous of the Civil War photographers was Matthew B. Brady. Trained by Samuel F.B. Morse, a man remembered primarily as the inventor of practical telegraphy, but who was also a painter, Brady combined an artist's sense of composition with a keen nose for business. By the outbreak of the Civil War he had opened a chain of photography studios, and although he was not personally present at Fort Sumter, several of his people were on hand to capture images of the fallen fortress and its garrison. However Fort Sumter was close enough to town that it was possible for these photographers to take the wet-plate glass negatives back to their regular studios. A more difficult challenge was posed by the Battle of Bull Run. Because wet-plate films had to be developed quickly, it was necessary to bring the darkroom to the site. Brady created two photographic wagons, mobile darkrooms custom-built with shelves and drawers to hold all the supplies a photographer would need in the field.

However the bulk of these wagons, nicknamed "Whatsits" by the soldiers, made them easy targets for enemy artillery. Sometimes they were mistaken for supply wagons, but often they were just convenient targets for artillery-men hungry for something to shoot at. More than once Brady or his assistants narrowly escaped with their lives when their photography wagons were destroyed in action. If they did not have a second mobile darkroom on hand, any pictures they had shot would have been lost to posterity.

Even with such primitive and often intractably limited technology, Brady and his colleagues still managed to have a powerful influence upon public opinion through the images they sent back to the population centers of the East Coast, particularly Washington, D.C. In the nation's capital, many civilians visited Brady's central studio to look at the photographs he had taken.

However these beginnings of photojournalism were stunted as a result of a simple fact: there was no practical, inexpensive way to incorporate images into text. The printing press was a monochrome process, creating spots of black ink on a white page, while the photograph was a continuous-tone process. Thus the printing press would destroy all the gradations of tone in a photographic image. A few photographers or newspaper publishers hired engravers to transfer the photographic images, but this greatly increased the expense. As a result, the only printed materials with photographs in them were a few very expensive books with separate photographic prints tipped in.

This technical bottleneck meant that Brady had no good way to translate his collection of history-making images into an income. Attempts to create a

Matthew Brady photographed in 1875. He is credited as the father of photojournalism.

traveling show and charge admission failed, as did negotiations for the government to purchase them for a historical gallery. Brady ended up dying in poverty and ill-health, shortly before the invention of the halftone process, which enabled the printing of photographic images by screening them into a mesh of tiny dots.

CONSTRUCTING THE TRANSCONTINENTAL RAILROAD

As early as the California Gold Rush of 1849 there were visionaries who saw the need for a railroad line running across the vast territory of the United States from east to west. Such a railroad would provide swift transportation between the established industrial cities of the east and the natural resources of the west. However the society of the time was not yet ready for the sustained effort required by such an undertaking.

The Civil War made Congress painfully aware of just how vulnerable the isolated states of California and Oregon were, separated by over 1,000 miles of unincorporated territory from the rest of the Union. Transcontinental railroad supporters argued that only a railroad could reliably transport

A Harper's Weekly 1869 illustration of the completion of the Pacific Railroad, showing a meeting of locomotives of the Union and Central Pacific lines, with the engineers shaking hands.

enough soldiers to defend them from attack, particularly the gold mines that would be a prime target in a society that still thought of money in terms of precious metals.

With support from Abraham Lincoln, now president of the United States, transcontinental railroad supporters were able to get bills passed granting enormous amounts of money and land for the building of a railroad. However the necessity of war meant that the actual construction of the railroad would be delayed until after the south was defeated.

The work would take five years, and was almost entirely performed by hand. There were no bulldozers or dragline shovels to move the vast amounts of earth that had to be shifted in order to create the level grade a railroad required for most efficient operation. Men with picks and spades and others with wheelbarrows did this work, occasionally assisted by draft animals such as horses and mules. Once the graders had created the roadbed, tie men laid down the wooden ties upon which the rails were laid and secured. Although a great technological achievement in its design and conception, much of the rail line was built using technologies such as the pick, shovel, and wheelbarrow, that were thousands of years old.

The vast majority of the workers on the transcontinental railroad were immigrants. The Central Pacific imported thousands of Chinese workers to force their way through the Sierra Nevada Mountains, while the Union Pacific hired thousands of Irishmen straight off the ships in New York City and shipped them to the Great Plains for the drive into the Rocky Mountains. As the two railroad companies' crews entered Utah and homed in on the meeting point, the rivalry between them became ferocious. Because each company stood to gain a considerable amount of money for each mile of track they were able to lay, it was to their advantage to work to the other company's despite. Teams from each company routinely sabotaged the other's work, even tearing up fresh-laid track and assaulting workers. More than once, ugly fights broke out.

Finally Congress stepped in and designated Promontory Point, Utah, as the location at which the two companies' efforts were to meet. On May 10, 1869 the transcontinental railroad was officially completed with the ceremonial driving of the golden spike. It activated a telegraph that sent the message of the line's completion to the great cities of the east. That night the actual golden spike was carefully removed and replaced with a regular iron spike, lest the historical artifact be stolen.

AMERICAN STEEL FOR AN AMERICAN LINE

The building of the transcontinental railroad not only helped rebound a broken nation. It also served as a spur for new development of the American iron and steel industry. Because of the political importance of the transcontinental railroad, Congress had stipulated that all materials used in building it must be of American manufacture. Although the American iron and steel industry had been producing railroad iron for decades, its capacity was sufficiently limited that many railroad companies augmented its output with rails imported from England.

However the dominant method of making rails at the time, using iron laboriously "puddled" in a boiling furnace and then beaten free of impurities, could produce only a limited amount of rails. As a result of the demand from the transcontinental railroad, the price of iron rails went from $70 a ton to $85 a ton. Heavier steel rails cost $120 a ton, largely because the crucible process then dominant could produce only very small amounts of this high-quality metal, which had previously been used primarily for such specialty items as knives and machine tools.

If America's industrial growth was to grow, such vital elements as railroad iron had to be made in sufficient quantities that its price remained manageable. The process already existed, developed in England as early as 1856 by Henry Bessemer. Using techniques developed while constructing a furnace for optical glass, he blew compressed air into a crucible for forming steel. It produced a fierce blow, compared by many observers to a volcano exploding, and the resultant steel was ready in far less time than when using previous methods. Within two years Bessemer developed the pear-shaped, tiltable converter vessel which would bear his name, and mass production of steel became a reality.

The Bessemer process was brought to America largely by the efforts of Alexander L. Holley. His father's work as a politician and a businessman showed him the inter-relationship between politics, business, and the economy, and he developed his own expertise in engineering to make him an expert respected by many leading politicians. In 1863 he secured a license to use Bessemer's patents in America, and began experiments in an abandoned grist mill on the Hudson River. When his financial backers were satisfied that the Bessemer process was not only practical, but profitable in an American context, he built an entire mill, incorporating improvements and optimizing it for the production of rails.

One of Holley's key inventions was the removable bottom, which greatly simplified the process of periodically relining a Bessemer converter vessel with refractory materials. Because the American steelmaking industry, largely driven by the demand of the railroads for rails, was a high-volume, rapid turnover industry; an apparatus that would reduce the time any converter vessel was out of operation for routine maintenance quickly showed a strong return on investment.

The railroads so heavily shaped the American steel industry in those early years that in many ways it would become a trap. When new uses for steel developed, causing the demand for steel to shift, American steelmakers would have difficulty adapting.

THE END OF RECONSTRUCTION

In terms of science and technology and of the effects upon American society, the division between the Reconstruction period and the Gilded Age that followed is arbitrary. The federal government's abandonment of Reconstruction, which permitted unrepentant southern leaders to establish segregation and Jim Crow laws, had its effects primarily in the impoverished south, not the industrial powerhouses of the north where most scientific and industrial development took place. In fact many of the same people who were major contributors to scientific and technological development in this period would continue as major figures in the Gilded Age.

LEIGH KIMMEL

Further Readings

Aldrich, Lisa J. *Cyrus McCormick and the Mechanical Reaper*. Greensboro, NC: Morgan-Reynolds, 2002.

Bray, John. *The Communications Miracle: The Telecommuniccation Pioneers from Morse to the Information Superhighway*. New York: Plenum Press, 1995.

Davis, L. J. *Fleet Fire: Thomas Edison and the Pioneers of the Electric Revolution*. New York: Arcade, 2003.

Fenichell, Stephen. *Plastic: The Making of a Synthetic Century*. New York: HarperBusiness, 1996.

Frizot, Michel, ed. *A New History of Photography*. Cologne: Könemann, 1998.

Galas, Judith C. *Plastics: Molding the Past, Shaping the Future*. San Diego, CA: Lucent Books, 1995.

Gernsheim, Helmut, *The Origins of Photography*. New York: Thames and Hudson, 1982.

Lemagny, Jean-Claude and André Rouillé, *A History of Photography*. Janet Lloyd, tr. Cambridge: Cambridge University Press, 1986.

Levin, I. E. *Inventive Wizard: George Westinghouse*. New York: Julian Messner, 1962.

Meikle, Jeffry L. *American Plastic: A Cultural History*. New Brunswick, NJ: Rutgers University Press, 1995.

Misa, Thomas J. *A Nation of Steel: The Making of Modern America, 1865–1925*. Baltimore: Johns Hopkins University Press, 1995.

Prout, Henry G. *A Life of George Westinghouse*. New York: Arno, 1972.

Sandler, Martin W. *The Story of American Photography*. Boston, MA: Little, Brown, 1979.

Shepard, Sue. *Picled, Potted and Canned: How the Art and Science of Food Preservation Changed the World*. New York: Simon & Schuster, 2000.

Wilson, C. Anne, ed. *Waste Not, Want Not: Food Preservation from Early Times to the Present Day*. Edinburgh: Edinburgh University Press, 1991.

Chapter 10

Entertainment

"Oh, Susanna, don't you cry for me
For I come from Alabama,
With my banjo on my knee."
— Stephen Foster's "Oh! Susanna," 1847

CULTURE IN THE form of music, art, and theater became increasingly important in the United States during the 19th century. Publishing had become a major industry. In New York City, two immigrant musicians, Bernard Beer and pianist Gustav Schirmer (1829–93) acquired the Kerksieg & Breusing music publishing venture on Broadway in 1861, becoming Beer & Schirmer. William Scharfenberg (1819–95) formed Scharfenberg and Luis, and sold tickets to the New York Philharmonic. Sheet music, particularly for the piano, was published in large quantities. This reflected the material culture of the 19th and early-20th centuries, when most residences had a piano and the music to perform, either publicly or for their private edification.

Athletic activities, including bicycling, baseball, tennis, racing (steamboat and horse), and yachting provided recreation and spectator sports for many Americans. By 1852 the Harvard-Yale boat race beckoned the beginning of intercollegiate sports. Colleges added baseball, football, and track during subsequent decades. In the first baseball game in 1859, Amherst College outscored Williams College 73 to 32. By the 1870s baseball was the primary college sport.

In the early 1860s New York City's German and Irish populations (not necessarily new immigrants) each comprised about 25 percent of the total. The Irish emphasized vernacular music, especially that of blackface minstrelsy. Among the most popular of these were Bryant's Minstrels, with Daniel D.

Emmett as a member, Campbell's Minstrels, Lloyd's Minstrels, and Sharply's Minstrels. Germans cultivated a more sophisticated tradition that included symphonic music. Many of these concerts were portrayed as "Sacred Con-

Music During the Civil War and Reconstruction

Many families owned a piano and sheet music during the 19th century. A wide variety of musical genres was played and heard throughout this time. Classical music was particularly popular in the cities, such as New York, Philadelphia, Washington, D.C., and New Orleans. There was the opera in New York, and the New York Philharmonic, its society served by George Templeton Strong and others.

Antebellum New Orleans became a fertile ground for opera production. Opened in 1835, the St. Charles Theatre seated 4,000, in a city with a population of 60,000. Those who listened included whites, free African Americans, and slaves. The French Opera House opened in 1859; Giacomo Meyerbeer's *Dinorah* was performed in 1861. Capture and occupation by Union troops in 1862 delayed operas until after the war.

Also popular was blackface minstrelsy, developed earlier in the 19th century by banjoist Joel Walker Sweeney (1813–60). His brother Sam Sweeney played banjo for Confederate Army General Jeb Stuart (1833–64). Thomas Dartmouth Rice (1808–60), "Daddy Rice," had first appeared as "Jim Crow" (1832). Folk music also prevailed, many musicians playing a banjo or similar chordal instrument, to tunes by Stephen Foster.

The Hutchinson Family of singers had performed since 1839, singing about temperance, women's suffrage, and abolition. In a recital for the Lincolns in January 1862, The Hutchinsons sang an arrangement of John Whittier's provocative abolitionist poem "We Wait Beneath a Furnace Blast" that nearly caused a riot. It eventually became one of the rally songs for abolitionists.

The Fisk Jubilee Singers, mostly former slaves, were founded at Fisk University in Nashville, Tennessee, by George White in 1871. They embarked on tours to New England in 1871 and to Europe in 1875, and sang before President Ulysses S. Grant in 1872. Much of their repertoire was classical music and sacred songs, but spirituals attracted the most attention. Their performances inspired other musicians to organize the Colored American Opera Company in Washington, D.C. in 1872. John Esputa directed "The Doctor of Alcanatara," an opera by Julius Eichberg (1824–93) to a packed theatre on February 3 and 4, 1873, in Lincoln Hall, in Washington, D.C. About one third of the audience was white. The troupe traveled to Philadelphia's Horticultural Hall for three performances before returning to Ford's Theatre in Washington, the site of President Abraham Lincoln's assassination.

certs," as they occurred on Sunday evening, a time decreed by law for only sacred events. During the opening months of the Civil War (April to December 1861), a majority of Union and Confederate families felt the war only in a limited manner. Pianist Louis Moreau Gottschalk performed 95 concerts 1862–64 in New York, and thought that city was immune to the ravages of war. But entrepreneurs were finding it difficult to sell concert tickets as the war progressed.

During the Civil War civilians often sang "Dixie," or Julia Ward Howe's poem the "Battle Hymn of the Republic" to the tune of "John Brown's Body." Based on their writings and diaries, soldiers, both Union and Confederate, favored songs that lacked wartime lyrics, like "Home Sweet Home" and "Lorena." In Union camps, "John Brown's Body" became an effective marching song. Union soldiers especially enjoyed the line "We'll hang Jeff Davis from a sour apple tree." Union troops also sang "Dixie," due to its northern origins, composed by Daniel Decatur Emmett (1820–1904), and abolitionist text supplied by Fanny Crosby (1820–1915) entitled "Dixie for the Union." Another popular tune was "The Battle Cry of Freedom" by George F. Root (1820–95), a composer of several war songs.

REGIMENTS AND BANDS

Band music became common in Washington, D.C., during the war. Several regiments had bands, which marched through the district. These ensembles performed a widely varied repertoire of patriotic songs, blackface minstrel tunes,

A wood engraving portrays preparation for the great national peace jubilee at Boston Music Hall. The members of the mammoth oratorio chorus, numbering 3,000, rehearsed on May 19, 1869.

Baseball provided exercise and a spectator sport for the Union troops, particularly those in prisons.

and operatic arrangements. The Marine Band presented regular summer concerts on the south lawn of the White House.

Baseball provided exercise and a spectator sport for the Union troops, particularly those in Confederate prisons. This game was then taught to the Confederates. On Christmas Day 1862 40,000 Union soldiers watched two teams of fellow soldiers play baseball on the island of Hilton Head, South Carolina.

While the war brought an increase in business for military bands, the New York Philharmonic Society retrenched in the wake of the Panic of 1857, and the increased competition they experienced from Italian opera singers and minstrel singers. The war only added to this stress. The New York Philharmonic Society, found in 1842, the nation's first permanent orchestra, moved its concerts from the Academy of Music to the smaller and less expensive Irving Hall for two seasons (1861–63). After selling out these two seasons the orchestra returned to the academy in late 1863. In spite of the war, opera thrived in cities. New York performances of 1862 included Giuseppe Verdi's *La Traviata* and *Il Trovatore*, Vincenzo Bellini's *Norma*, and Christoph Willibald Gluck's *Orefo ed Euridice*.

During the war censorship extended to music. When Major General Benjamin Butler took control of New Orleans, he censored the southern song "The Bonnie Blue Flag." He arrested the song's publisher, Armand Edward Blackmar, destroyed all existing copies, and threatened to fine anyone who sang or whistled the melody.

TECHNOLOGY AND SPORTS

After the Civil War communications technology and transportation influenced the growth of sports. Due to shortened travel time, baseball teams used the railroads; racers also shipped their horses by rail. In addition sporting news could be transmitted instantaneously with the telegraph, and then used by newspapers. The late 19th century saw the bicycle grow in popularity. In 1866 Pierre Lallement's velocipede, also called the "boneshaker," provided city residents a means of escape from densely populated areas. In 1866 New York's Jerome Park reinstituted horse racing. In 1867 the park hosted the first running of the Belmont Stakes, a 1.5-mile race for three-

Baseball Emerges as a Professional Sport

Baseball, an urban game, became popular after 1845, mostly in northeastern cities. Alexander Cartwright (1820–92) organized a game on June 19, 1846 in Hoboken, New Jersey. His rules included the diamond shape for the field, nine players, and the duration of nine innings, with three outs per inning. Some specific activities had different names: "strikers" (batters) attempted to score "aces" (runs); the first team scoring 21 aces won. Outfielders were labeled "scouts" and the pitcher's mound was known as the "pitcher's point." Fans were called "cranks."

The National Association of Base Ball Players was organized in 1858. Its membership fell from 54 teams in 1860 to 34 teams in 1861, the group later suspending all games. During the Civil War captured Union troops in Confederate prison camps often played baseball, spreading the game to the south. On Christmas Day 1862 40,000 Union soldiers watched two teams of fellow soldiers play baseball on the island of Hilton Head, South Carolina. Amateur baseball spread across the nation after the war.

In 1869 major league professional baseball's first team, the Cincinnati Red Stockings, were founded by Harry Wright (1835–95), achieving a 57-0-1 record their first season. This was the first all salaried team, players earning $600–$1,400 annually. By the end of 1870 there were five all-salaried baseball teams. In 1870 William A. Hubert (1832–82) founded the Chicago White Stockings, a team that eventually became the Chicago Cubs. This team was part of the National Association of Professional Ball Players (1871–75). It consisted of the Boston Red Stockings, Chicago White Stockings, Cleveland Forest Cities, Fort Wayne Kekiongas, New York Mutuals, Philadelphia Athletics, Rockford Forest Cities, Troy Haymakers, and the Washington Olympics. The fire in Chicago in October 1871 destroyed the White Stockings's ball park and uniforms. The team finished in second place, but did not resume play until 1874. The Philadelphia Athletics achieved the pennant in 1871. Boston's Red Stockings captured that trophy the following four years (1872–75).

Pitcher Albert G. Spalding (1850–1915) played for the Boston Red Stockings 1871–75; in the final year in Boston, the team compiled a 71-8 record behind Spalding's 56-4 pitching record. He then jumped to the White Stockings in Chicago in 1876. In February 1876 he organized his sports equipment enterprise, A.G. Spalding & Brothers, in Chicago. After playing and managing the Chicago team, he retired after the 1878 season to the sports equipment business of his name. The National League of Professional Base Ball Clubs formed in 1876. Dominated by owners instead of players, investments increased, and for the first time, umpires were paid. That year the standings were Chicago, St. Louis, Hartford, Boston, Louisville, New York, Philadelphia, and Cincinnati.

Velocipedomania, Bicycling as a Leisure Activity

An 1869 issue of Scientific American *declared "the art of walking is obsolete."*

In 1863, a Parisian machinist, Pierre Lallement (1843–91) developed the first successful bicycle. In 1866 he traveled to America and patented his velocipede. Due to poor sales, he returned to France in 1867. Calvin Witty, a carriage maker in New York City, bought the patent in 1869 and several velocipedes were sold during 1869–70.

Also in New York City, the Hanlon Brothers, a troupe of traveling gymnasts and acrobats, created a touring show, the *Hanlon Superba*, which featured cycling with the sound of lively music. They later owned the largest velocipede hall in the city. Outdoor road conditions were poor, and most cyclists rode indoors, especially where winter weather was severe. By winter 1868–69, riding schools had 10,000 students each in New York and Boston, with thousands more in Philadelphia, Chicago, St. Louis, and San Francisco. Some terms for these halls were *velocipedarium* or *velocinasium*, taught by *velocipedagogues* or instructors.

Materials used for American velocipedes varied. Cast iron proved hazardous and was quickly discontinued. Pickering and Davis used steel tubing. Even the clergy presented views on the moral use of velocipedes. Henry Ward Beecher, pastor of Plymouth Congregational Church of Brooklyn, hoped to see many riding to his services, but Shakers suspected the devil in this machinery.

In spring 1869, many riders went to Central Park. Non-asphalt roads in New York caused damage to several bicycles. Riders, accustomed to smooth surfaces, used sidewalks. Protests from pedestrians and legislation halted this, and eventually velocipedes were banned from Central Park.

Velocipedomania lasted only until late 1871. An exhibit at the Philadelphia Centennial Exposition of 1876 would attract former Civil War officer Colonel Albert Augustus Pope, who later formed the Pope Manufacturing Company to sell pistols and a cigarette rolling machine.

year- old thoroughbreds. That year's winner was Ruthless. In 1866 William Steinway (1835–96) built Steinway Hall as an extension of his piano show-room in New York. It was preceded by other music halls, the Academy of Music, and Irving Hall. William Scharfenberg was president of the New York Philharmonic 1864–67. George Templeton Strong was president of the Philharmonic Society 1870–74.

In 1867 Gustav A. Dentzel, an immigrant from Germany, remodeled his shop in Philadelphia to aid in his manufacture of carousels. His were the first in America to use steam energy. About 1870 Frederick Savage, an English mechanic, mounted a steam engine to a wooden carousel.

POSTWAR ARTS AND SPORTS

In 1869 Rutgers and Princeton universities played a soccer-style version of football. In professional baseball's first season, the Cincinnati Red Stockings, founded by Harry Wright (1835–95), achieved a 57-0-1 record their first sea-son. This was the first all-salaried team, players earning $600–$1,400 annu-ally. By the end of 1870 there were five all-salaried baseball teams.

Caledonian societies, largely of Scottish descent, had formed in the 1850s to sponsor professional track and field events. By the 1870s these drew up to 20,000 spectators. In 1870 the Baltimore Pimlico Park opened for horse rac-ing. Another sport, bicycling, finally increased in popularity about this time. In New York, due to poor road conditions outdoors, most cyclists rode in-doors in velocipede halls, especially during the winter. The arts and sciences offered leisure when the Metropolitan Museum of Art was organized in 1869. In 1871 the museum was built. The American Museum of Natural History, also built in 1871, is adjacent to Central Park. The Fisk Jubilee Singers, mostly former slaves, were founded at Fisk University in Nashville, Tennessee, by George White in 1871. They embarked on tours to New England in 1871 and to Europe in 1875, and sang before President Ulysses S. Grant in 1872, sing-ing classical music, sacred songs, and spirituals. Another ensemble was the Colored American Opera Company, organized in Washington, D.C. in 1872. They performed in that city and in Philadelphia.

In post-Civil War New York, Anthony Comstock (1844–1915) became a dominant figure in American censorship. The 1865 Postal Act had banned ob-scene materials from the mail. In 1873 Comstock founded the New York Soci-ety for the Suppression of Vice, serving as its secretary until his death. Also in 1873, Congress passed the Act for the Suppression of Trade in and Circulation of Obscene Literature and Articles of Immoral Use, the Federal Anti-Obscenity Act that was commonly referred to as the Comstock Law. Distributing printed materials deemed "obscene, lewd, or lascivious," including birth control litera-ture, could result in five years in prison. After one year as a special agent in the Post Office, Comstock had seized 130,000 pounds of "bad books," 194,000 indecent pictures and photographs, and other paraphernalia.

City Parks as Places of Leisure

During the middle of the 19th century city parks were created as diversions to the chaos and high tempo of urban life. In the 1850s landscape architect Frederick Law Olmsted and Calvert Vaux designed Central Park, an 843-acre park in New York City, America's first major city park. This included 136 acres of woodlands, 250 acres of lawns, and 150 acres of water in four man-made bodies of water. Construction began in 1858, displacing 1,600 people from their residences. Laborers, mostly German and Irish, worked 10 hour days, at wages of $1.00 to $1.50 per day. Early guidebooks invited citizens to observe the construction. Olmsted and Vaux used the name "Greensward," an English term meaning "unbroken stretches of turf or lawn." By winter 1858 the principal lake of New York's Central Park was used for skating, and by 1865 the park saw seven million visitors a year. By 1873 10 million cartloads of material, comprising 4,825,000 cubic yards of stone and dirt, had been hauled through the park, including 270,000 trees, shrubs, and plants, representing 1,400 species. In addition the Metropolitan Museum of Art organized in 1869, building its museum within Central Park. The American Museum of Natural History, also built in 1871, is adjacent to the park.

In 1869 Olmsted designed Riverside, a suburb of Chicago. Central Park served as a model for later parks, including Philadelphia's Fairmont Park by James Sidney and Andrew Adams. Begun in 1859 to protect a water supply, by the 1870s its size far exceeded that of Central Park. Others following the model were Washington Park in Chicago (1869) and a park in Tacoma, Washington (1873). Golden Gate Park, 1,107 acres built on reclaimed sand dunes, began development in 1871. The design by William Hammond Hall shows the influence of Olmsted. President Grant declared Yellowstone a National Park in 1872, although in the early years, travel there was affordable primarily to the wealthy.

A lithograph from the 1860s depicts families and ice skating on Jamaica Pond, West Roxbury, Massachusetts. Parks and recreation areas became popular in the mid-19th century.

By 1870 yacht racing had become popular in America. Nineteen years earlier, on August 22, 1851, the schooner *America* had defeated the British in the One Hundred Sovereign Cup. George Templeton Strong thought that the headline was overblown, describing it as "intolerable, vainglorious vaporings that make every newspaper I take up now ridiculous."

The America's Cup yacht race was held in New York until the 1920s. The winner of the first in 1870 was *Mag-ic*, commanded by Captain Andrew Jackson Comstock. Subsequent American winners included *Columbia & Sappho* (1871) and *Madeleine* (1876).

Yacht racing became popular in 1870, as the year witnessed the first America's Cup race.

Sheet music provided an avenue for advertising. In St. Louis, the Wm. Barr Dry Goods Company published complimentary sheet music of Johann Strauss (1825–99) and others. On the back cover was a catalog of materials for sale, including silks, dress linings and loopers, and Marseilles quilts. The store claimed the largest inventory in the West.

During the Civil War and Reconstruction, sports, whether amateur, college, or professional, grew in popularity. Baseball emerged as a national pastime and in 1874, modern football was played using modified rugby rules. Yacht racing and horse racing attracted not only participants, but thousands of spectators.

The arts and sciences became a point of leisure for many, with the openings of the Metropolitan Museum of Art and the American Museum of Natural History in New York, and the Smithsonian Institution in Washington, D.C. For the popular magazine *Harper's Weekly*, artist Winslow Homer and printer L. Prang produced a series of collectible souvenir cards that depicted life in the camps. People read several serialized novels published in monthly or weekly periodicals. Poetry by Walt Whitman appeared in *Harper's Weekly*. Games occupied many, including solitaire, cribbage, and checkers. Women developed such hobbies as needlework, knitting, and crocheting.

RALPH HARTSOCK

Further Readings

Cornelius, Steven H. *Music of the Civil War Era*. Westport, CT: Greenwood Press, 2004.

Cross, Gary S., ed. *Encyclopedia of Recreation and Leisure in America*. Detroit, MI: Charles Scribner's Sons, 2004.

Dodge, Pryor. *The Bicycle*. New York: Flammarion, 1996.

Fahs, Alice. *The Imagined Civil War: Popular Literature of the North and South, 1861–1865*. Chapel Hill: University of North Carolina Press, 2001.

Graziano, John, ed. *European Music and Musicians in New York City, 1840–1900*. Rochester, NY: University of Rochester Press, 2006.

McGurn, James. *On Your Bicycle*. New York: Facts on File, 1987.

Miller, Sara Cedar. *Central Park: An American Masterpiece*. New York: Harry N. Abrams, 2003.

Riess, Steven A. *City Games: The Evolution of American Urban Society and the Rise of Sports*. Urbana: University of Illinois Press, 1989.

Rogers, Elizabeth Barlow. *Frederick Law Olmsted's New York*. New York: Praeger, 1972.

Ryczek, William J. *When Johnny Came Sliding Home: The Post-Civil War Baseball Boom, 1865–1870*. Jefferson, NC: McFarland, 1998.

Schuyler, David. *The New Urban Landscape: The Redefinition of City in Nineteenth-Century America*. Baltimore, MD: Johns Hopkins University Press, 1986.

Simpson, Jeffrey. *Art of the Olmsted landscape: His Works in New York City*. New York: New York City Landmarks Preservation Commission, 1981.

Strong, George Templeton. *The Diary of George Templeton Strong*, edited by Allan Nevins and Milton Halsey Thomas. New York: Macmillan, 1952.

Trager, James. *The New York Chronology*. New York: HarperResource, 2003.

Ward, Andrew. *Dark Midnight When I Rise: The Story of the Jubilee Singers*. New York: Farrar, Straus, and Giroux, 2000.

Wiley, Bell Irvin. *The Life of Johnny Reb: The Common Soldier of the Confederacy*. Baton Rouge: Louisiana State University Press, 1978.

Chapter 11

Crime and Violence

*"We sometime didn't get enough to buy oats for our horses.
Most banks had very little money in them."*
— Frank James, outlaw and brother of Jesse James

CRIME DROPPED THROUGHOUT the 19th century. This may come as a surprise to people who grew up listening to tales about the wild west as well as those who learned in school about the rise of the American city. The conventional wisdom once held that a correlation existed between urban growth and criminal behavior of all kinds. More people led to more crime. Examinations of historical crime trends have demonstrated that such a belief is false. For the majority of people, life in the Civil War and Reconstruction era proved relatively peaceful and safe, except of course, for those involved in the war.

Then as now, Americans debated the causes of crime. While there are isolated cases in which the devil is blamed for criminal conduct, the age generally reflected rational thinking. In the 19th century science assumed a significant place in the American value system. Although science did not displace God, it did generate its own set of beliefs about the origins and meaning of human life. Science profoundly affected thinking about crime.

The doctrine of phrenology had just about passed its heyday by 1860. Phrenology determines human behavior by examining the shape of the skull. It encouraged Americans to think about crime in terms of biological abnormality, not simply moral failing. Degeneration theory succeeded phrenology as another biological explanation of crime. The theory held that socially problematic people devolved from normality and that degeneracy could be identified as poverty, drunkenness, chronic illness, or mental retardation. Accordingly criminology took root in a United States that already had some familiarity with the idea that criminality is a form of sickness; that there is something significant about the criminal's brain, that biology mirrors morality, and that crime can be addressed through science. The classical school of criminology represented the emergence of modern criminology, superseding the earlier view that crime was a supernatural phenomenon. Much of the machinery of the American criminal justice system of the 1860s and 1870s can be traced to the teachings of this school.

Classical thought offered the first naturalistic explanation for crime and, as such, represented a tremendous humanitarian advancement. People make decisions in a logical, calculating way by estimating the costs and benefits of a particular act. Having free will, they can act as they choose. At the heart of classical thought is the idea that it is better to prevent, than punish crime. Deterrence can be employed to influence behavior through threats. Classicists argued that the essence of crime was harm to society. A killing is not an act to be avenged by the bereaved family, but by society as a whole. Criminal law should be employed only to control behavior that is harmful to society. Punishment can be justified only as it is proportionate to the harm done.

Neoclassical thought modified the teachings of the classical school in the first decades of the 19th century. Neoclassical theorists introduced a number

A pre-Civil War lithograph portrays the night-time raid on the Charleston, South Carolina, post office by a mob of citizens and the burning of abolitionist mail, including magazines and newspapers.

Jesse James, Outlaw and Folk Hero

Tales of gunfighters of the old west have captured the imagination of readers since the 1870s. Jesse James, who came to prominence in this era, is probably the most famous American outlaw. Jesse and his older brother, Frank, became folk heroes for joining with their cousins, the Youngers, to rob banks and trains across the plains. Other men, just as lawless and violent, also helped give the west its wild image. Like the James brothers, most of these men were forged into killers in the bloody crucible of the Civil War.

Jesse Woodson James was born in Clay County, Missouri in 1847. Raised in a rural Missouri county by slave-owning parents, James witnessed many violent clashes between antislavery elements in nearby Kansas and proslavery groups in Missouri before the outbreak of the Civil War. At 17 years old, Jesse and Frank joined Bloody Bill Anderson's Confederate guerillas. Jesse saw several battles, gaining a reputation for skill and courage.

Beginning in 1866 the James-Younger Gang robbed banks and held up trains across several states. It was not until December 1869, however, that the men were publicly identified as suspects following a bank robbery in Gallatin, Missouri. Unlike most bandits, James recognized the power of public opinion and worked to shape it. He wrote several letters to local newspapers, sympathetic to the Lost Cause, which proclaimed his innocence and suggested he was the victim of political persecution by Radical Republicans in Missouri for his wartime service to the Confederacy.

Good planners and organizers, the James brothers were also notably vicious, despite their reputations as latter-day Robin Hoods. Jesse James, while fleeing the scene of one robbery, pivoted on his horse and put a rifle bullet through the head of an unarmed 17-year-old boy standing in the street. The James and Youngers never hesitated to gun down anyone who got in their way, including innocent bystanders. While they may have shared some of their loot with the poor, much of it ultimately went to finance gambling, drinking, and carousing. Jesse James died in 1882 when one of his gang, Robert Ford, shot him in the back of the head. Frank James lived into old age, publicly regretting his days of violence.

An 1864 photograph of Jesse James.

The New York City draft riots in 1863: Many of the deaths, often through vicious lynchings of African Americans, apparently were not recorded.

of shifts in criminal policy. There was an identification of degrees of criminal responsibility. Juveniles and the mentally ill were deemed incapable of forming intent to commit crime. Consequently the absence of criminal intent meant absence of responsibility for criminal acts. This shift from a focus on the harm inflicted, to the intent of the offender, represents the most important distinction between *classical* and neoclassical thought.

THE PROBLEM WITH STATISTICS

In the 19th century guns were fewer and poverty more widespread. These factors made a difference in crime rates. However the exact amount of crime in the Civil War and Reconstruction era is unknown simply because statistics were not kept. Reasonably consistent annual data about crime was not systematically gathered and published prior to 1930, when the Federal Bureau of Investigation began issuing its Uniform Crime Reports. Although there is good evidence to suggest that rates of criminal violence declined through the era, historians have had difficulty in proving this conjecture.

Homicide is generally considered one of the firmest indices of criminal behavior, because it is least subject to the vagaries of differing labeling procedures and definitions. Barring the relatively rare, calculated offense, it may be assumed that all but a handful of killings become known to the police. Nei-

Female Victims of Crime

Chivalry and gallantry towards women in the 19th century did not necessarily extend to female victims of crime. For women who were raped, religious and cultural attitudes often blocked the reporting and prosecution of sexual criminals.

Stories about women who sexually tempt men and incite men's desire to be sinful are part of Christian theology. The stories support religious views that hold women responsible for men's lustful conduct toward them. In the view of some Christian theologians, women who had been raped were tainted beyond repair. Jerome, an early medieval writer, advised women to commit suicide after rape because Christ did not have the power to crown one who had been so corrupted. By the 19th century Christian leaders still had clearly not consistently condemned the practice of rape or rape theories that harmed the victim.

Further complicating the situation of rape victims, legal treatises cast doubt on the believability of women. Sir Matthew Hale, a 17th-century English judge and legal scholar, influenced American law until the 20th-century. In his 1736 *The History of the Pleas of the Crown,* Hale took a suspicious stance toward female complainants by famously warning that rape is an accusation easily made, but hard to prove and hard to defend. He also asserted that rape in marriage was legally impossible because the wife had contractually agreed to perform sexual services.

English jurist William Blackstone built upon Hale's work with his classic 1765–69 four-volume treatise *Commentaries on the Laws of England.* Blackstone stated that the husband and wife become one by marriage. His assertion of the legal non-status of women lent further support to common law's long-standing non-recognition of rape in marriage. Blackstone also showed skepticism of the motives of women charging rape. He focused on the requisites of appropriate female response, imposing the greater burden on raped women in order to protect potentially innocent men from the threat of lying accusers.

These blaming attitudes created shame, guilt, and confusion for women victims. The courts did not help, appearing uninterested in protecting women from sexual assault. In *People v. Abbott,* an 1838 New York decision, the court ruled that a rape victim must meet three conditions to prove a charge. The woman must be of good reputation, must show evidence of physical resistance, and must have tried to call for help. In *People v. Morrison*, an 1854 New York State case, the court declared that the woman must resist a sexual attacker by using all of her natural abilities. In the absence of such resistance, there is no rape. In the presence of such social and legal attitudes, few women risked their reputations by making a charge that would not likely result in punishment for their attacker.

ther assumption holds true for the 19th century, as the best official statistics greatly underestimate the actual number of homicides committed.

For this era of the Civil War and Reconstruction, the coroner's office in several cities, including New York City and Philadelphia, published annual counts of homicides. The coroner's jury played a major role in determining how the deaths were reported. When the jury decided that the cause of death was not one man hitting another in a saloon, but rather the fall to the floor or that the victim had a weak heart, the case would be tallied in the annual reports as an accidental death.

Similarly a number of men were found with skull fractures in streets or alleys outside of saloons and were declared to have fallen on the pavement while drunk. A dying declaration about robbers might be ignored. In Philadelphia, an enormous number of people were reported as dying from drowning. In about 40 percent of these cases, the evidence for drowning was merely that the body had been found in the water. As one historian, Roger Lane, found, the fact that both hands were found tied behind the back was no sure key to a homicide verdict. There appears to have been considerable pressure on coroner's juries to reach verdicts that were not homicide.

The result of this fuzzy data is an unclear picture of crime in daily American life in the 19th century. The best available statistics for the period come

Perhaps the most impactful crime of the mid-19th century was the assassination of President Abraham Lincoln, portrayed above at Ford's Theatre being shot by John Wilkes Booth.

John Wilkes Booth, Assassin

Arguably the most famous murder of the 19th century, the 1865 assassination of President Abraham Lincoln by Confederate sympathizer John Wilkes Booth placed a period at the end of the massacre known as the Civil War. By his actions, Booth became the first presidential assassin in American history. By removing Lincoln, who could have overseen Reconstruction with mercy and justice, Booth also severely wounded his beloved south.

Born into wealth in Maryland in 1838, the temperamental and charismatic Booth grew up in a theatrical family. He followed his father and two older brothers onto the stage in 1855, making his professional debut in Baltimore. A specialist in Shakespearean tragedy, he earned $20,000 a year at the peak of his popularity.

Taking the side of the south in the Civil War, Booth publicly denounced both President Lincoln and the north. Toward the end of the war, Booth began to assemble a small band of conspirators in Washington, D.C. His group included David Herold, George Atzerodt, and Lewis Powell, also known as Lewis Payne. By this time Booth had become acquainted with a young southern sympathizer, John Surratt, and his mother, Mary Surratt, who operated a boardinghouse in Washington, D.C., in which the group would meet from time to time. Whether or not Booth had any official mandate from the Confederacy remains unclear.

On April 14, 1865 Booth learned that President Lincoln planned to attend *Our American Cousin* at Ford's Theatre. Booth assigned Atzerodt to assassinate Vice President Andrew Johnson and Payne to kill Secretary of State William Seward while Booth murdered Lincoln. Atzerodt made no attempt on Johnson, but Payne nearly killed Seward. Booth entered Ford's Theatre at about 10 P.M., moving across the rear of the balcony to the president's box. Lincoln's security was notably lax and no one challenged Booth. He entered the box and fired a single .44-caliber bullet at point-blank range into the back of Lincoln's head. He shouted "Sic semper tyrannis! The South is avenged!" before leaping 12 feet to the stage, breaking his left leg. He escaped from the theater to a waiting horse, and, accompanied by Herold, fled Washington.

They stopped at the home of Dr. Samuel A. Mudd in Bryantown, Maryland, to have Booth's leg set, then hid in neighboring woods for six days while federal troops vainly searched for them. By April 23 Booth and Herold reached the Virginia farm of Richard H. Garrett, 78 miles from Washington. The men hid in one of Garrett's tobacco barns. When federal troops surrounded the building in the early morning of April 26, Herold surrendered, but Booth chose to fight. The troops set fire to the barn and Sergeant Boston Corbett felled Booth with a bullet as he attempted to use a crutch to stand. Booth died and the government eventually hanged the other conspirators, including Mary Surratt, who may have been innocent of the plot.

from indictments presented to a jury. In 1860 New York City was exploding into America's largest metropolis with a polyglot immigrant population. The city held 800,000 people on the eve of the Civil War, including 12,000 African Americans. In 1860 there were 58 homicides recorded by newspapers. Of these cases, 32 went to trial and 29 resulted in convictions.

The New York City homicide rate remained fairly steady over the next 15 years, except for an unexplained jump to 100 corpses in 1864. Many of the deaths, often vicious lynchings of African Americans during the 1863 New York City draft riots, were not recorded. In Philadelphia, another major metropolis, there were 100 homicides 1860–66, while 156 people were murdered 1867–73 for an annual homicide rate of 2.85 per 100,000 people.

In 1870, as the murder rate dropped, the suicide rate rose. This pattern continued to the end of the century. Perhaps not coincidentally, the greatest historical increase in those employed in factories and bureaucracies occurred during the 1860s and the proportion increased steadily after that. Educational figures are parallel. Martin Gold, a social psychologist who developed the Suicide-Murder Ratio, argues that the process of socialization inclines individuals toward either the internalization or externalization of violence.

Those individuals inclined to be suicidal are trained to be cooperative, rational, and the extreme, repressed. Products of public schools learned to sit still, take turns, mind the teacher and listen for the bell—all ideal training for later factory or bureaucratic work. Progress for the United States accidentally brought higher suicide rates.

FAULTS IN THE CRIMINAL JUSTICE SYSTEM

Juries in this era were part of a society and criminal justice system that still accepted physical violence between men as an ordinary part of social discourse. Homicides occurring during brawls and drinking bouts inevitably carried minimal manslaughter charges.

A New York City man who beat his drinking buddy to death with a metal pipe received only one year in the penitentiary for fourth-degree manslaughter. A forger sentenced on the same day by the same court received 15 years. Given the nearly universal view that murder was the most serious crime, and the public awareness of such deaths, the courts simply appear to have been uninterested in prosecuting vigorously the most elemental criminal behavior.

Plea-bargaining was such a regular practice that the *New York Times* railed in December 1866 about murderers receiving light punishment. In San Francisco, a young Mark Twain (Samuel Clemens), a reporter for the *Morning Call*, complained bitterly when a vicious criminal received a year in state prison for brutally beating and robbing a man. Some mobs lynched killers because they knew that the judicial system would be lenient. A Monterey, California deputy sheriff who hanged a convicted murderer despite a postponement from the governor was commended in the local newspaper for allowing law and order to triumph.

The intake part of the criminal justice system also had serious faults in the 19th century. Many of the statistics fail to include a form of murder very common in the 19th century—infanticide—because of the lack of scientific procedures. With birth control and abortion inaccessible, many infants were killed shortly after birth. The mothers were typically unmarried women, in an era when the sexual double standard made the social penalties for child-bearing outside of wedlock especially severe. Virtually undetectable by the forensic techniques then available, infanticide was easy to hide under cover of any number of infantile diseases or mishaps. Some fraction of the total in Philadelphia can be measured by the number of anonymous newborns found unburied in the city's streets, empty lots, and privies. These infants, typically identified as dying from "unknown causes," numbered 12.3 per 100,000 cases in the 1870s. If they were counted as homicides, they would have greatly multiplied the available homicide figures.

Wholly without any technological aids, the police often were unable to capture suspects. Any attempt at flight or concealment was often enough to baffle an investigation. In 1860 photography was in its infancy. Without photographs, police had little reliable identifying information. Additionally, while they could collect masses of information on criminals, no systematic organization system existed so that the information could be accessed. Further complicating matters, assaults or killings by strangers or in the streets were characteristic of 19th-century crimes.

RACE, CLASS, AND CRIME

Racial and class discrimination, an element in much violence, proved especially intense in the 19th century. Life in many 19th-century immigrant urban neighborhoods was squalid and mean. Immigrants were disproportionately represented among the ranks of the inner-city poor. By 1860 nearly 90 percent of New York City's paupers were immigrants. When not begging for food or accepting charity, they lived in dank, dark, filthy, crowded tenements. Such conditions served as a breeding ground for alcohol abuse and crime. In 1870, 65 percent (32,322 of 49,423) of those in New York City's prisons were foreign-born, with 68 percent hailing from Ireland. The immigrants generally preyed on one another, with Irish and German males, in particular, slaughtering one another.

Racial hatred triggered the most infamous riot in American history. The New York City draft riots of July 1863 were sparked by the refusal of Irish men to be drafted to fight for the liberty of African Americans. Class resentment was an additional factor in the violence. Already at the bottom of the economic ladder, the Irish feared the competition that would be offered by freed African Americans. They resented the ability of rich men to pay $300 to hire a substitute to

A late 19th-century lithograph by Currier & Ives portraying African-American crime in the west. The American public hungered for pulp novels about bandits, outlaws, and desperadoes.

serve in the military. The fighting began on July 13, when an Irish mob stormed a building housing a draft office. By mid-morning, they controlled the streets. With the militia away with the Union army, only a few hundred police officers were available to take on a mob that frightened authorities estimated at 50,000. The rioters fought everyone, attacked every symbol of authority, beat surrounded cops to a pulp, and nearly killed the Irish-American police chief. Above all, they targeted African Americans. Over the course of several days, African Americans were lynched all over lower Manhattan. The size of the crowd cheering on the rioters inhibited most bystanders from intervening to help the victims.

As the draft riots indicate, crime has a structural cause. After the Civil War white homicide rates declined while African-American rates increased. Racial discrimination created a city that was structurally different for African Americans, as opposed to the one inhabited by whites, immigrants included. These structural differences accounted for the crime differences. Neither antebellum African Americans nor southern slaves were notable for interpersonal violence. Yet the homicide rate for urban African Americans rose steadily during this era because they were constant victims of race riots, dangerous trades, and menacing neighborhoods. Accordingly, African American men came to the logical conclusion that guns and knives were indispensable survival tools. Proportionately far more African Americans than white killings involved knives and guns. However necessary as protection, the carrying of weapons tended to escalate otherwise harmless arguments into deadly affairs.

THE WILD WEST

The image of the western frontier as a violent place where young men and the occasional young woman would pull a gun and shoot it out over the slightest provocation has endured through the decades. In the 19th century the number of pulp novels dealing with bandits, outlaws, and desperadoes soared as the reading public hungered for accounts of crime and violence in other parts of the country. Frontier crime is very much a part of American culture, if not actual history.

Reality may not have been as bloody as the image of the west, though. The press had an appetite for blood. Crime sold newspapers. The media reported minor killings that occurred both locally and in other parts of the country. As the frontier pushed steadily westward, correspondents provided eastern newspapers with a steady stream of accounts of shoot-outs and vigilante action. The

The Murder of "Wild Bill" Hickok

James Butler Hickok (1837–76), better known as "Wild Bill," was a frontiersman, lawman, scout, and especially a gunfighter, who became a legend through self-aggrandizing interviews he gave to eastern newspapers and magazines. His exploits were recounted and embellished to the point where he claimed to have killed "more than 100 men" in shootouts. His days came to an end in a Deadwood, Dakota Territory saloon when he was shot in the back of the head by John McCall, who later claimed the murder was in revenge for Hickok's killing of McCall's brother—a claim found untrue. Legend has it that Hickok, playing poker at the time of his death, held a pair of aces and a pair of eights, now known as a "Dead Man's Hand."

Martha Jane Cannary, better known as "Calamity Jane," wrote in 1897:

My friend, Wild Bill Hickok, remained in Deadwood during the summer with the exception of occasional visits to the camps. On the 2nd of August, while setting at a gambling table in the Bell Union saloon, in Deadwood, he was shot in the back of the head by the notorious Jack McCall, a desperado. I was in Deadwood at the time and on hearing of the killing made my way at once to the scene of the shooting and found that my friend had been killed by McCall. I at once started to look for the assassin and found him at Shurdy's butcher shop and grabbed a meat cleaver and made him throw up his hands; through the excitement on hearing of Bill's death, having left my weapons on the post of my bed. He was then taken to a log cabin and locked up, well secured as every one thought, but he got away and was afterwards caught at Fagan's ranch on Horse Creek, on the old Cheyenne road and was then taken to Yankton, Dak., where he was tried, sentenced and hung." (Life and Adventures of Calamity Jane) use of language tended to result in over reporting, as "fatal" or "mortal" did not mean that a person had died, only that it was likely that the person would succumb. The newspapers typically failed to follow-up on these presumed murders. In the west territorial newspapers regularly carried accounts of shootings, robberies, assaults, murders, and trials. While the number of killings remained low, the concern and anguish caused by these acts of violence shaped popular attitudes toward law enforcement and crime.

However the west was undoubtedly a violent place. The years after the Civil War were marked by lawlessness. In the mining region of the west, such as Idaho and Colorado, miners flocked to gold and silver fields in the 1860s. Fortunes were made and lost quickly, often illegally. The precious metals were packed out by stagecoach or on horseback, making the gold or silver vulnerable to thieves and the miners easy targets for violence. Also contributing to the blood atmosphere, most men and many women had at least one gun.

Settlers simply poured into the region too quickly for the legal system to adapt. The nearest courts and sheriffs were often two or more days away. In 1870 the *Idaho Tri-Weekly Statesman* reported that 200 men had been murdered in the past eight years, but only five killers were apprehended, found guilty of first-degree murder, and hanged. The absence of law enforcement forced westerners to create their own form of policing. Vigilante justice became common. In a typical episode, three robbers were grabbed by vigilantes and hanged in Montana Territory in the 1860s to end their reign of terror. The corpses were left to swing from trees as a warning to others.

BLOODY FAMILY FEUDS

Many westerners chose the age-old system of an eye for an eye. As a result, bloody feuds between two families or factions became common. Feuds happen whenever the law is absent or powerless and conditions become intolerable. In centuries past, it was a family obligation to avenge the killing of a relative. Anglo-Saxons could substitute money for blood (*wergeld*) and prevent the killing, but the English had to wait until the Middle Ages for murder to be defined as a crime against the state. Relics of these old attitudes appeared in more civilized times and places such as west of the late 19th century. Texas was the leading state for personal wars, with the region between San Antonio and Houston labeled the Pure Feud Belt. However all of the western states had episodes of such violence.

The violence in the west became intolerable as more people moved into the territory. As late as 1873, immigration to California was seriously hampered by the widely-publicized exploits of the notorious bandit, Tiburcio Vasquez. Demands for the control of serious offenses grew more common and vociferous, as citizens and political leaders called for greater protection in their new communities. For the sake of the safety of their families and their possessions, westerners, like the people of the east, south, and midwest, wanted law and order. They sought some sort of codified justice. Although weapons remained widespread, people became less willing to use them to settle an argument or dispute. Few westerners preferred the independent, man-against-man model of law maintenance. The rate of crime in the west dropped by 1876 as it already had throughout the rest of the United States.

CARYN E. NEUMANN

Further Readings

Brown, Richard Maxwell. *No Duty to Retreat: Violence and Values in American History and Society.* New York: Oxford University Press, 1991.

Brown, Stephen E., et al. *Criminology: Explaining Crime and Its Context.* Cincinnati, OH: Anderson, 1991.

Culberson, William C. *Vigilantism: Political History of Private Power in America.* New York: Greenwood Press, 1990.

Dedera, Don. *A Little War of Our Own: The Pleasant Valley Feud Revisited.* Flagstaff, AZ: Northland Press, 1988.

Kauffman, Michael W. *American Brutus: John Wilkes Booth and the Lincoln Conspiracies.* New York: Random House, 2004.

Lane, Roger. *Murder in America: A History.* Columbus: Ohio State University Press, 1997.

———. "Urban Homicide in the Nineteenth Century: Some Lessons for the Twentieth." In James A. Inciardi and Charles E. Faupel, eds. *History and Crime: Implications for Criminal Justice Policy.* Beverly Hills, CA: Sage, 1980.

Monkkonen, Eric H. *Crime, Justice, History.* Columbus: Ohio State University Press, 2002.

Reasoner, James. *Draw: The Greatest Gunfights of the American West.* New York: Berkley, 2003.

Secrest, William B. *Lawmen and Desperadoes: A Compendium of Noted, Early California Peace Officers, Badmen, and Outlaws.* Spokane, WA: Arthur H. Clark, 1994.

Settle, William, Jr., *Jesse James Was His Name.* Columbia: University of Missouri Press, 1966.

Waite, Robert G. "Violent Crime on the Western Frontier: The Experience of the Idaho Territory, 1863-90." In Louis A. Knafla, ed. *Violent Crime in North America.* Westport, CT: Praeger, 2003.

Chapter 12

Labor and Employment

"Labor is the superior of capital, and deserves much the higher consideration."
— Abraham Lincoln

ONE WAY TO look at the Civil War and its aftermath, Reconstruction, is that these events were a struggle over what kinds of labor or work Americans preferred to accomplish in a good society. By the mid-19th century American society stretched from the Atlantic to the Pacific Ocean, a breathtaking expansion taking only a few decades to acquire. But west of Mississippi River, even by the time of the Civil War, the land was inhabited largely by some one quarter of a million Native Americans, not American citizens. The fate of these western lands, particularly in terms of whether they would be open to slavery, largely inspired the hostile, sectional organization of the country, north and south, by the eve of war in 1860.

By 1860 most northerners believed in "free labor," meaning either self-employment by farmers or proprietors, independent work by skilled laborers who traveled from place to place or job to job, independent work by rooted skilled laborers, or dependent work by workers laboring under an employer or boss. Free labor ideology, in which workers were independent, or expected to become so, and were rewarded the fruits of their labor, was prevalent in the 23 northern states where slavery was non-existent or not widespread, which remained in the United States when war broke out in 1861. Among the 11 states that seceded and formed the Confederate States of America, there was no such consensus around free labor. Within these states there were

149

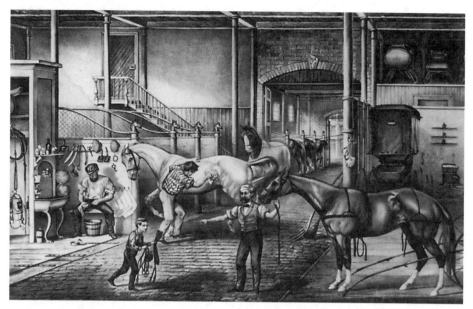

An 1893 lithograph shows common work in a stable: race horses being groomed, with a boy brushing a horse, another boy carrying reins to man, and a man cleaning bits.

3.5 million African-American slaves, nearly 40 percent of the total population of the Confederacy. In Mississippi and South Carolina, slaves outnumbered free people. Protection of white southerners' rights to own slaves and to benefit from the products of slaves' work—the defense of slave labor—was a primary reason the Confederacy waged war. In areas of the south in which there were relatively few slaves, such as in the mountains of Virginia, Tennessee, and even Alabama, and in the border states of Delaware, Maryland, Kentucky, and Missouri, which practiced slavery but did not secede, slave owners did not have strong support. In these areas pro-Union and pro-Confederate southerners fought during the war, and this division hurt the Confederacy's war effort. But Abraham Lincoln shortly before he became president described the United States as "half slave, half free," thus capturing the doctrines of labor that collided in the Civil War.

NORTH AND SOUTH BEFORE THE WAR

The Civil War had roughly opposite effects on American work and employment, north and south. In the north labor became more industrialized and productive; in the south, with the end of slavery and emancipation of four million slaves, or freedpeople, labor became more primitive and inefficient. After the Civil War the U.S. government and military sought to reconstruct the south in accordance with the doctrine of free labor, but the effects of the war's destruction of the southern economy, as well as white resistance to freedpeople's capacity for and right to free labor, limited the achievements of Reconstruction.

The Draft Riots and Employment

In March 1863 the U.S. government passed a conscription law that made all men between the ages of 20 and 35 and all unmarried men between the ages of 35 and 45 liable to military duty. Drafted men who provided an acceptable substitute, or paid $300 (equivalent to about $6,000 today) were exempt. The law pertained only to U.S. citizens, so only white men were liable. New York City was the country's largest seaport, where new poor immigrant workers felt especially threatened by anti-abolitionist warnings that emancipation would bring low-wage freedmen to compete with white laborers for employment.

On Monday, July 13, four hours before the city's draft selection was to begin, workers in the city's railroads, shipyards, iron foundries, and construction projects, including immigrants from Germany and Ireland, Catholics, and native-born Protestants began marching. They rallied briefly in Central Park, then converged on the draft office, where, shortly after names began to be drawn, city firemen ironically set the building on fire. By noon crowds numbered over 12,000, and by evening rioters were hunting various officials identifiable with the draft, and their property. By the middle of the week the rioters were more heavily Irish Catholics, and more common laborers, others having turned against the insurrection. These persisting rioters targeted not only the draft apparatus, but also anyone suspected of sympathizing with it, including policemen, Republican Party officials and supporters, supporters of the Emancipation Proclamation, and African Americans, whom many rioters apparently assumed the draft secretly sought to protect. At least 11 African-American New Yorkers were murdered, and hundreds of others were wounded and/or fled the city. Property was destroyed, including houses, telegraph lines, bridges, ferries, and a firearms factory in the industrial district of the Upper East Side. Working people, men and women, battled against policemen and U.S. infantry troops before the factory was burned down.

By the fourth day of the riots regiments returning to New York from the Battle of Gettysburg seized key streets and factories of the Upper East Side, and troops moved door-to-door, arresting or bayoneting protesters. The riots did not persist, aided by the Lincoln administration's modest reaction to declare that the draft must go forward, but giving local Democratic officials authority for best how to enforce it, and not declaring New York City under martial law.

The New York City draft riots reflected the collision of free labor politics asserted by the U.S. national government during the Civil War, and the on-the-ground wartime pressure and fears felt by urban workers, many, if not enslaved, then "unfree" and new to the United States. Elite organizations in the city sought to reform city politics, run perennially by corrupt and racist politicians of Boss William Tweed's Tammany Hall city government. But for many Americans the riots ingrained an image of a "dangerous class" of urban proletariat in an America becoming at once more socially rigid and more ethnically diverse.

Americans in 1860 shared many common working conditions. For many American farmers corn and cattle were staple products they grew for the market, and for their own sustenance. Most northerners and southerners alike made their living in farming, either as landowners or hired hands. Many children 10 to 16 years old were hired out to work on farms.

Most urban workers, northern and southern, slave and free, worked in small shops, rather than factories, in trades such as blacksmithing, carpentry, tailoring, masonry, and plumbing. Class structure across the United States also was similar, in that small groups of wealthy men—merchants and some industrialists in the northern states, large plantation owners in the southern states—strode atop society. When the Civil War began, the richest one percent of Americans owned 27 percent of the nation's property, while roughly half the population, consisting of working class industrial and agricultural workers, owned no property.

On the other hand some important differences existed in work patterns between the north and south. The most obvious difference was slavery. Most slaves, from when they were small children until they reached old age, worked as field hands, planting and harvesting crops, sometimes on large plantations, but more often on small farms. The rarity of large slave plantations, such as portrayed in the film *Gone With the Wind*, suggests those planters' wealth and impact on the American social structure.

The richest Americans of all on the eve of the Civil War were large southern slave owners, while successful but less wealthy merchants and farmers created a relatively large middle class in the northern states. Differences in climate and soil influenced northerners to grow wheat and oats, and southerners to grow cotton, and to a lesser extent tobacco, sugar, and rice, as their main cash crops. The success of the slave economy in the south influenced the region away from urban and industrial development; there were far more and larger cities in the north than in the south in 1860. Southern industry produced about one-fifth that of northern industry before 1860.

THE EFFECTS OF THE CIVIL WAR

The Civil War increased these differences. Industrial labor existed before the war, such as within the iron industry in a northern city like Pittsburgh and a southern city like Richmond, which employed slave labor and free labor working together. The iron industry resisted mechanization, relying through the 1870s on skilled laborers, many immigrants from England, shoveling iron ore onto railcars from boats and into furnaces from the railcars, "puddling," or using poles to stir molten pig iron into crystallized balls, and rolling the balls into plate or bars.

Elsewhere however, northern mechanization and industrial sophistication increased during the war, especially in boot and shoe production, meat-packing, railroads, and farming. Demand for products and skilled labor grew dramatically for needs of the Union military. Although most northern farmers at the end of the Civil War still turned the soil with a plow and seeded and harvested it by hand, the number of mowing machines manufactured tripled 1861–64. In the postwar years, a time when southern farmers of tobacco, rice, and sugar continued to rely on manual labor, and the cotton gin had mechanized only the deseeding of harvested cotton, not its planting and picking, wheat farmers came to rely on mowers, reapers, and harvesters. The war thus damaged the standing of unskilled northern workers, whose wages did not keep up with the wartime rise in prices. Labor organizations formed in many northern cities, and strikes for higher wages were common. The most tragic moment in labor militancy during the Civil War was the 1863 New York City draft riot, when largely immigrant mobs for nearly a week destroyed property and hunted down African American civilians in the city.

If the Civil War accelerated northern industrialization, its effect in the south was to make the economy more primitive, due to loss of usable property and labor. Practically the entire war was fought in the south, and fields, pastures, markets, and harbors were laid waste by battles, marches, and camps. Southern civilians supplied food for Confederate soldiers and animals throughout the war. By the end of the war even northern armies, such as Ulysses Grant's during the 1863 Vicksburg campaign and in particular William Sherman's during the

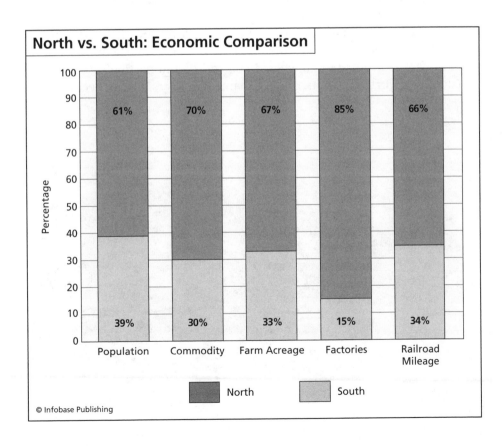

1864 "march to the sea" confiscated southern civilian food and livestock and intentionally destroyed agriculture, railroads, bridges, factories, and other usable property. Meanwhile the Union naval blockade reduced southern imports and exports by sea, worsening the shortage of domestic goods caused by southern factories' conversion to production of war materials, not goods for civilian consumption. In April 1862 the Confederacy enacted a military draft, requiring all men between 18 and 35 years old, not owners of at least 20 slaves, to serve in the military. Because the Confederacy's population was only some nine million, compared to some 23 million in the Union, the war required a greater proportion of white laborers for military service in the south than in the north; three of every four white men of military age—by 1864, 17 to 50 years old—served in the Confederate army. This left agricultural and industrial jobs much in the hands of white women, and slaves with diminishing incentive to remain loyal.

FEMALE LABOR

The most common form of labor outside the home for American women in the 19th century, constituting about eight percent of the American labor force in the 1870s, was domestic service, as maids, cleaners, child minders, and cooks. But the Civil War brought changes to American women's labor, the change most profound in the south.

Among northern working women, new opportunities to work outside the home emerged in clerical work and teaching, previously dominated by men, as well as in nursing fallen soldiers, considered particularly suited to female skills. Northern women also became teamsters, bridge keepers, and

A wood engraving published in 1863 depicts laborers building a levee on the Mississippi River, below Baton Rouge, Louisiana.

undertakers. Northern military needs also increased women's jobs in sewing and in textile mills, although women's place in these forms of work had gained acceptance in the north long before the Civil War. Sewing women were paid by "the piece," working either in their homes or in large mass-producing warehouses. America's first factories, the textile mills of New England, had long employed large numbers of women. This continued during and after the war, but working conditions worsened as power looms and yarn sizing "slashers" reduced need for laborers and made human labor more routine and deskilled.

An 1877 issue of Harper's Weekly features women and men working in a gun cartridge factory.

In the south, where white slaveholding and non-slaveholding families alike were organized socially around authority of the father and husband, and which was heavily agricultural, the departure of men for the military forced many women (if they did not soon become refugees—during the war, most white refugees were female) to undertake new kinds of labor for the first time. In the antebellum south, white women did not work outside the home without experiencing a degree of social scorn. But after the war began women became shopkeepers, teachers, government clerks, waged workers in wartime factories, and nurses, although, especially in the latter category, not in numbers necessary to meet the Confederacy's acute need for medical care for wounded and sick soldiers. Care in hospitals and infirmaries, in fact, became a small province for new labor of slaves, female and male.

More broadly, southern white women had to perform demanding field labor for the first time, or, if they were slave owners, at least to make new decisions about administering slave or hired labor for planting and harvest. Household management in the United States of the 19th century, in general, compared to today, required more skill and much more effort in food preparation, laundering, cleaning, and repairs. In general however, the Civil War forced southern women to become more self-reliant than their northern counterparts. Confederate policy-makers urged women to produce and wear "homespun," clothing sewn, woven, and spun by themselves, not bought. This encouragement, made on the basis of practicality as well as southern patriotism, was not widely embraced, however. Poorer women often resorted to recycling bed and table linens and curtains for clothes, and women unaccustomed to home production

The Transcontinental Railroad

In 1832 a Michigan newspaper called for a railroad from New York City to Oregon, and in 1859 Abraham Lincoln, one of the country's foremost railroad lawyers and an aspiring candidate for the U.S. presidency, asked Grenville Dodge, a railroad engineer, about the best route for a railroad to the Pacific Ocean. In 1862 Congress, absent southern members who had argued that a transcontinental railroad should terminate at the southern city of New Orleans, passed legislation for the Union Pacific Railroad (UP), a private company, to begin at the Missouri River, and to meet the Central Pacific Railroad (CP), another private company, originating in Sacramento. A follow-up act in 1864 specified that the UP's eastern terminal would be Omaha. No meeting point of the two railroads was designated. Both corporations were to receive financial aid, land grants, and all building materials, and were to complete the entire road by July 1, 1876.

Many of the railroads' first workers were Irish immigrants brought west from New York and Boston. Prodded by strikes, the CP leadership asked the U.S. War Department for Confederate prisoners of war, freedmen, and Mexican immigrants, but was unsuccessful. When the CP reached the Sierra Nevada Mountains the railroad decided, despite concerns that white laborers would desert, to hire Chinese, called "coolies," a Hindu term meaning unskilled labor. Chinese men had come to California in the gold rush, but facing white discrimination in mining by the 1860s had migrated to domestic service. Most Chinese immigrants, like Irish immigrants, did not come to the United States at this time to work on the railroads, but Chinese laborers, working in gangs but less prone to strikes, came to dominate the lower paid elements of the railroad's construction. Their tasks included grading, blasting, felling trees, and hanging suspended in baskets for work in the mountains, drilling holes for and igniting black powder for driving tunnels. Although nitroglycerin was adopted by 1867, its components were hauled separately and mixed on the spot by a Scottish chemist. White, usually Irish bosses supervised the gangs, and whites performed the skilled work of masonry and rail-laying. In tunnels, a foot a day was normal progress.

Many of the workers on the UP railroad continued to be Irish, and the UP's workforce became labeled as such. The UP's workforce generally was more diverse than the CP's, with workers from across Europe and the United States, including some 300 freed slaves. Mormon laborers joined the work in Utah. UP workers were plagued not by mountains, but by the heat of the Great Plains, as well as harassment by hostile Native Americans.

By 1869 the CP crew consisted of native-born white men, former slaves, European and Chinese immigrants, as well as a few Mexicans and Native Americans. On May 10, 1869, seven years ahead of schedule, the two railroads met at Promontory Point, Utah, a golden spike driven into the line to commemorate the moment.

before the war sought clothing through smuggling goods either through the Union blockade or from Union occupied areas of the south.

White women's ability to manage slaves was crucial to the fate of the Confederacy, given slavery's importance to the south's economy. Slave owning women did attempt to take many of the tasks of slave owning, including exhorting slaves to work efficiently, manipulating slave labor by rewarding good work and berating or beating slaves who worked inefficiently; buying and selling slaves; worrying about the possibility of slave uprisings, or, with increasing frequency, witnessing slaves running away. Southern women in general did not believe themselves capable of controlling slaves, and their letters to the Confederate government and, more significantly, to men in the Confederate military probably contributed to declining military morale and increasing desertion rates.

FREEDPEOPLE

Ironically Confederate deserters headed south sometimes might meet with runaway slaves generally going north, because, even before Lincoln issued the Emancipation Proclamation of 1863, slaves began to abandon their owners' farms and plantations, headed for the nearest Union army. Initially some Union generals ordered that the runaways be returned to their masters, but as much for practical impossibility as moral imperative, the Union's policy in 1861 became that any slave coming within Union lines would be considered "contraband of war," not returnable to their owners. Through slave initiative and government policy, by 1865 millions of slaves across the south were becoming refugees. In the short run runaway and contraband slaves were put to work by the Union army as cooks, launderers, and teamsters, earning monetary wages, or more frequently given food and clothing as compensation.

In March 1865, shortly before the end of the war, Congress attempted a comprehensive plan to accommodate the freedpeople and white refugees alike, in its creation of the Bureau of Refugees, Freedmen, and Abandoned Lands, or Freedmen's Bureau, the most prominent if not only U.S. government agency committed to helping American workers before the 20th century. The bureau was to distribute clothing and food to former slaves and whites displaced by the war pledging loyalty to the Union, and even to divide land previously owned by white planters, now, after the war, considered abandoned, into 40-acre plots for rental and sale to these groups. Land transfer happened in a few areas in the south, where freedmen settlers attempted as much as possible to create and maintain farms self-sufficient by or at least as independent of white oversight.

The most storied case of African-American land settlement during Reconstruction happened on the initiative of General William Sherman, whose march through Georgia and South Carolina brought to his control thousands of acres of coastal rice plantations and the Sea Islands. Early in 1865 Sherman ordered that these lands be set aside for the exclusive settlement of African

The Welsh in America

Samuel Ab Thomas was a Welsh immigrant miner who worked in the coalmines of eastern Pennsylvania. He wrote the letter, excerpted in part below, a few months before the miners began their "long strike" (December 1874–June 1875) over long hours, low wages, compulsory patronage of the company stores and housing, and the required level of production.

There are four large coal works in Tioga County by the names of Morris Run, Fallbrook, Antrim, and Arnot. You all know about the bankers' debts a few months ago which caused the new railroads to be stopped, mills and furnaces to be blown out, and the coal works to be stopped, etc., so that thousands of craftsmen, puddlers, and laborers have been thrown out of work to live or die as best they can. Also, to show us their power, they forced us to sign the contract law, which was against the law of the state government, that is that if any misunderstanding occurred between master and workman, the latter had to leave his house with ten-days' notice according to the contract law, whereas the state government allowed three months.

But, although we suffered the above without grumbling throughout the years, it was not enough to satisfy the greed of our masters, for early this winter they rushed on us with the fierceness of a lion on its prey, lowering us to 20 percent and also threatening us with 10 percent and forcing us to bind ourselves not to accept money for our labor until May 20, 1874.

In the face of such tyranny and oppression, we called a meeting of the workmen for the purpose of drawing up some plan to withstand the continuance of such tyranny and oppression. We resolved to form a branch of the National Miners and Laborers Benevolent Association of Pennsylvania, which was backed by the government a few years ago and gave it a charter. As I understand it, this same union pays well throughout the country, and we hope it will be the same here.

Americans. Each family would receive 40 acres of land, and Sherman also indicated that the Union army could loan mules for assistance.

Neither Sherman nor military policy used the expression "forty acres and a mule," but the expression gained life with this event, although today its usage has come to mean the failure of Reconstruction and the general public to assist African Americans in the path to freedom. This meaning is grounded in the action of President Andrew Johnson, a white southerner, former slave owner, and Lincoln's vice president, who thus became president upon Lincoln's assassination. Johnson did not share his predecessor Lincoln's support for strong federal government, and especially for African Americans' right to participate in southern Reconstruction, after having slavery abolished. He believed that

A mid-1860s photograph of military railroad operations in northern Virginia of African-American laborers twisting rail. To destroy the enemy's supply lines, both sides often tore up railroad track and bent the rails, preventing rapid repair.

the freedpeople would compete with white yeoman farmers and mechanics, whose cause he had championed for decades. In May 1865 Johnson pardoned southerners who had sympathized with the Confederacy, but who would now swear loyalty to the U.S. Constitution and abolishment of slavery, and required that the U.S. Army restore these individuals' lands to them. He thus rescinded attempts to provide land to freedpeople by ownership or lease by Sherman as well as other Union commanders and the Freedmen's Bureau. Most freed-people, too poor to buy any farmlands they then occupied, were evicted.

SHARECROPPING AND THE FAILURE OF "FREE LABOR"

The return of most land in the south to its previous owners forced the bureau toward the more conservative program of encouraging or forcing the freed-people (but not unemployed or displaced white farmers) to sign annual labor contracts to work on plantations reclaimed by former owners or purchased by northern businessmen come south.

Under these contracts, and because of a scarcity of cash money in the south, the system of sharecropping emerged, in which tenant farmers received land on which to live and work, tools, and seed, and received a portion of the crop harvested at the end of the year. Actually many poor whites fell into sharecrop-ping, but the system was open to abuse especially of African-American tenants by wily planters, who might write contracts that called for African Americans, most of whom were illiterate (although illiteracy was widespread among whites also), to work for unreasonably small crop portions, or even nothing, and re-sorted to corporal punishments of uncooperative African-American workers,

The Cowboy

The most storied American laborer that emerged shortly after the Civil War was the western cowboy, great numbers of whom flocked first to Texas to herd cattle toward railroads for transport to market. Cowboys were of various ethnic backgrounds, European, African American, and Mexican, a diversity reflected in the *Buffalo Bill's Wild West* Show of the famous William F. Cody, started in 1883, which probably first launched the glamorous image of the cowboy, subsequently embraced by Hollywood.

Actually cowboys' daily lives functioned similarly to those of other 19th century systematized laborers. Most cowboys were illiterate. They spent most of their time herding, rescuing animals lost or in distress, mending fences, repairing equipment, gathering dried manure for fires on the plains, and fighting brush fires. As in other detailed organizational hierarchies emerging in American business at the time, cattle drives had various labor components. Foremen experienced with the land led the way, followed by the chuck wagon and the herd. Then came the most experienced drovers, riding either flank both to prohibit straying and to watch for Native Americans, who, reflecting the onset of labor for money in the west, sought as frequently to scare cattle into running away, and then to collect pay for catching them, as to attack the cowboys. A wrangler leading spare horses rode to one side of the herd. The remainder of the outfit brought up the rear. An average herd of cattle numbered about 2,500 head and was tended by about a dozen cowboys.

In conjunction with the extension of the railroads, by the early 1870s new ranches were established on the northern plains, in Kansas, Nebraska, Colorado, Wyoming, and Montana, closer to Chicago and markets east. Some cowboys at the conclusion of a cattle drive would stay for work in northern shipping yards. Yard workers used prods to jab cows' flanks to direct them onto railroad cars, thus becoming known as "cowpunchers," a play on words reflecting the homogenization of American workers through connection of western plains with eastern cities.

Photograph of a late 19th-century cowboy. Most cowboys were illiterate and spent their time herding and mending fences, among other duties.

many of whom resented dependent conditions they believed too reminiscent of slavery, or were more interested in locating family members sold under slavery than in labor tied to land.

The Freedmen's Bureau acted vigorously in protecting African-American workers' rights against exploitation, prosecuting landlords shown to be abusive. Nonetheless, the system of annual contracts restricted freedpeople from seeking better working conditions elsewhere, unless emerging industries were very nearby, a violation of basic free labor economics that the bureau was established to apply in the south.

RAILROADS AND THE WEST

An explosive industry that could draw, at least temporarily, many poor laborers from agricultural doldrums was the steam-powered railroad. More railroad track was laid in the decade after the Civil War than existed before the war began. Reflecting the birth of American big business at this time, the Pennsylvania Railroad Company, the nation's largest corporation, possessed more track than most foreign countries. The railroads extended beyond the Mississippi River after the Civil War, a connection between east and west symbolized by the celebrated meeting of the transcontinental railroad at Promontory Point, Utah. The extension of the railroad system beyond the Mississippi River brought the free labor system into the west.

The railroad industry created a whole new organizational work force: engineers, firemen, conductors, brakemen, station agents, switchmen, baggage porters, dispatchers, repairmen, and mechanics. Railroads also spawned other large-scale industries, including meat-packing, lumbering, and mining, operated like the railroads by large interstate corporations employing hundreds of waged workers. The federal government expanded its power considerably during the Civil War, mainly under the Republican Party. To maintain this authority and hasten national development, federal policymakers especially beginning with the presidency of Ulysses Grant in 1868—again, Andrew Johnson had opposed an active federal government—granted millions of acres of western land for development, a policy of enormous benefit to railroad and mining companies.

Thus farmers, ranchers, cowboys, miners, immigrants, sheep, and cattle poured into the Great Plains and onward to the Pacific Coast during the Reconstruction period, bringing the west into the free labor system. This transformation, destroying buffalo herds that had provided food and clothing for the Native Americans of the Plains, effectively ended the Native-American way of life, forcing them to accept settlement on reservations and farming as a means of survival. The Pawnee people submitted to living on reservations relatively peaceably, and were actually hired on to protect workers of the Union Pacific railroad from attacks by hostile Native Americans. But the Sioux, Cheyenne, and Arapaho proved hostile, and fought and were pursued by U.S. military for the rest of the century. Large estates, similar to southern plantations, emerged in California, which utilized Chinese and Mexican immigrant labor in ways similar to African-American sharecropping in the south. Overall, however, it was possible for many western farmers to own their own land.

Labor independence was more the case in the post-war west than east. In the east an industrial capitalist class emerged, as well as an entrenched working class, especially in New England. There dramatic rates of income inequality appeared, as much as in the pre-Civil War south. Such disparity strengthened the growth of unions as workers struggled against periodic wage cuts, hazardous conditions, long working hours, and child labor—by the 1870s perhaps 300,000 children less than 16 years old worked in factories, mills, and mines, or as domestic servants.

The Great Strike of 1877 by railroad workers, protesting wage cuts, however, spread north and west from West Virginia, and was joined by workers in other industries. The Great Strike eventually required U.S. federal troops, many quickly transferred from garrisons in the south, to put down the strikers by force from Buffalo to St. Louis. Dozens of people were killed and thousands of railroad cars were destroyed. By the mid-1870s there were more nonagricultural workers than farmers in the United States. Perhaps reflecting this change from before the Civil War, the U.S. government, forced to act against wage laborers in the north rebelling against the industrial class system there, stopped its attempt to put southern agriculture on a free labor path. The south thus saw redemption by politicians who championed states' rights and largely were committed to wiping out economic and political opportunities for the freedpeople. By 1875 truly free labor existed in the United States largely west, not east, of the Mississippi River.

TIMOTHY M. ROBERTS

Further Readings

Ambrose, Stephen. *Nothing Like it in the World: The Men Who Built the Trans-continental Railroad 1863–1869*. New York: Simon & Schuster, 2000.

Bernstein, Iver. *The New York City Draft Riots*. New York: Oxford University Press, 1990.

Faust, Drew. *Mothers of Invention: Women of the Slaveholding South in the American Civil War*. Chapel Hill: North Carolina Press, 1996.

Foner, Eric. *Reconstruction: America's Unfinished Revolution*. New York: Harper & Row, 1988.

Paludan, Philip. *"A People's Contest": The Union and the Civil War 1861–1865*. Lawrence: Kansas Press, 1996.

Pessen, Edward. "How Different From Each Other Were the Antebellum North and South?" *American Historical Review* (v.85, 1980).

Sutherland, Daniel E. *The Expansion of Everyday Life 1860–1876*. New York: Harper & Row, 1989.

Chapter 13

Military and Wars

"There is many a boy here today who looks on war as all glory, but boys, it is all hell."
— William Tecumseh Sherman, 1879

FROM 1861 TO 1865 the United States was locked into a devastating civil war between the northern and southern sections of the nation. The crisis that led to this split had many roots, but the central issue was the extension of slavery into territories not yet organized into states. It was feared widely in the south that if free states ever outnumbered slave states, the institution would eventually be ended by constitutional amendment. Even though the vast majority of white southerners did not own slaves, the idea was potentially devastating to the region; not only was the south's agricultural economy dependent upon slavery, but its domestic and political institutions rested upon it and the racial hierarchy which supported it. The rise of the Republican Party in the north during the 1850s, which was devoted to the principal of the spread of free labor and had many abolitionists among its ranks, was considered by many white southerners an ominous sign for their region's future.

Following the election of Republican President Abraham Lincoln in November 1860, the states of the deep south seceded. In February 1861 they came together to form the Confederate States of America. A crisis meanwhile brewed over the continuing presence of U.S. troops at Fort Sumter in Charleston harbor, which the federal government refused to give up. On April 12 Confederate forces opened fire on Fort Sumter, forcing the garrison to surrender the next day. Lincoln's call for 70,000 volunteers to crush the rebellion

163

resulted in the secession of the wavering upper south states, which joined the Confederacy in turn. It would take four years before the crisis was resolved on the battlefield, by the end of which slavery had been eliminated. Questions over the role that the former slaves would play in the new America, however, would lead to more controversy and violence during the Reconstruction. The failure of the Civil War generation on how to deal with this issue would haunt the nation for many years.

Both the United States and the Confederate States of America were forced to improvise their war efforts. On paper the north passed the advantage in resources, as it had the greater industrial strength and manpower base, an agricultural system devoted to food production over staple crops, a much larger and better integrated war railroad network, and a regular army and navy. Nevertheless the U.S. Army was small, and most of it was scattered at various posts in the west, so like the Confederacy it would have to raise a large number of troops to put into the field. Furthermore a number of former and active officers of southern origin would lend their services to the Confederacy. The south also possessed a major advantage in the size of its territory, which would take time to subdue if properly defended. Thus to some extent both sides were starting on a relatively even level, although over time the north's superior resources would play a greater role.

Both sides developed strategies to implement their respective goals. For the United States the object was to defeat the Confederacy's military forces in order to reunite the nation. The initial plan, devised by General-in-Chief Winfield Scott, was dubbed the Anaconda Plan. It called for a naval blockade of the south's ports to prevent war supplies and other goods from entering the Confederacy,

A wood engraving shows the floating battery in Charleston Harbor, South Carolina, during the bombardment of Fort Sumter, marking the start of the Civil War on April 12, 1861.

The Enlisted Troops

The vast majority of U.S. and Confederate troops were not regular soldiers, but citizens who enlisted voluntarily or involuntarily for service. During 1861, when patriotism and optimism were at a premium on both sides, large numbers of northerners and southerners volunteered for the conflict. The U.S. government had long practiced the raising of volunteer companies for military crises to supplement the usually rather small standing army. This had happened on a large scale in the War of 1812 and the Mexican War.

During the antebellum era the often feeble state militias were supplemented by volunteer companies raised and equipped by local communities or wealthy individuals. There had been a particular increase in such units in the south following John Brown's Harpers Ferry Raid in 1859. Many such volunteer companies, both north and south, along with new ones organized during the secession crisis or after the outbreak of the war, formed into state volunteer regiments and battalions and were accepted for national service. Each of these units belonged to one of the three main branches of land service at that time: infantry, cavalry, or artillery. Soldiers who entered the Union or Confederate regular armies, both of which were small in comparison to the provisional or volunteer forces, might serve in other types of units, such as the military engineers.

As the war continued and it became obvious that quick victory was not around the corner, enthusiasm waned among those who had not yet joined up. Because enlistments sharply declined and many early volunteer units were raised only for service of from six to 12 months, something had to be done. The result was that both governments instituted conscription, with the Confederacy taking the lead in April 1862. The draft proved hugely unpopular in both sections. Many efforts were devised to circumvent it, including various exemptions offered at the state or national levels, or the hiring of substitutes to serve in a draftee's place. Such methods only served to promote cynicism among those who could not take advantage of the system, and opposition to the drafts increased, including the outbreak of anti-draft riots in New York.

Although the majority of the soldiers, whether volunteers or conscripts, served out their terms unless felled by death, injury, or disease, some chose to desert. The reasons for desertion were many, and by no means limited to simple cowardice; instead, soldiers left the army for a variety of reasons, including war weariness and opposition to the conflict (or at least their section's role in it). Anti-war dissent was in particular a major problem in some sections of the south, especially in eastern Tennessee, where pro-Union sentiment was high, and it is not surprising that many desertions came from such regions. Health problems were another reason for desertion, as were troubles at home. The latter was a particular problem for Confederate armies as the war progressed, and more and more territory was threatened by advancing federal soldiers, causing worries for the safety of loved ones among the ranks.

Federal Treatment of Confederate Civilians

It has become an established part of Civil War mythology, especially in the south, that federal armies behaved in a uniformly barbarous manner towards southern civilians. The central villain in this body of lore is Major General William Tecumseh Sherman, whose troops on their march through Georgia and the Carolinas in late 1864 and early 1865 supposedly committed arson, vandalism, rape, and other atrocities unprecedented in all of human history, or at least in all of American history.

In fact the actual picture was in many ways quite different. Atrocities certainly occurred in the war, and some of Sherman's soldiers would have to be included among the guilty. In general however, Civil War armies on both sides practiced restraint in regards to civilians, and in terms of official practice Sherman was no exception. Hardships inflicted on civilians were usually the result of armies attempting to feed themselves by living off the land, or were the results of efforts to shorten the war by targeting the transportation and communication systems on which both the army and the public depended.

The gathering of food from a local populace in an area which either a hostile or friendly army was occupying or passing through was a time-honored method used by military forces to supplement their food supply. Transportation systems and food preparation and preservation prevented them from having the majority of their sustenance brought up to them from their home bases. In addition, other things necessary for the functioning of an army might be requisitioned, such as horses to replace broken-down cavalry mounts. There were general rules to manage such conduct, and some form of compensation was usually promised (whether or not it might be received was another matter). In addition to this, hungry soldiers on the march in both armies would take what they needed to fill their bellies. If caught, they might be punished, but officers and even army commanders might wink at such behavior.

A more deliberate policy evolved during the war in terms of striking out at what might be called today the enemy's infrastructure: railroads, canals, telegraphs, industry, supply depots, and the like. Such willful destruction would hurt the opposition's ability to resist, not only by making it difficult to wage war, but also by striking a blow to enemy morale. Ideas related to such conduct were not related to the north alone: Thomas J. "Stonewall" Jackson was an early advocate of such a "hard war" policy in regards to the north, even if he was never really able to personally put it into practice. The fact that some officers on both sides advocated such methods should hardly be surprising, as they shared not only a common American military background, but also a common western military inheritance, where such ideas were hardly novel. As the war progressed and the chances of a quick victory proved elusive, the U.S. commanders moved to implement them as their armies progressed deeper into Confederate territory.

while a major joint Army-Navy advance down the Mississippi River would split the Confederacy in two. Scott optimistically thought that these measures would cause the Confederacy's collapse. Political pressure for a quick victory led to the first modification of Scott's plan: the decision to march the primary federal army in the east, the Army of the Potomac, from Washington, D.C. to Manassas Junction, Virginia, as a prelude to the capture of the Confederate capital of Richmond.

The poorly-trained Army of the Potomac suffered a major defeat at the First Battle of Bull Run on July 21. The outcome greatly boosted Confederate morale, and produced a corresponding damper in the north.

For the Confederate government, the primary strategy was defensive: to defeat whatever forces were sent into its territory. Confederate leaders also hoped that the blockade would provide unintentional assistance, forcing Britain and other nations dependent on southern cotton for their textile industries to intervene on their behalf. The Confederacy also hoped to circumvent the blockade by sending out blockade runners, fast ships to evade federal warships, and bring both military supplies and civilian goods into southern ports. Finally the government commissioned the construction of commerce raiders. Often in foreign ports, these ships would prey on U.S. merchant vessels and hopefully inflict as much or more havoc on the northern economy as the blockade would on the south's economy.

The engagement between the Union Monitor *and the Confederate* Virginia (*former U.S. naval ship* Merrimac), *represented a revolution in naval warfare as the first clash between two ironclad ships.*

The conduct of the war was not just determined by manpower, strategy, or generalship, but by technology. Like other wars of the mid-19th century, the Civil War was fought during a period of technological innovation that both sides sought to take advantage of with varying degrees of success. Innovations included better and deadlier firepower, to ironclad naval vessels, to the use of railroads for moving supplies and troops, and the telegraph for communication. The Civil War was one of several conflicts that marked a transitional phase in western warfare between the Napoleonic Wars of the beginning of the century and the world wars of the next.

The war also produced many changes within American society. Women volunteered in heavy numbers to assist their respective war efforts in a variety of ways, including serving in hospitals. Many others bore the burdens of warfare in more personal ways, taking care of families in the absence of

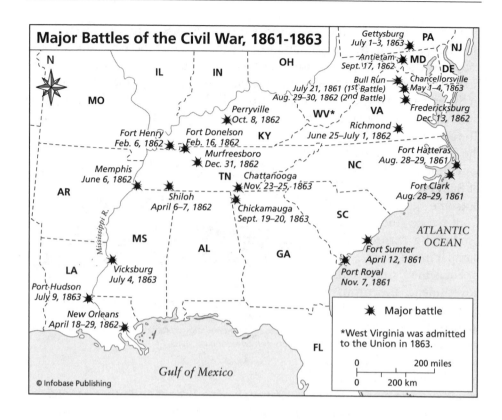

Major Battles of the Civil War, 1861-1863

husbands. For African Americans, the changes would be the most profound, as the war brought an end to slavery. Further the presence of a large African American population, both slave and free, proved to be a trump card for the Union as a potential manpower source.

THE PROGRESS OF WAR

Following the first battle of Bull Run, command of the federal armies passed to Major General George B. McClellan, a brilliant strategist and organizer. McClellan added an important revision to Scott's original strategy, the idea of a simultaneous advance by all major federal forces to prevent the Confederates from shifting reinforcements from one sector to another. Under McClellan the army also began a series of joint operations with the U.S. Navy along the southern coast, designed to establish bases for operations into the hinterland and close off or capture major ports. McClellan's tenure as federal commander ended unsuccessfully, however, due to a variety of issues, the chief being that his meticulous approach to preparation and training and his textbook brand of warfare by maneuver did not sit well with the more aggressively-minded Lincoln administration. McClellan came close to capturing Richmond in summer 1862, but a savage counteroffensive from

General Robert E. Lee's Army of Northern Virginia forced the Army of the Potomac to withdraw.

Like McClellan, Lee introduced a degree of modification to this government's military strategy: a mix of the offensive with the defensive. Although the primary Confederate strategy remained defensive, under Lee and like-minded generals this would not mean waiting behind prepared positions to be attacked; instead they would seek out and attack federal forces as they moved southward. Confederate armies might also make limited excursions in the north to shift the burden of the war upon the northern populace and perhaps seek a major battle that might lead to decisive victory, or at least impact enemy morale. These ideas fit in with the thinking of Confederate President Jefferson Davis. While Lee became the dominant military figure east of the Appalachians, federal military efforts began to pay off further west. A series of combined Army and Navy operations on the river systems cleared major parts of Tennessee of Confederate forces and gave the United States control of much of the Mississippi River. These campaigns featured two officers who rose to prominence as the war continued, Ulysses S. Grant and William T. Sherman.

In the east, an excursion by Lee into Maryland was turned back following the battle of Antietam on September 17, 1862. The campaign led to the final fall of McClellan for his failure to mount a counteroffensive. More significantly it led to the issuance of the preliminary Emancipation Proclamation by Abraham Lincoln on September 22. It declared all slaves free in Confederate-held territory if the southern states did not return to the Union by January 1, 1863. The announcement marked the culmination of an evolving attitude toward the use of African Americans in the Union war effort.

Although Lincoln had long been opposed to slavery, he was not an abolitionist, believing before the war that the institution would eventually fade if its further progress was halted. During the first months of the war Lincoln reacted quickly against some commanders who freed local slaves or encouraged them to run away to Union protection, primarily to avoid antagonizing the slave-holding Border states. Nevertheless as more slaves streamed into Union lines, a policy shift occurred. Runaway slaves were recognized as "contraband" whose loss would hurt the southern economy.

Union General Burnside's troops forced their way across this bridge over Antietam creek with great loss of life on September 17, 1862.

The Second Battle of Fort Fisher, January 13–15, 1865: Union Army and Naval forces attacked the fort near Wilmington, South Carolina, taking the Confederacy's last remaining seaport.

EMANCIPATION AS STRATEGY

Meanwhile some commanders began recruiting runaway slaves as soldiers. Although this was originally done without administration approval, gradually it became clear what this might mean for the Union army's manpower pool. Thus Lincoln began to contemplate the idea of emancipation as a war effort that would seriously injure the Confederacy, and have the by-product of ending the despised institution. Following January 1, slaves would automatically be freed whenever Union forces entered their vicinity, and the proclamation would encourage even more to flee their masters. Meanwhile Union military recruitment of both slaves and northern and southern free African Americans continued, with eventually some 186,000 serving. Thus emancipation was not only a major social development, but an important component of federal military strategy.

Although the issuance of the Emancipation Proclamation signaled the determination of the Lincoln administration to call upon all available resources, there were many months of hard fighting left. Lee remained the Confederacy's most successful general, winning major victories at Fredericksburg in December 1862, and Chancellorsville in May 1863. A second advance northward, however, came to grief at the battle of Gettysburg in July.

Federal success continued along the Mississippi River. After a long campaign, forces under Grant captured the city of Vicksburg in July, virtually completing the task of gaining Union control over the river. A major setback in September to a promising federal campaign in Tennessee and northern Georgia led to Grant's elevation to command of all western federal armies to resolve the crisis. His victory at Chattanooga in November sealed his reputation as the north's greatest general.

In March 1864 Grant became federal general-in-chief. He took up McClellan's idea of a simultaneous federal advance upon all fronts, but pursued the strategy more aggressively. Overseeing operations against Lee himself, Grant's slow advance southward was marked by several major battles, with high casualties on both sides; by the end of June a stalemate had ensued, with the Army of Northern Virginia besieged at Petersburg.

In the west, Atlanta fell to Sherman in September, who succeeded Grant in that region; along with federal victories in the Shenandoah Valley later in the same month and in October, its capture ensured Lincoln's reelection. Sherman then embarked on a bold move in November, cutting loose from his base operations and living off the land as he pushed for the Atlantic Coast as

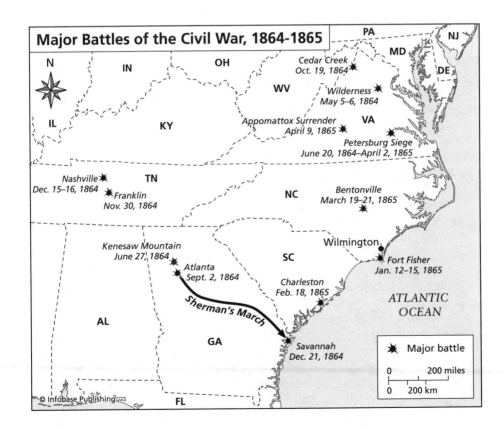

Major Battles of the Civil War, 1864–1865

Reconstruction Violence

By 1867 a growing pattern of violence was emerging in the former Confederate states. The targets were the freedmen; a variety of northern reformers and speculators lumped derisively together as "carpetbaggers" and "scalawags," white southerners who, for one reason or another, sided with the federal government in its Reconstruction policies.

Ex-Confederates watched in rage as former slaves asserted their rights, a reaction often shared among other white southerners who had remained loyal to the Union, but were growing uneasy about what promised to be a major upheaval in the region's social system. Violence became the means of choice to resist Reconstruction, opening up what was in many ways a new phase of the Civil War. In this situation, the U.S. Army and various state forces played an uneven role in efforts to suppress the violence, a situation complicated by the fact that policy on the use of troops in such cases was not firmly established.

A forecast of what was to come occurred on July 30, 1866, at a time when a new state constitutional convention for Louisiana was meeting in New Orleans. Among the issues up for debate were the possible extension of the voting franchise to African Americans, and the prohibition of voting rights for former Confederates. A riot erupted near the meeting place when a collision between African-American marchers in support of the franchise and a crowd of whites led to shots being fired. The riot, which included the participation of some members of the police, left around 40 African Americans killed and many others injured.

Urban race riots were not the only type of violence used against freemen and their allies. A number of paramilitary groups tormented those who threatened the old status quo. The most famous group, and one that served as a prototype of others, was the Ku Klux Klan, organized in Pulaski, Tennessee, in 1866. The Klan originally began as an association of bored local veterans looking for diversion, but soon moved to harassing African Americans and acts of often brutal violence.

The response to the Klan and similar groups by state and federal authorities was uneven. Following the establishment of military rule in the south in 1867, the U.S. Army had more power on paper to act. The relatively small size of the federal occupation forces were often limited in their ability to respond. As a result, governors sometimes relied on their own state militias to put down the night-riders, with mixed results.

By 1871 the Klan and similar groups were fading away due to dissension within their ranks between the more ideologically driven members, and those devoted to mayhem for mayhem's sake, as well as a major congressional investigation. Their members and supporters were able to achieve their goals through the ballot box, with the aid of intimidation, vote-counting fraud, and terror tactics, as the south was restored to white rule by 1877.

a preliminary move to joining Grant in Virginia. Savannah fell to Sherman's forces in December. He resumed his march northward in February, reaching North Carolina by early March.

Grant finally broke the siege of Petersburg on April 2. The Army of Northern Virginia surrendered at Appomattox Court House on April 9. Other Confederate forces surrendered in the following weeks. Over a million lives had been lost in the conflict to battlefield deaths, wounds, and disease. One of the last casualties was Lincoln, assassinated by Confederate sympathizer John Wilkes Booth on April 14.

END OF HOSTILITIES

Following the end of regular hostilities, decisions had to be made in regards to the fates of both the south and of the freedmen. The role that the army would

The Freedmen's Bureau

The Bureau of Freedmen, Refugees, and Abandoned Lands was created by Congress in March 1865. Known generally as the Freedmen's Bureau, it operated as a part of the War Department under the leadership of General Oliver O. Howard.

Among the many important tasks with which the Freedmen's Bureau concerned itself was education for the former slaves, with nearly 3,000 schools established by 1869. The bureau also gave its support to the construction of hospitals and providing limited medical care. It also was involved in the struggle for legal justice for the freedmen, initially running its own courts before southern courts regained jurisdiction over African Americans in 1866. The bureau also sought to arbitrate labor disputes for African Americans, an important issue given the efforts of former masters to have conditions arranged in their own favor as much as possible. Bureau tribunals reviewed labor contracts and enforced them, undoing attempts by hirers to cheat the former slaves. At the same time the bureau attempted to impose labor standards that were of more benefit to the landowners than the freedmen.

A major point of controversy in which the bureau was involved was its mandate to decide on the fate of lands confiscated or abandoned by their owners during the war. Initially there was some thought of distributing at least some of this land to former slaves. Although the policy was carried out on a limited basis in certain areas, the government eventually decided to give the land back to its original orders. The Freedmen's Bureau was allowed to lapse out of existence in 1869. Given its uncertain funding and the political controversies that accompanied Reconstruction in both the south and the national government, it is perhaps not surprising that the bureau achieved only limited achievements. Nevertheless, what it did accomplish was very impressive.

play in Reconstruction was equally uncertain. Most people assumed that occupation of the former Confederate states would be brief. The army was quickly demobilized. Officers in charge of the small occupation forces had little authority to draw upon to enforce law and order or protect themselves and their men, and vacillated in their reaction to growing violence by ex-Confederates in the form of urban race riots and the night-riding activities of groups such as the Ku Klux Klan. Many former slaves decided to help themselves, joining the army or African-American militia companies raised by Reconstruction governments.

The policies of President Andrew Johnson added to the confusion, as he favored a lenient reconstruction policy and turned a blind eye to abuses against the freedmen. As a result, a conflict emerged between Johnson and Congress, dominated by Radical Republicans who were against an easy admittance of

President Johnson and the Radical Republicans

During Reconstruction, Congress, led by the Radical Republicans and President Johnson, fought over which branch of government would control policy. On March 2, 1867 Congress amended the Army Appropriation Act to undermine the president's position as commander-in-chief of the Army. The amendment required the president to channel military orders through the general of the Army and required consent of the Senate prior to removing or reassigning the general of the Army. Reprinted below is an excerpt of that act.

An Act making appropriations for the support of the Army for the year ending June 30, 1868, and for other purposes . . . .

Section 2. And be it further enacted, that the headquarters of the General of the Army of the United States shall be at the city of Washington, and all orders and instructions relating to military operations issued by the President or secretary of war shall be issued through the General of the Army, and, in case of his inability, through the next in rank. The General of the Army shall not be removed, suspended, or relieved from command, or assigned to duty elsewhere than at said headquarters, except at his own request, without the previous approval of the Senate; and any orders or instructions relating to military operations issued contrary to the requirements of this section shall be null and void; and any officer who shall issue orders or instructions contrary to the provisions of this section shall be deemed guilty of a misdemeanor in office; and any officer of the Army who shall transmit, convey, or obey any orders or instructions so issued contrary to the provisions of this section, knowing that such orders were so issued, shall be liable to imprisonment for not less than two nor more than twenty years, upon conviction thereof in any court of competent jurisdiction.

the southern states back into the Union, or the restoration of former Confederate officials to national and state office.

With the assistance of Congress, Grant and Secretary of War Edwin M. Stanton did what they could to circumvent Johnson's policies. These efforts culminated in the First Reconstruction Act, which divided the south into military districts and gave the army the legal backing it needed to enforce order through martial law if necessary. Nevertheless the army ultimately had little effect on anti-Reconstruction violence. During the latter part of Grant's administration, troops were pulled out of the south in increasing numbers, the result of a desire on the part of the northern public to put the war behind them and a loss of interest in the fate of the freedmen. The last occupying troops were withdrawn in 1877, the result of the political deal that brought Rutherford B. Hayes to office in the contested election of the previous year. Although it would be years before southern African Americans lost all of the political gains that they made during the Civil War and Reconstruction, white supremacy ruled in the region once again, and the door was open for the gradual implantation of the policies of segregation.

MICHAEL W. COFFEY

Further Readings

Coffman, Edward M. *The Old Army: A Portrait of the American Army in Peacetime, 1794–1898.* New York: Oxford University Press, 1986.

Foner, Eric. *Reconstruction: America's Unfinished Revolution 1863–1877.* New York: Harper & Row, 1988.

Franklin, John Hope. *The Militant South 1800–1860.* New York: Beacon Press, 1970.

Grimsley, Mark. *The Hard Hand of War: Union Military Policy Toward Southern Civilians 1861–1865.* Cambridge: Cambridge University Press, 1995.

Hollandsworth, James G., Jr., *An Absolute Massacre: The New Orleans Race Riot of July 30, 1866.* Baton Rouge: Louisiana State University Press, 2001.

Millet, Allan R., and Peter Maslowski. *For the Common Defense: A Military History of the United States of America.* New York: The Free Press, 1994.

Trelease, Allen R. *White Terror: The Ku Klux Klan Conspiracy and Southern Reconstruction.* Baton Rouge: Louisiana State University Press, 1995.

Chapter 14

Population and Migration

*"Immigration, which even the war has not
stopped, will land upon our shores hundreds of
thousands more per year from overcrowded Europe."*
— Abraham Lincoln

THE YEARS BETWEEN 1860 and 1876 were some of the most difficult years
in American history. The Civil War had lasted from 1861 to 1865 at a cost
of over 600,000 lives. Reconstruction had gone on through the early 1870s,
as the south tried to recover political and economic power and four million
newly-freed slaves tried to find a new role in the world. Immigration dipped
briefly during the war years, but quickly regained momentum. Urban areas
grew at rates often exceeding 600 percent annually. It was also a period of
tremendous economic growth, with the Industrial Revolution taking hold
with the expansion of mills and factories; at the same time the 1870s would
bring about a severe economic depression whose effects would be felt into
the early 1900s. This was also the great age of westward expansion, with millions of people moving onto the distant frontiers. As a result, thousands of
Native Americans were forced into a war of resistance that ended in their
defeat and removal to reservation lands by the mid-1880s.

A good approach to the study of population and migration within the United States from 1860 to 1876 is to look into the censuses conducted in 1860,
1870, and 1880. The Bureau of the Census complied data on far more then just
the number of people in the country. Each census was an increasingly in-depth
attempt to capture a picture of life in America, from the number of people living in each county down to the number of pounds of beeswax produced on its

An 1866 engraving of an afternoon of leisure. "General good health prevailed, and peace reigned throughout the country," the U.S. Census noted for the period.

farms, and to compare these statistics to the decade before as a way to measure the nation's progress.

The growing sophistication of the country, its population, economy, and government, can be clearly seen in the development of the census itself. In 1860 all the data collected fit in two volumes, and the report had been completed in a matter of months after the final returns from the field were received. By 1880 it had grown to to 22 volumes and took almost the entire decade to compile the returns. For the 1890 census, the bureau began using punch-cards and automatic tabulating machines, direct ancestors of modern computers.

THE CENSUS: 1860

The Eighth Census of the United States was delivered to Congress in May 1862, having taken more then two years to tabulate and arrange the data. Collecting the information had taken the work of 64 marshals and 4,417 assistants, at a cost of $1,045,206.75 in salary and payments. With the nation on the brink of war as the final returns were coming in from around the country, another $247,000 was held back "on account of the presumed or known disloyalty of officers, or the existence of some good reason for suspending payment."

Paddy's Lamentation

The Irish were a critical part of the Union war effort, with more than 150,000 donning the uniform 1861–65. But as the war dragged on, the U.S. government was facing declining volunteer enrollments, and turned to the military draft to fill the ranks. Because it was possible to buy one's way out of conscription, for the price of about $300 to hire a substitute to go in one's place, the draft hit the poor and the immigrant community particularly hard. Many of the estimated 50,000 protesters of the New York City Draft Riots of June 1863 were Irish-born men. Some Irish immigrants barely made it off the boats before being conscripted into service, an experience commemorated in a song probably written during the war era. Originally known as "By the Hush," the tune is also known as "Paddy's Lamentation":

> Well it's by the hush, me boys, and sure that's to hold your noise
> And listen to poor Paddy's sad narration
> I was by hunger pressed, and in poverty distressed
> So I took a thought I'd leave the Irish nation
>
> Chorus:
> Here's to you boys, now take my advice
> To America I'll have ye's not be going
> There is nothing here but war, where the murderin' cannons roar
> And I wish I was at home in dear old Dublin
>
> Well I sold me ass and cow, my little pigs and sow
> My little plot of land I soon did part with
> And me sweetheart Bid McGee, I'm afraid I'll never see
> For I left her there that morning broken-hearted
>
> Well meself and a hundred more, to America sailed o'er
> Our fortunes to be made [sic] we were thinkin'
> When we got to Yankee land, they shoved a gun into our hands
> Saying "Paddy, you must go and fight for Lincoln"
>
> General Meagher to us he said, if you get shot or lose your head
> Every murdered soul of youse will get a pension
> Well meself I lost me leg, they gave me a wooden peg,
> And by God this is the truth to you I mention
>
> Well I think meself in luck, if I get fed on Indian buck
> And old Ireland is the country I delight in
> With the devil, I do say, it's curse Americay
> For I think I've had enough of your hard fightin'

Loosely translated, this means most southern census-takers did not get paid for their services. Still the Census Bureau had collected information from all 34 states and five territories, enough to build a complete picture of the 31,403,321 people that called America home.

The Panic of 1873

The Panic of 1873 was one of a series of financial depressions in America during the 19th century. The immediate cause was the collapse of financier Jay Cooke's banking empire in September 1873. Cooke and his investors had poured millions into the development of the Northern Pacific Railroad, only to find themselves forced into bankruptcy. This sent shockwaves through financial community, even leading the New York Stock Exchange to close its doors for 10 days. Over the next two years around 18,000 American businesses failed, and unemployment rose to 14 percent. Even those who remained employed saw their wages depressed. The Panic, also known as the Long Depression, was particularly hard on poor urban dwellers. Unskilled laborers in New York City made about $1.75 a day in 1874. A tailor earned around $2.26 in 1874 (or about $14 a week), but many saw drops in wages over the height of the depression. The average working family with one child living in New York City in 1874 was faced with weekly expenditures nearly equal to their weekly income:

Flour & Bread	$0.84
Meats	$2.82
Butter	$0.50
Lard	$0.08
Cheese	$0.22
Sugar & Molasses	$0.34
Milk	$0.49
Coffee	$0.19
Tea	$0.25
Fish	$0.15
Soap, starch, salt, pepper, vinegar	$0.40
Eggs	$0.25
Vegetables	$1.00
Fruits	$0.28
Fuel	$1.00
Oil & other light sources	$0.06
Beer & tobacco	$0.50
Rent	$3.60
Educational & religious material	$0.15
Clothing	$1.79
TOTAL	**$14.91**

Since the 1850 census, the county had added three new states and organized five new territories. The borders of America were now firmly set, with the census noting that the only new land acquired since 1850 was "a narrow strip to the southward of the Colorado River, along the Mexican line, not yet inhabited." The Gadsden Purchase had added 45,535 square miles to the United States at a cost of around $10 million. The treaty had been signed by President Franklin Pierce in June 1854.

"As general good health prevailed, and peace reigned throughout the country," the census report noted, "there was no apparent cause of disturbance or interruption to the natural progress of population." The states were only growing in population, with none losing in population from a decade earlier. Vermont, which saw its population increase by only one-third of one percent, was almost an exception to that rule, while the neighboring state of New Hampshire grew at only two percent. Texas, little more than a empty wilderness in 1850, was now home to 604,215 people, an increase of 184 percent. New York was the most populous state in the Union, with 3,880,735 residents; Pennsylvania was close behind with 2,906,215. At the other end of the population spectrum was Dakota Territory, with just 4,837 inhabitants, and Nevada Territory, with 6,857.

SLAVE STATES AND FREE STATES: 1860

The 15 slaveholding states of the south had a total population of 12,240,000. This was broken into three categories: 8,039,000 whites, 3,950,000 African-American slaves, and 251,000 free African Americans. The population of the region had grown by 27.33 percent since 1850. By comparison the 19 free states and

An 1867 wood engraving by Winslow Homer. Coming to America by ship, many immigrants to the United States basically walked off the pier and vanished into society.

seven free territories of the north and west had a total population of 19,203,008. Here, too, demographers could break the total into three categories: 18,920,771 whites, 237,283 free African Americans, and 41,725 "civilized" Native Americans (those who owned land or were considered to be assimilated). The population of the free states had increased by 41.24 percent, or 5,624,101 people, largely due to the higher rate of immigration into northern and western communities.

IMMIGRATION: 1860

Counting the number of immigrants arriving in the United States was tricky business. There was no centralized bureau to document each person as they stepped off the boat in American ports; immigrants basically walked off the pier and vanished. For purposes of the census, it was easier to ask people where they were born. The number of foreign-born Americans in 1850 was 2,210,839. By 1860 it had almost doubled, to 4,136,175.

A total of 1,611,304 gave their country of origin as Ireland, and 1,301,136 came from Germany. Another 431,692 were British, and 249,907 were Canadian. There were also 109,870 Frenchmen, 108,518 Scots, 53,372 Swiss, and 35,565 Chinese. New York had seen the biggest influx in its foreign-born population, with close to a million of its 3.9 million residents hailing from abroad. Illinois, Pennsylvania, Wisconsin, and Ohio also experienced significant increases.

URBANIZATION AND POPULATION DENSITY: 1860

America was getting more and more crowded. In 1850 population density in the New England states was 43.92 per square mile. By 1860 it had climbed to 50.47 per square mile. In the middle states, which included New York, Pennsylvania, and Ohio, density rose from 56.36 to 69.83 per square mile. Even distant California had seen its density jump—from 0.87 inhabitants up to 2.01 per square mile.

More and more Americans were living in cities and towns. Urbanization had risen from six percent in 1815 to over 20 percent in 1860. New York, Philadelphia, Brooklyn, Baltimore, Boston, New Orleans, Cincinnati, St Louis, and Chicago all had populations over 100,000 in 1860. New York City was still America's largest, having grown 56 percent over the decade to 805,651 people. So many people were moving into New York that the population spilled out past the borders of the city. Brooklyn grew 175 percent, from 96,838 to 266,661 inhabitants. Jersey City, New Jersey, saw a 326 percent increase, from a village of 6,850 to a city of 29,963 people. Newly-founded cities saw the highest growth rates, sometimes exceeding 600 percent—although in the case of towns like La Fayette, Indiana, the 672 percent increase moved the population from a tiny 1,215 to a still-modest 9,387. Chicago grew 265 percent in a decade, from 29,963 in 1850 to 109,260 in 1860, mostly due to the development of the 15 separate railroad lines running into the once sleepy lakeside town.

INTERNAL MIGRATION AND SEX RATIO: 1860

In general, about three-fourths of Americans lived in the state of their birth, with one-fourth removing to other states or territories. Most internal migrants did not go too far, usually just moving across the border to an adjacent state. Residents of Alabama, for example, were most likely to move to Mississippi, Texas, Arkansas, or Louisiana. New Yorkers tended to head for the open lands of Michigan, Illinois, Wisconsin, or Ohio. A few years later, the same people might move over by another state, as the landscape filled up. For every American that packed up the wagon and trekked to the distant Pacific Coast in one epic move, there were probably 10 who made the same journey in fits and starts over a period of a decade or more.

In 1860 males outnumbered females in America by about 730,000, although deaths of men in the Civil War soon brought the overall proportions quite a bit closer. In some areas, particularly on the frontier, the gender disparity was significant. In Colorado Territory, there were 20 men to every one woman. In California there were 67,000 more men than women, about a fifth of the total population, and it would take some years of settlement to equalize the ratios there. The average age in the United States in 1860 was 23.53 years—a young population in the prime of their reproductive life. The census tallied 224,682 marriages that year. There were 933,721 recorded births. The young states of

An 1866 photograph of Telegraph Hill in San Francisco. Immigration was not just an East Coast phenomenon—many came to America via West Coast ports.

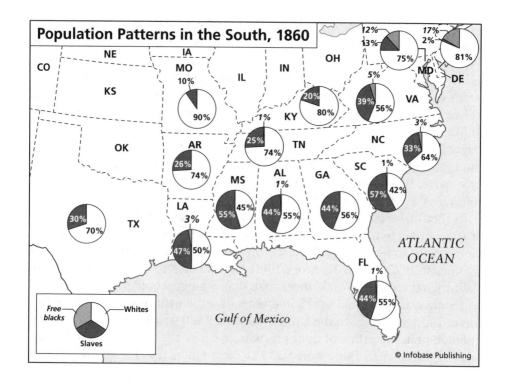

Population Patterns in the South, 1860

Oregon, Iowa, Minnesota, Missouri, and Texas had the highest birth rates per capita, while the older New England states like New Hampshire, Vermont, and Maine had the lowest, along with California, which was suffering from a shortage of females.

The same period saw 394,123 deaths. Major causes of death included consumption, pneumonia, and "dropsy" or edema (a swelling of the tissues often indicative of congestive heart failure). The major infectious diseases included scarlet fever, typhoid fever, common fevers, croup, and dysentery. The number of violent deaths jumped from 12,174 in 1850 to 20,115 in 1860. Some of these deaths were murders, but most were accidents in the home, including falls and burns, or industrial or railroad accidents. There were about 1,000 reported suicides. A total of 466 deaths in 1860 were in people over 100 years of age. The census was somewhat skeptical of some of the claims. Two Alabama slaves were said to be 130 years old at their death, while a slave in Georgia was allegedly 137 years old. A Mexican in California was reportedly 120 at her death, while two southern women were said to be 115 years old.

WORK AND WEALTH: 1860

Financially, the population of 1860 seemed to be doing well. Americans owned $6,973,106,049 worth of real estate and $5,111,553,995 worth of personal property. Per capita incomes were also on the rise, in some places to a staggering degree. In 1850 Iowans earned $123 per capita. In 1860 it had jumped to $366, an increase of 197 percent. In Pennsylvania, income rose by a more modest 46 percent, from $312 to $487 per capita.

America was still an agricultural nation. The total assessed value of farms in 1860 was $6.65 billion; farm implements added another $247 million. These farms were home to six million horses, one million mules, 8.7 million cows, 2.2 million oxen, over 20 million sheep, and 32 million hogs. Crop output was equally staggering.

In 1860 American farms produced 830 million bushels of corn, 171 million bushels of wheat, 172 million bushels of oats, and 21 million bushels of rye. Southern farms produced 187 million pounds of rice and 429 million pounds of tobacco. Cotton production had jumped 110 percent over the decade, with the 1860 crop totaling 5,198,077 bales of ginned cotton—over two billion pounds of fiber.

This bounty did not stay on the family farm. It traveled to the great cities through an ever-expanding network of railroads. In 1850 there had been just about 8,539 miles of track laid in the entire United States. A decade later there were 30,794 miles. The climbing population had also spurred a huge boom in construction.

There were five million dwellings in the United States in 1860, an increase of almost 50 percent in less than a decade. The population was hard at work in a variety of occupations, with close to 600 different job categories listed in the census tables, including 2.4 million farmers and 800,000 farm laborers, down to nine "globe-makers" and 104 lightning rod makers.

The census did not tabulate the size of the Regular Army in 1860, but it did calculate the number of men of military age—that is, between the age of 18 and 45—on the eve of the Civil War. It reported a military-age population of 5,624,065. Of this number, 898,831 lived in the 11 Confederate States. By comparison, New York State alone had 796,881 military-age residents, and Pennsylvania had 555,172. Since most immigrant males

Poverty crossed racial lines: An 1863 photograph shows two African Americans, one with a soup ladle, the other with a cigar.

were in the 18–45 age range, and most ended up in the north, they too were expected to increase the Union war effort.

THE CENSUS: 1870

Much had changed by the time Francis Walker, chief of the Census Bureau, transmitted the Ninth Census to Congress in August 1872. The Civil War had been over for seven years; immigration rates had returned to normal; and the whole population seemed to be on the move. The Homestead Act of 1862 had promised 160 acres to anyone willing to claim a piece of frontier land and live on it for a period of years, and tens of thousands of Americans were ready to take the challenge.

The 1870 Census had proven quite a challenge in itself. The country was more complex than it had been, and the amount of data had also increased.

Death and the Centennial

July 4, 1876 was supposed to be a joyous Independence Day in America—the 100th anniversary of the signing of the Declaration of Independence. But this was also the day many Americans learned of a terrible tragedy in their morning newspapers: Lieutenant Colonel George Armstrong Custer's entire detachment of the 7th Cavalry had been wiped out in a desperate battle with a large force of Native Americans in the Little Bighorn Valley of the Montana Territory on June 25. The 7th had lost 268 men, including 16 officers, 10 civilian scouts, and 242 enlisted men; among the dead were the 37-year old Custer, his younger brothers Thomas and Boston, his 18-year-old nephew Henry Reed, and his brother-in-law James Calhoun. The news hit the small community of Monroe, Michigan, with particular force. Custer had lived in Monroe in his youth, and his wife, Elizabeth, had grown up there. "Libbie" Bacon and "Autie" Custer were well known in town, particularly after his heroics during the Civil War. Sixty-two years after the fact, a Monroe resident told a newspaper reporter about the scene that July morning:

I was sitting upstairs by the window mending. I saw Father coming up the street, his coat off, his vest off, his hat in hand, waving a paper, the old Tribune. It was about eleven o'clock in the morning. He came in and called "Minnie! Minnie!" Minnie was not my name but Father often called me by it. I flew downstairs for I knew something awful had happened. There he stood, white and chalky, with the paper shaking in his hands. "General Custer's entire brigade has been wiped out," he gasped. "Think of it Autie, Lieutenant Calhoun, Ross, Tom, they're all gone!" A great silence came over Monroe, then all the bells began to toll—church bells, firehouse bells, every bell in the town. To this day, I never hear a bell toll that it does not bring back the memory . . .

Information had been delayed for more than six months in some cases. Since the census determined the apportionment of congressional seats, and with new states up for grabs, along with a reapportionment of southern seats due to the emancipation of slaves, the political community must have been waiting for the final report with bated breath. "These delays," said Walker in his official report, "most vexatious and most discreditable in a national work of such importance . . . were, as you are aware, absolutely unavoidable, with existing census machinery."

U.S. territory had expanded once again with the purchase of Alaska from Russia's Tsar Alexander II in 1867. The final asking price for the 600,000 square miles of northern wilderness was $7.2 million, or about 1.9 cents per acre. The public was divided over the wisdom of the buy. "Already, so it was said, we were burdened with territory we had no population to fill. The Indians within the present boundaries of the republic strained our power to govern aboriginal peoples," wrote the powerful editor of the *New York Tribune,* Horace Greeley. "Could it be that we would now, with open eyes, seek to add to our difficulties by increasing the number of such peoples under our national care?" But the land was rich in fur, timber, fish, and mineral deposits, and Congress ultimately approved the treaty in July 1868.

Since the 1860 census the number of states had increased, with Nevada and Nebraska moving from territorial status to full statehood, and West Virginia having split off from Virginia proper during the Civil War. The new territories of Alaska, Arizona, Dakota, Idaho, Montana, Wyoming, and New Mexico had been formed. There had been talk in the north immediately after the war of abolishing the states of the Confederacy, breaking them up and reforming them into new states with new names, but in the end, cooler heads had prevailed, and the old slave states had retained their names and their borders. Even with the upheaval and displacement caused by the war and Reconstruction, no state or territory lost population between 1860 and 1870.

THE MISSING TWO MILLION: 1870

The total population of the United States in 1870 was 38,558,371, or 22.22 percent higher than it had been in 1860. This was a respectable rate of growth, but about two or three million short of what demographers had predicted a decade earlier. Most had believed the 1870 population would easily top 40 million, but, said Walker, he and others "took counsel rather of their patriotism than their judgment." Simply put, the Civil War had caused a ripple effect through the population for most of the decade. The war had killed or seriously wounded around 500,000 northern soldiers and 350,000 Confederates—the majority of them young men who would have likely gone on to father many children had they lived to old age.

Then there were the potential children not born during the four years that an average of 1.25 million men were off fighting. There had also been a sharp drop

An 1869 engraving showing emigrants crossing the Plains. Prior to the railroads, the only option most Americans had to reach the western frontier was an overland trip by wagon.

in immigration during the war years, again robbing the population pool not just of adults, but of the native-born children they might have had. More worrisome to Walker was the overall drop in the birth rate that had continued even after the soldiers had returned home. "Luxury, fashion and the vice of 'boarding' combine to limit the increase of families to a degree that in some sections even threatens the perpetuation of our native stock," he fretted in his report.

Of the 38.6 million Americans alive in 1870, 33,589,377 were white, 4,880,009 were African American, 63,254 were Chinese or Japanese, and 25,731 were Native American. For the first time in 80 years, the column for "slaves" was blank in the census tables. The number of Native Americans had dropped by about 18,000 from 1860, but the census-takers generally counted only those Native Americans who were landowners or taxpayers. The ratio of males to females was more balanced that it had been in 1860, having dropped to only 429,000 more men than women over the decade. This might reflect the impact of the large number of men killed during the war.

In some frontier areas, the disparity between men and women remained high. Most notably, the Chinese community was comprised of 58,680 men, but only 4,574 women. The 1870 census found 5.6 million immigrants in the United States, with two million hailing from Ireland and the British Islands and 1.7 million from Germany.

INTERNAL MIGRATION: 1870

The war had slowed, but hardly stopped westward migration. The Homestead Act, passed in 1862, had brought 15,000 new settlers to the frontier in its first three years. Between 1860 and 1870 the number of Americans living in the territories had grown from 184,496 to 311,030. The movement from the countryside to the cities also continued. In 1860 the urban population had been about 16 percent of the total United States population. In 1870 it was close to 21 percent. The number of cities had grown from 141 to 226.

WORK AND WEALTH: 1870

The assessed value of American farms had risen from $6.65 billion to $9.3 billion in a decade. Farm implements added another $337 million. In terms of bushels or pounds produced and the number of work animals and livestock dotting the landscape, increases over 1860 outputs were minimal. That being said, the cash value of crops and livestock in 1870 was still over $310 billion.

The census tables recorded the ongoing struggle to recover southern agriculture in the aftermath of war and the traumas of Reconstruction. The 1870 cotton crop was 3,011,996—more than two million bales short of what it had been in 1860. Rice and tobacco production had fallen by more than half. Figuring out what constituted a farm in the south in the post-war era had been nothing but a headache for census-takers. "The plantations of the old slave States are squatted all over by the former slaves, who hold small portions of the soil, often very loosely determined as to extent, under almost all varieties of tenure." The sharecropping system, in which a landowner parceled out their fields to a former slave or landless white farmer in exchange for a portion of the crops they produced, had been born. The manufacturing sector continued to grow. The total product of the mills, factories, and shops of America was $1.9 billion in 1860; by 1870 it was up to $4.2 billion, or about a 108 percent increase. Unfortunately even census statisticians could not really say how much of this was due to real growth, and how much this reflected the depreciation of currency in the country in the late 1860s. After studying the numbers, they reported the real increase in manufacturing over the decade was 52 percent.

In all there were 232,148 manufacturers operating in 1870, almost double the number in 1860. These factories employed 2,053,996 people, including 323,770 women and 114,628 children under the age of 16. In 1870 they paid out $775,584,343 in wages. American factories were churning out an enormous amount of stuff, with 23,428 shoe manufacturers and 33,207 producers of building materials (including glass, paint, and roofing tiles). Reflecting the growing ranks of the leisure class, there were 53 producers of children's sleds. There were also 24 factories in the United States producing artificial limbs for the hundreds of thousands of amputees arising from the war years.

Unemployment was low. Of the 10.4 million American men between the ages of 16 and 59, the census-takers found that 9.5 million were gainfully employed.

"American Homestead Spring"—An 1869 Currier & Ives lithograph offering an idyllic view of the American migration west and the rewards that awaited homesteaders.

Of the 980,000 men over the age of 60, at least 635,000 were still at work. Women were not as much of an oddity in the working world as they had been. Of 9.75 million women aged 16 to 50, fully 1.6 million were employed.

Agriculture was still the main occupation of Americans in 1870, totaling 5,922,471 farmers and farm laborers that year. Industrial workers came next, with 2,707,421 employed in manufacturing in some capacity. Those engaged in professional and personal services had grown to 2,684,703 workers, running the gamut from one million common laborers and 985,000 domestic servants, to 62,383 physicians, 40,736 lawyers, 2,653 actors, and 35,185 restaurateurs. The trades and transportation workers were also on the rise, mostly due to the expansion of the railroads and shipping; of the 1,191,238 workers in this category, at least 168,000 were working for the rail companies.

POPULATIONS SHIFTS
The development of the railroads, particularly the establishment of the first transcontinental railway in 1869, made internal migration an easier process for many Americans. Prior to the railroads the only option most people had to reach the frontier was an overland trip by wagon—a long and dangerous proposition. Where once a family might only move over to an adjacent state, it was now possible to get on a train in Chicago and be standing in a boom town in Arizona in a matter of days. From there, it was a relatively simple mat-

ter to collect the supplies needed to form a homestead and head out in search of a new home. Blank spaces on the map were becoming increasingly rare. The northwest Pacific Coast was seeing rapid settlement, and settlers were quickly fanning across Dakota, Nebraska, Kansas, and Texas. Railroads were

Come to South Carolina

The loss of slave labor created an unstable labor force throughout the south following the Civil War. Southern states, forced to compete with industrial centers in the north and renewed western expansion, often passed laws creating commissions charged with advertising the benefits of living in their state. Excerpted below is legislation passed by the state of South Carolina designed to increase immigration to the state.

An Act for the encouragement and protection of European immigration, and for the appointment of a commissioner and agents, and for other purposes therein expressed.

1. Be it enacted by the Senate and House of Representatives, now met and sitting in General Assembly, and by the authority of the same, that for the purpose of encouraging, promoting, and protecting European immigration to and in this state, the sum of $10,000 be appropriated from the contingent fund, to be expended under the direction of the government, for the purposes and in the manner hereinafter provided.

2. That the governor, by and with the advice and consent of the Senate, shall appoint a commissioner of immigration, who shall open an office in the fireproof building in Charleston, to perform such duties as may appertain to his office, and shall be paid for his services the salary of $1,500 per annum out of the fund aforesaid in quarterly payments.

3. That it shall be the duty of said commissioner of immigration to advertise in all the gazettes of the state for lands for sale; to cause such lands, after having been duly laid off, platted and described, at the expense of the owner or owners of said lands, to be appraised by three disinterested persons, and their title to be examined by the attorney general or solicitors of the state, and endorsed by them, as the case may be; to open a book or books for the registry of the same, together with the price demanded and the conditions of payment. And in case such lands be selected by an immigrant, to superintend the transfer of title and other necessary instruments and proceedings of conveyance.

4. That the said commissioner shall periodically publish, advertise, and cause to be distributed in the Northern and European ports and states, descriptive lists of such lads as have been registered and offered for sale, together with this act, and a statement of such advantages as this state offers in soil, climate, productions, social improvements, etc., to the industrious, orderly, and frugal European immigrant.

helping bring populations into once isolated parts of Michigan, Wisconsin, and Minnesota. Even long-settled eastern states were seeing the population penetrate into areas that had always been ignored, including the interior of Maine and the Adirondacks of New York. Most of the Florida peninsula and the Gulf Coast were free of vacant spaces. Urbanization had also continued to build in the 1870s, rising to 22.5 percent of the total U.S. population. Over 11.3 million Americans lived in urban areas by the end of 1879.

The country was just beginning to recover from the Panic of 1873. There were 17.4 million workers in America in 1880, including 2.6 million women and just over one million children between the ages of 10 and 16. Agriculture was still the primary occupation of most Americans, with a total workforce of seven million. Another four million worked in professional or personal services, while three million worked in manufacturing and mining, and 1.8 million worked in trades and transport.

HEATHER K. MICHON

Further Readings

Anderson, Margo J. *The American Census: A Social History*. New Haven, CT: Yale University Press, 1990.

Ambrose, Stephen E. *Undaunted Courage*. New York: Simon & Schuster, 1996.

Brandon, William. *The Rise and Fall of North American Indians: From Prehistory Through Geronimo*. Lanham, MD: Taylor Trade Pub, 2003.

Haines, Michael R., and Richard H. Steckel, eds. *A Population History of North America*. Cambridge: Cambridge University Press, 2000.

Klein, Herbert S. *A Population History of the United States*. New York: Cambridge University Press, 2004.

The Library of Congress. 2005. *The African-American Mosaic: Colonization*. Available online, URL: http://www.loc.gov/exhibits/african/afam002.html (Accessed December, 2007).

Mintz, Steven, and Susan Kellogg. *Domestic Revolutions: A Social History of American Family Life*. New York: The Free Press, 1988.

Rossiter, W.S. *A Century of Population Growth. From the First to the Twelfth Census of the United States: 1790–1900*. Washington, D.C.: GPO, 1909.

Taylor, Colin F. *Native American Life: The Family, the Hunt, Pastimes and Ceremonies*. New York: Smithmark, 1996.

Chapter 15

Transportation

*"Old men, who predicted that the road would be built,
but 'not in our time,' may have the opportunity of
bathing in the Atlantic one week and the Pacific the next . . ."*
— reporter commenting on the transcontinental railroad, 1868

IN THE EARLY 19th century a major transportation revolution occurred in the United States. While the lion's share of the revolution occurred between the War of 1812 and the Civil War, the evolving needs of a country at war with itself created an environment in which the effectiveness of transportation often decided the fate of the entire nation, calling for innovation and technological advancement. Because the south was agrarian, the Confederate states began with a transportation disadvantage on land and sea. In the north, where the Industrial Revolution was in its early stages, merchants had already begun to recognize the need for reliable rail and water modes of transport and were able to take advantage of emerging technologies. Southern states used steamboats chiefly for exporting cotton and tobacco. The northern transportation advantage was instrumental in the establishment of effective blockades of southern ports, which prevented the entry of essential goods, including medicine and food, into the Confederacy where the struggle for survival outweighed everything else during the Civil War.

Even in the mid-19th century the United States was a sprawling geographic area; and the ability to move troops and supplies in and out of contested areas was vital. The quickest method of transport was by rail, which allowed troops to travel further from their supply bases and ensured a steady replenishment of essentials. Both armies turned to water travel when long distances were necessary, and access to steamboats linked to railroads was a distinct advantage. Northern and midwestern states were able to transport troops and supplies using a private system of canals and turnpikes built in the 1820s.

In some southern states, slaves made up the majority of the population. In the north, the free male population outnumbered those of the south more than fourfold. The north had a tenfold advantage in factory production, and a 30 to one advantage in the production of coal, which was essential to both industry and transportation. Non-southern states had advantages in other ways also, claiming more textiles, corn, wheat, livestock, and draft animals. Northern railroads outnumbered their southern counterparts seven to one. Navy tonnage was recorded at a ratio of 25:1 and merchant ship tonnage at 9:1. When war broke out in 1961, the south's lone locomotive was used in the manufacture of munitions in Richmond, Virginia.

CIVIL WAR: OCEANS AND RIVERS

Throughout the Civil War, both the Confederate and Union armies understood the importance of maintaining access to inland as well as coastal waterways and of obtaining reliable methods to transport troops and supplies. The Union entered the war with a few dozen ships, but had sufficient resources to buy and charter others. Some 600 vessels and 70,000 sailors were requisitioned from the merchant marine to supplement the military might of the Union. These extra resources were essential in maintaining the southern blockade that prevented basic supplies from coming into the south and kept cotton from being exported to foreign markets. The Union Quartermaster's rail and river transport division had 139 boats and 352 steamers at its disposal. Bulk cargoes could be moved cheaply along waterways in riverboats and barges. The Union entered the war with superior firepower, and northern gunboats were quick to seize control of important waterways that prevented southern vessels from moving troops and supplies.

The Pacific Mail Company's steamer Golden Gate, burned at sea July 27, 1862.

Only 819 ships sailed out of southern ports during the year that ended on June 30, 1861, as compared to 11,079 that left northern ports. The disparity was also reflected in differences in shipping tonnage, with the south recording only 286,445 tons of a total of 4.889 million American tons. Of 10,586 ships that left the United States for foreign lands in 1861, only 220 sailed from the south. In order to compensate for such deficiencies, the Confederacy authorized privateers, but most Confederate raids were carried out by the Confederate Navy on sail or steam commerce raiders, which included the *Alabama*, the *Shenandoah*, and the *Florida*. Without ship yards of its own, the Confederacy purchased British ships that were crewed chiefly by British seamen who received high wages and were promised prize money once the war was over. During the war Confederate raiders were successful in capturing 200 Union ships, not only in the Atlantic and the Caribbean but as far away as Cape Horn and Australia. In order to bypass privateers, the Union resorted to flagging some 1,600 ships as foreign. At war's end America's flag-fleet was greatly diminished.

The south had a distinct advantage in privateer raids early in the war, capturing a total of 40 Union vessels. The north fought back by capturing privateers and refusing to honor southern Letters of Marque and Reprisal. The United States had entered the war of 1812 in large part to protest the failure of warring European nations to recognize the freedom of the seas. Ironically the Union repeated these actions during the Civil War, arresting captains and crews of captured southern vessels and treating them as pirates.

On July 6, 1861 the crew of the *Jefferson Davis* captured the *Enchantress*, a merchant schooner sailing near Delaware. On July 22, Union forces sailing on Cape Hatteras, North Carolina, reclaimed the *Enchantress* and threatened to hang the captain and crew, who had been found guilty of treason. Officials swore that the captain and crew of the *Savannah*, which had been captured the previous month, would suffer a similar fate. The south began making plans to

Pittsburgh: Suburban Evolution

While suburbs are generally associated with 20th-century America, the first suburbs emerged in cities such as Pittsburgh during the Reconstruction era when steel cities with important railways became essential to propelling the United States into a position of industrial prominence. Pittsburgh had all the ingredients for a successful role in this process. The existence of the Pennsylvania Railroad, virtually a city with a wide range of assets and support enterprises that ranged from foundries and mines to hotels and sea vessels, was essential to Pittsburgh's industrial growth. Furthermore the city was built where the Allegheny and Monongahela Rivers converged, and possessed plentiful natural resources of coal and gas.

Outside the south, in large cities with ready access to railroads and waterways, small factories had been converted to large mass production enterprises by the 1870s. As industries expanded, factory owners ventured away from the confines of cities, creating the first suburbs, along with mill and mining towns. Over time this pattern was repeated in cities throughout the country, spawning vast metropolitan areas containing large segments of the American population.

A view of Charleston, South Carolina, in the distance, with a Northeastern Railroad train making its way to the southern city in the mid-19th century.

kill an equal number of high-ranking northern prisoners for every southern privateer executed. The Union did not carry out the proposed executions.

CIVIL WAR: RAILROADS

By the end of the Civil War dependence on water vessels had begun to decline, and the Union turned to railroads to move troops and supplies. In this area also, the south trailed behind. In 1860 the south had 8,541 miles of railroad track as compared to 22,000 in northern states. With 1,771 miles, Virginia led southern states in rail mileage. Even before the war northern railroads had been linked together to speed the transfer of goods and facilitate travel. By contrast the South had only one east-to-west railroad, running from Richmond to Chattanooga and on to Memphis.

Despite the importance of waterways to both the Union and the Confederacy, railroads were the essential mode of transportation during the Civil War. An examination of all major battles reveals that either a railroad junction or a river port was within 20 miles. Union strategists, who well understood the significance of controlling rails, targeted railroad junctions in southern cities, including Manassas, Petersburg, Atlanta, Nashville, Corinth, and Chattanooga. The fact that the Union had sufficient resources to ensure superior management of railroads was instrumental in their ultimate victory. Union officials paid railroad owners two cents per mile to move troops and supplies. Freight charges were based on a sliding scale. As the war drug on, railroad owners raked in huge profits, which grew even larger during Reconstruction and intensified industrialization.

With its vast resources, the Union army was able to create special units to run and maintain Union railroads and destroy southern rail lines. Abraham Lincoln, who became known as "the constitutional dictator" because of the extensive powers he amassed during the war, received congressional authority to federalize railroads to benefit Union interests. The government

American Canals

As early as the late 18th century progressive Americans had determined that it was necessary to build a waterway to connect the Great Lakes with the eastern United States in order to facilitate transportation and industry. In the early 19th century New Yorkers unsuccessfully attempted to obtain federal funding for a canal to connect Lake Erie with the Hudson River, the city's major waterway. After the State of New York agreed to finance the canal, construction began on July 4, 1817 in Rome, New York. A section connecting Rome with Utica was navigable within two years. By 1825 the Erie Canal was completed at a cost of $7,144,000, covering 363 miles. The success of the canal spawned a surge of canal and bridge building in the United States.

The same year the Erie Canal opened in New York, construction began on the Chesapeake and Ohio Canal to build a trade route from Washington, D.C.'s Potomac River to the Ohio River in Western Pennsylvania. The C&O Canal played a direct role in the Civil War since it separated the Confederacy from northern lands. Both sides understood the importance of the C&O Canal for transporting troops, supplies, and fuel resources. Because the canal was officially under Union protection, it became the scene of frequent Confederate attacks, many planned by legendary cavalrymen such as Jeb Stuart, the hero of several major battles. When fighting broke out in Maryland, both armies used the C&O Canal towpath, and locals used the path to reach safe havens during battles.

Canals in the south also played a role in the Civil War. In 1863 the Union Army made several attempts to create a supply route that would bypass the City of Vicksburg, located at the mouth of the lower Mississippi, and a Confederate stronghold. Workers were assigned to create diversion canals to divert the flow of the river, but they proved unsuccessful. Later that same year Ulysses S. Grant finally took Vicksburg through a combination of land and water attacks.

also established the United States Military Railroad (USMRR) as an independent agency to oversee and maintain all captured Confederate railroads. This agency played a major role in a number of Union victories. By the time the war ended in 1865, the USMRR was the largest railroad system in the entire world, covering 2,100 miles of track and employing 25,000 workers.

Railroads were also essential to military strategy in the south, beginning with the first Battle of Bull Run (Manassas) in which General Rene Beauregard was able to quickly move his troops through the Shenandoah Valley by rail. In 1862 General Braxton Bragg stalled a Union advance by transporting 30,000 troops by rail from Mississippi to Tennessee. The following year General James Longstreet moved 13,000 men from Virginia to Georgia and ensured a Confederate victory at Chickamauga, even after one-half his delegation was late in arriving. Union forces transported by rail to eastern Tennessee and Chickamauga assisted General Sherman with the burning of Georgia on his march to the sea, devastating the land between Atlanta and Savannah.

Unlike northern railroads designed to quickly move passengers and freight over long distances, southern railroads were intended for seasonal transport of agricultural products. Consequently they did not always meet standard gauge requirements. When the Confederate government ordered owners to meet specific guidelines, they were ignored, in part because funds were not always available for improvement and expansion in the war-torn south. Like their Union counterparts, Confederate officials paid railroad owners two cents a mile to move troops and supplies, but this rate proved insufficient to

Profits and Profiteers

Like most wars, the Civil War produced its share of profiteers who used the war to feather their nests. Though southern profiteering history emphasizes the so-called "carpetbaggers" who flocked to the south during Reconstruction, many profiteers viewed themselves simply as astute businessmen who were able to meet the needs of a nation at war and assist in rebuilding afterwards. Many of those who made excessive profits during the war and Reconstruction had founded large railroads in the decades before the first shot was fired at Fort Sumter on April 12, 1861. The Baltimore and Oriole Railroad, for instance, expanded at that time through the efforts of Johns Hopkins, a liquor merchant, and John Work Garret, a merchant banker.

Even before the war, some railroad owners had seen the advantage of consolidation, and the first significant railroad merger took place in 1853, creating the New York Central and making shipping magnate Cornelius Vanderbilt even wealthier. Vanderbilt sold his ships to the Union Navy at the beginning of the war and invested in New York's rail system, building a line that connected the states from New York City to Buffalo. Later Vanderbilt expanded his holdings with a line that ran from New York City to Chicago, earning him the title of the world's richest man.

Built by the Credit Mobilier Construction Company, the Union Pacific had become one of the leading railroads in the country by the mid-1860s. It earned a solid place in American history and increased the profits of its owners by participating in the construction of the first transcontinental railroad. Even enterprising Americans with limited cash flows sometimes seized on opportunities to amass fortunes. One New Yorker, for example, turned a $12,000 ship investment into $833,000 by offering his ship for charter during the war. The construction of the transcontinental railroad provided a wealth of opportunity for railroad owners who were able to build rail lines and support towns on land ceded them as part of the federal government's official efforts to expand domestic trading and passenger routes.

cover operating costs. Repairs were difficult because essential materials remained under Union control. Railroad owners also discovered that payments made in Confederate government bonds rapidly became useless. As the war went on, many railroads were captured, and the condition of railroads still under southern control deteriorated rapidly, limiting the south's ability to move troops and receive supplies.

Union soldiers working on repairing the Grapevine Bridge over Chickahominy River, Virginia, 1862.

With vastly superior resources to draw on, the north continued to easily move men and supplies throughout the Civil War, and foreign trade continued to flourish despite the activities of southern commerce raiders. On the other hand, vessels going in and out of the south were forced to bypass the substantial blockade of southern ports. The result was that trading profits mounted in the north even as the south was being forced to depend on its own resources for survival.

At the beginning of the Civil War the north had 20,000 miles of railroad track and the south 9,000. After years of fighting and devastation in the south, most tracks were destroyed or inoperable. This situation was a major factor in General Robert E. Lee's surrender in 1865.

CIVIL WAR: ANIMAL POWER

In addition to railroads and waterway, animal power was an essential element in fighting the Civil War. In 1860 the United States claimed 6.1 million horses, but only 1.7 million of those were found in the south. Mules were more plentiful than horses in the South because even poor farmers used mules in their agricultural endeavors. Southerners owned 800,663 of 1,129,554 mules and 856,645 of 2,240,074 oxen in 1860.

Horses were very much a part of military life. While both the Union and Confederate cavalries used horses in battle, larger numbers were used to haul ammunition, weapons, food, and supplies. A group of animal-drawn wagons known as a "train" accompanied both armies as they moved from one camp to another. Horses were expensive to keep because they required feed and hay. The superior resources of the Union allowed them to maintain a steady supply of replacement horses. Since they were better cared for, Union horses were far healthier than those in the south, where horses remained with their owners indefinitely. Union horses were supplied by the government and were generally replaced after four months of service. However as the war continued, it was impossible to supply the 500 replacements needed each day. Horse prices had risen from $125 to $185 by war's end.

Fewer Confederate records are available, but Civil War scholars estimate that southern horse prices rose faster than those in the north because of the extensive price gauging that existed in much of the south during the war. The long years of the war eventually took its toll on the southern cavalry, sapping its legendary superiority.

RECONSTRUCTION: THE TRANSCONTINENTAL RAILROAD

After the Civil War ended in 1865 a transportation revolution occurred in the United Sates. The merchant marine, which had been instrumental in the Union victory, was abandoned, and young American men no longer sailed the ocean to see the world. Instead they struck out for the American west in increasing numbers.

Vast fortunes had been made during the war, providing ready capital for expanding rail lines and the establishment of new businesses and cities. The number of immigrants coming to the United States increased just in time to furnish the cheap labor that was needed to settle western lands, and the reunited government was eager to provide aid through land grants and cash subsidies.

After gold was discovered in California in 1848, plans for a transcontinental railroad had begun to be thought of as a necessity rather than a luxury. As Secretary of War, Jefferson Davis had determined that a southern route for the new railroad was preferable to one in the northern or central United States. When war broke out, Davis left to become the president of the Confederacy, and President Abraham Lincoln's attention was diverted into preserving the Union. Lincoln did not, however, forget the idea of a transcontinental railroad. He signed the Pacific Railroad Act in 1862, authorizing the construction of a transcontinental railroad to connect the United States from the Atlantic to the Pacific. With great ceremony, the first continental railroad was completed on May 10, 1869, when Union Pacific and Central Pacific workers, who had been constructing rail lines from opposite ends of the country, met in Promontory Point, Utah, to drive in the now legendary "golden spike." By 1900 four other transcontinental railroads had been built, increasing American rail mileage from 30,000 in 1860 to 201,000 in 1900.

Instead of spending two or three months at sea, American travelers could now reach the opposite coast in less than two weeks. This availability of relatively comfortable and speedy travel across the country encouraged European immigrants to leave the east for the west, where they helped to destroy the cultures of Native Americans who had lived on the Plains for centuries. By the end of the Civil War railroad pioneers had been fine-tuning the industry for a generation, learning how to serve their own interests as well as those of the rapidly growing nation. Unlike railroads in most other industrializing countries, American railroads for the most part were built by private investors. Those investors did, however, accept government aid, particularly in the form of land grants. Railroads such as the Baltimore and Oriole, which had built a line across the Appalachian Mountains, had expanded by using joint funding from private investors in the State of Maryland. Foreign investors who had become wealthy during the industrialization of Europe turned their attention to investing in American railroads after the Civil War. Together they funded some 25 percent of American rail expansion.

EXPANDING HOLDINGS

Throughout the 1870s the American railroad industry continued to grow steadily. In 1870 there were 45,000 miles of track in the United States. Over the next three decades mileage expanded to 215,000. By 1875, 70,000 locomotives were regularly traveling 160,000 miles of railroad tracks. Millions of acres of public lands were ceded to large railroad companies to make this advancement possible. Railroads sold extra lands to finance additional construction. Smaller companies, on the other hand, were forced to bear the costs of purchasing their own land, and frequently had to haggle for rights of way over private land.

Republican Rutherford B. Hayes entered the White House after the election of 1876, agreeing to end Reconstruction in exchange for Democratic support in the contested election. Once in office, Hayes used his executive power to call up the National Guard to force an end to a railway strike and continued to throw the weight of the federal government into assisting railroad magnates in expanding their holdings.

Technology also played a role in railroad expansion, as indicated by Andrew Carnegie's use of Bessemer steel converters to turn iron into the large quantities of steel needed to build railroads. The fact that railroad owners agreed to comply with a single standard gauge also facilitated post-war growth. Neither the federal nor state governments exercised much

Aiken's Landing, Virginia: the steamer New York waiting for exchange of prisoners. Steamboat transportation served where roads were non-existent.

oversight over the railroad industry. Consequently, the freewheeling capitalism that developed frequently led to cutthroat competition.

While much industry exploded in the rest of the country, transportation advances in the devastated south moved at a much slower pace. There were few animals left for use in either transportation or agriculture. Roads, bridges, levees, wharves, rolling stock, and steamboats were in various stages of disrepair. In order to rebuild the transportation infrastructure, it was first necessary to reopen blocked rivers and repair roads and passageways that had been destroyed. With large sums tied up in defunct Confederate bonds, many transportation companies went bankrupt. Railroad companies faced an almost insurmountable task in rebuilding rail lines. In Alabama, for instance, all bridges and trestles had been destroyed on a 114-mile stretch of railroad. Buildings were burned, water towers were destroyed, and weeds and bushes covered the tracks. Sherman's destructive path through the south had left hundreds of miles of track in ruins. It took a generation and an infusion of outside capital before southern railroads began to recover.

CIVIL WAR AND RECONSTRUCTION: MAIL

Because the United States covers such a large geographic area, reliable ways to communicate among cities, states, and territories has always been vital. In the first half of the 19th century the federal government generally depended on stagecoaches to deliver mail. The first major roads, known as "post roads," were built for this purpose. Steamboats transported mail in areas where stagecoaches could not travel. By the 1830s eastern railroads had sped up mail delivery, tra-

An 1865 photograph of what is probably a Civil War camp. The wagon in the center served as transport for officers' luggage and saddle equipment.

versing 4.5 miles in only 35 minutes. Lacking the extensive railroad system of the east, mail delivery in western areas tended to be slower and less reliable. Mail delivery by wagon trains presented easy targets for thieves, and accidents were common. The federal government dealt with the logistics of mail delivery by awarding contracts to private companies, such as the Pacific Mail Steamship Company in California and John Butterfield's Overland Mail Company, which delivered mail along a 2,757 stretch between El Paso and San Francisco. Under optimal conditions, the Overland line, which also carried passengers, could complete a one-way trip in 25 days. However a trip could, and often did, take several months. The United States military filled in gaps left by private companies, delivering mail between Leavenworth and Santa Fe.

In 1860 William H. Russell solved the problem of slow mail delivery in the western United States by establishing the Pony Express. He initially advertised for "young, skinny, wiry" expert riders under the age of 18 to transport mail as quickly as possible. His preference for orphans underscored the seriousness of his warning that those who were hired would be putting their lives on the line. Such restrictions were later lifted, and riders from 11 to 49 signed up to deliver mail. Originally the Pony Express route traversed 2,000 miles, crossing the lands of hostile Native Americans on a path from St. Joseph, Missouri, to Sacramento, California. Traveling among nearly 200 relay stations where horses were changed every 10 to 15 miles, a rider could cover 100 miles a day, receiving a salary of $50 to $100 per month. In the early days customers paid up to $5.00 an ounce to send mail. This amount was later reduced to $1 for a half ounce. In 1861 Lincoln's Inaugural Address became the fastest piece of mail in the history of the Pony Express, reaching California in seven days, 17 hours.

Within 18 months of its creation, the transcontinental telegraph line had rendered the Pony Express obsolete. The line was bought by Wells Fargo. A decade later the first experiment with airmail took place. On September 23, 1870, more than 500 pounds of mail was lost when postal balloons failed to reach their delivery point. By 1911 the United States had begun experimenting with traditional airmail.

The federal mail service was unable to operate along southern routes during the war. Confederate raids on mail stages were so common that they forced mail carriers onto a more central route. By the 1880s railroads had relegated stagecoaches to history.

TRANSPORTATION AND MIGRATION

Unlike arduous and unsafe stagecoach journeys, railroads allowed passengers to travel more safely and in relative comfort. As a result, settlers, miners, adventurers, and entrepreneurs flocked to the western United States after the Civil War. These western immigrants settled the west, building towns and communities and raising families. For instance, after the Union Pacific laid track in Wyoming 1867–68, settlers established the towns of Cheyenne, Laramie, Rock

Springs, Rawlins, and Evanston. Cheyenne, which later became the state capital, emerged as a shipping and maintenance hub. Many western cities also began as 30-day railroad camps, developing into market towns and, ultimately, into commercial centers as lands were settled around them. These railroad towns attracted eastern settlers who eventually learned to exploit the rich supply of raw materials. Fertile western lands also spurred production of agricultural products, first for domestic use, and later for export.

In 1862 the Homestead Act provided for the settlement of 160-acre farms to all individuals willing to occupy and improve the land. By 1880, the Indian wars had ended; and life on the frontier was much safer. Large mining communities were thriving in Nevada, Montana, Wyoming, the Dakotas, and Colorado. Huge tracts of grassland attracted wealthy ranchers and cattle barons to the western United States. Cowboys drove herds of cattle from Texas to the Great Plains where cattle could graze unrestricted on open ranges. More than 55 million acres of public lands were ceded to western immigrants. Within three decades of the end of the Civil War, more than five million individuals had relocated to the west.

The arrival of ranchers in the west created a new meat industry. Ranchers moved large herds of longhorn cattle across inhabited public areas to railroads in Kansas. From that point, meat was shipped to the east and midwest, which was industrializing and urbanizing at a rapid pace. After cattle ranching expanded into Colorado, Wyoming, Kansas, Nebraska, and the Dakotas, railroads provided quick export prepared meat.

RECONSTRUCTION: STEAMSHIPS
After the Civil War Britain and Germany introduced steamships, which soon became the chief method of transporting products for trade and for carrying emigrants to other parts of the world. By steamship, immigrants came from Canada, Europe, Australia, New Zealand, South America, and other parts of the United States to help industrialize and expand the country. In the 1870s many of those immigrants came from Britain, Ireland, Germany, and the Scandinavias, where industrialization had resulted in a decline of agriculture as lands had been given over to industrialization. In the "melting pot" that made up life in 19th-century America, all immigrants brought elements of their own cultures, making life more diverse.

Steamships had a distinct advantage over earlier water transportation, cutting the trip from Europe from a month to 10 days by 1880. Between 1860 and 1924 steamships brought more than 25 million immigrants into the United States. Wealthy Americans and Europeans also used steamships to travel, and shipping lines rushed to meet their needs. Ships such as the Cunard line's *Mauritania* and the White Star line's ill-fated *Titanic* offered luxurious state and public rooms and elaborate entertainments for the affluent. Poor immigrants were relegated to steerage in the lower level of the ships where they were crowded into

An 1870s lithograph of the steamships Egypt *and* Spain *that regularly sailed the transatlantic route between New York City and Liverpool, England.*

poorly ventilated and overcrowded areas that were either too hot or too cold. While the wealthy enjoyed opulent feasts on luxury ships, steerage passengers often went hungry. Germs flourished, and sicknesses spread rapidly.

Steamships regularly crossed the Pacific Ocean too, bringing immigrants from Asia to the United States and transporting goods between the western and eastern hemispheres. The first Pacific crossing took place on December 8, 1866. A year later the *Celestial Empire*, later rechristened the *China*, set sail with room for 1,300 passengers.

TRANSPORTATION TECHNOLOGY

Between 1866 and 1888 Texas ranchers brought six million head of cattle to winter in the grasslands of Colorado, Wyoming, and Montana. By 1885 the western ranching boom had peaked as a result of overgrazing. Remaining open lands had been taken over by railroad companies, and homesteaders had enclosed their lands to keep cattle away from crops and animals.

Once cattle arrived in the west, railroads offered ranchers the opportunity to ship live cattle to eastern processing plants in stock cars that had been ventilated by removing slats. Cattle that had traveled hundreds of miles to reach stock cars did not always arrive in good condition. Animals lost substantial amounts of weight along the way. On the trip to the processing plants, many animals were hungry and thirsty, and some were injured. Because of their weakened conditions, many animals did not survive the journey to the east.

As early as the 1830s, railroad owners had begun adding passenger cars for livestock handlers. Once refrigerated cars were introduced, cattle were slaughtered before being shipped, and the drovers' car was no longer necessary. By the mid-20th century this car had become the familiar caboose that trailed all other cars. In the pre-Civil War era, cattle and poultry had generally been transported in open-roofed boxcars. In the 1880s railroads introduced humane stock cars. Improved conditions allowed larger numbers of animals to arrive safely at their destinations. Normal loss rates were calculated at six percent for cattle and nine percent for sheep.

The carcasses of animals that did not survive were tossed out, taken to glue factories, or used by unscrupulous butchers.

This wood-burning engine, on display at the Pennsylvania Railroad Museum, was built for the Virginia and Truckee Line in 1875.

RECONSTRUCTION: URBAN TRANSPORTATION INNOVATION

Urban transportation developed during the 19th century in response to the rapid industrialization that brought large numbers of workers into cities and allowed commuters to live in the suburbs. One of the first innovations was the horse-drawn trolley, or omnibus, which had been introduced in France in 1828. These privately-owned trolleys could hold from 25 to 50 passengers each. In 1832 New York City installed rails along city streets to make cable cars run smoother and become more energy efficient.

As early as 1800 a twice-daily city stage coach service had opened in the nation's capital, but the venture failed. Three decades later, the first horse-drawn omnibuses appeared in Washington, D.C. and continued to operate until they were replaced in 1854 by streetcars. The electric trolley was introduced in the city in the 1880s. Technology continued to expand transportation alternatives in the late 19th century.

By the 1870s experiments with trolleys pulled by steam engines were underway. Steam engines had a significant advantage over earlier urban modes of transportation because they could pull several cars in one trip, could travel greater distances at faster speeds, and were considerably more reliable. Transit lines were built in major cities to bypass urban congestion caused by pedestrians, vendors' carts, and horse-drawn carriages.

In 1868 New York became the first city to construct an elevated rail transit line, which opened on Greenwich Street between Dey Street and Battery Place. The elevated had a maximum speed of 15 miles an hour. The railroad reorganized its services in 1870, expanding service into other areas and adopting steam-powered equipment.

Within three years New Yorkers were introduced to their first pneumatic-powered subway. This 22-seat innovation was operated by a steam engine, which used a giant fan to suck in air and force it into a 312-foot tunnel. In 1871 Andrew S. Hallidie introduced his "endless wire ropeway" that created power by using a system of weights and pulleys that were propelled along a wire rope.

CABLE CARS

By 1873 San Francisco had begun using a cable car pulled by steam that was able to navigate its steep hills, becoming the first city in the world to use a cable-powered railroad. San Francisco's trolley system remains in operation in the 21st century, drawing tourists from around the world to the city that was known in the 19th century as the "Queen of Pacific" because of the vast number of ships that entered and left its port. Other cities, including Chicago, followed San Francisco's innovative experiment with cable cars, and older forms of urban transportation became obsolete. During the following decade, many cities replaced cable cars with electric trolleys.

Indicative of southern economy recovery, Richmond, Virginia introduced its first electric streetcar in 1888. In the south transportation technology was often intertwined with social change, frequently tainted by the Jim Crow laws that had been passed after Rutherford B. Hayes agreed to end Reconstruction in 1876 in his quest for the presidency.

Most southern cities segregated all forms of transportation, a practice that also existed in a number of northern cities. In Louisville, Kentucky African Americans were forced to sit in rear trolley seats or stand on exterior platforms. When trolleys were full, African Americans were not allowed to board at all.

In the 1870s African Americans rebelled and forced desegregation in a number of cities. Nevertheless segregated transportation continued in much of the south for almost another century. In 1896 the Supreme Court upheld the right of southern states to continue this "separate but equal" way of life in *Plessy v. Ferguson* (163 U.S. 537). It was not until the mid-20th century that African Americans won the legal right to equal access to public transportation.

In all large urban areas, transportation technologies operated in conjunction with industrial development. In Pittsburgh, for instance, development occurred alongside the Pennsylvania Main Line and Beaver canals. Transportation magnates such as Andrew Carnegie continued to play a large role in both urban and transportation evolution, establishing industries beside major railroads and waterways.

ELIZABETH PURDY
JOHN BARNHILL

Further Readings

Abdill, George B. *Civil War Railroads: A Pictorial Story of the War between the States, 1861–1865*. Bloomington: Indiana University Press, 1999.

"A Cradle on Wheels: Stagecoach Travel in the Wild West." Available online, URL: http://americanhistory.about.com/library/weekly/aa120501a.htm. (Accessed August 2007).

Bankston, Carl L., and Danielle A. Hidalgo, eds. *Immigration in U.S. History*. Pasadena, CA: Salem Press, 2006.

Bianculli, Anthony J. *Trains and Technology: The American Railroad in the Nineteenth Century: Bridges and Tunnels Signals (Bridges and Tunnels, Signals)*. Newark: University of Delaware Press, 2003.

Ezell, John Samuel. *The South Since 1865*. New York: Macmillan, 1963.

Fleming, Maria. "Freedom's Main Line." Available online, URL: http://www.tolerance.org/teach/printar .jsp?p=0&ar=366&pi=apg. (Accessed August 2007).

Longfellow, Rickie. "Back in Time; Transportation in America's Postal System." Available online, URL: http://www.fhwa.dot.gov/infrastructure/back0304.htm. (Accessed August 2007).

Luraghi, Raimondo, et al. *The Confederate Navy: The Ships, Men, and Organization, 1861–65*. London: Conway Maritime Press, 1997.

Muller, Edward K. "Industrial Suburbs and the Growth of Metropolitan Pittsburgh, 1870–1920," *Journal of Historical Geography* (v.27/1, 2001).

U.S. Postal Service. "Moving the Mail; The Pony Express." Available online, URL: http://www.usps.com/postalhistory/the_pony_express.htm. (Accessed August 2007).

Chapter 16

Public Health, Medicine, and Nutrition

*"Give a man health and a course to steer;
and he'll never stop to trouble
about whether he's happy or not."*
— George Bernard Shaw

DURING THE CIVIL War years Americans in both the north and south were focused on the war and all that was entailed in abolishing slavery and restoring the shattered Union. Nevertheless important lessons in health and nutrition were learned in the course of the Civil War. Widespread mobilization of troops precipitated an influx of enteric and respiratory diseases, and soldiers who were sent home from the battlefield to recuperate often spread infectious diseases along their way. Between 1820 and 1875 the populations of all large American cities suffered outbreaks of smallpox, cholera, and typhoid fever. Infants were particularly susceptible to diseases and unsanitary conditions, and tuberculosis, diarrhea, and enteritis were the leading causes of death among this age group. At the end of the Civil War in 1865 the death rate in the United States was estimated at 25 deaths per 1,000 of the population. Beginning in 1850 physicians and scientists were involved in formulating the germ theory of disease. Findings from this research led to major reforms in the management of water supplies and basic sanitation. As a result, permanent health departments were created around the country.

From the end of the Civil War to the 1930s the United States entered a period in which production, communication, transportation, business, and industry were completely transformed. In 1870 the Public Health Service, created by President John Adams (1735–1826) in 1795, was reorganized into a network of hospitals under the leadership of the surgeon general, giving the federal government the chief role in checking the spread of infectious diseases. As a result, the federal government took over the quarantine responsibility, particularly on ships coming into and going out of the country.

Overland transportation routes reduced the cost of food imported into other areas of the country, and increased the range of available foods. After the construction of the Erie Canal in 1821, the United States began building a series of other canals to facilitate transportation of goods. The advent of railroads further revolutionized life in America, increasing the speed at which food could be transported. At the end of the 17th century, the French had discovered that ice could be used in liquors and frozen juices. By 1800 ice houses were scattered around the United States. In 1860 Boston shipped 97,211 tons of natural ice. Refrigerated produce was shipped for the first time in 1836. By 1865 an improved design allowed strawberries, and later peaches, to be shipped in refrigerated rail cars. Three years later, the first commercial refrigeration unit for meats was installed in Louisiana. Life in many American homes had also been transformed, and there were 1,285,177 heating stoves, 15,351 hot-air furnaces, and 5,450 cooking ranges in use in the United States during this period.

An 1862 wood engraving by Winslow Homer portrays an army surgeon tending to wounded soldiers at the rear during an engagement in the Civil War.

The Slaughterhouse Cases

During Reconstruction the Republican-controlled Congress approved the Fourteenth Amendment, establishing constitutional protections for former slaves that theoretically included due process of law and equal protection from legal discrimination. Although ratification of the amendment was made a condition of reentry into the Union, most southern states tended to see the Fourteenth Amendment as an infringement on states rights. In 1873 the Supreme Court addressed the first challenge to the amendment with the Slaughterhouse Cases (83 U.S. 36). The challenge arose out of an 1869 Louisiana law passed by a corrupt Reconstruction Congress that had awarded a 25-year monopoly of the slaughterhouse industry to a group of white butchers who operated the only slaughterhouse in the New Orleans area. The suit challenging the law was instituted by a group of butchers and livestock dealers in the area who were being forced to pay to have their slaughtering done at the designated facility. In a five to four decision, the court upheld the Louisiana statute, determining that the amendment could not be used to protect private property from state government regulation.

The local government had justified the 1869 law on the grounds that government control of the slaughterhouse industry was essential to protect public health. At the time New Orleans was considered the dirtiest and unhealthiest city in the entire country. More than 300,000 animals were slaughtered each year in the city, which had no public sewer system. Hotels frequently discarded wastes in gutters or directly onto city streets. Wastes and animal carcasses were dumped in uninhabited areas or in local waterways, including the levees along the Mississippi River. Despite its claim of protecting public health, the New Orleans slaughterhouse industry was a major participant in local pollution, regularly dumping enormous barrels of entrails, liver, blood, urine, and dung into the river. As a result, both the air and water around the city was heavily polluted. The humid subtropical climate of New Orleans ensured that, under existing conditions, diseases such as cholera and yellow fever would flourish.

NUTRITION IN MILITARY HOSPITALS

During the Civil War nurses in hospitals in both the north and south set up diet kitchens inspired by nursing pioneer Florence Nightingale (1820–1919), working to ensure that soldiers received nutritional food. In an era of primitive medical care, proper nutrition helped to save many lives. Mortality rates in some hospitals declined from five to 10 percent in response to improved diets for convalescing soldiers. In Richmond, Virginia Sally Tompkins boasted that her hospital had a 95 percent survival rate. Tompkins, who was commissioned as a captain of cavalry, was the only southern woman to hold military rank in the Confederate army. In 1862 Congress agreed to fund the hiring of hospital matrons and nurses in Union hospitals and placed them in charge of food, laundering, and the dispensing of medicine. In the south, nurses tended to be volunteers or slaves.

Toward the end of the war ensuring proper diets for soldiers became extremely difficult, as food became scarce and prices rose drastically. Confederate records document a severe shortage of the salt needed to preserve meat and fish. Cooks resorted to Native-American methods of preservation such as drying the food by fire, smoke, and sunlight. Southern cooks also devised various substitutes for favorite foods and beverages. Molasses was used to sweeten food. Acorns poached, shelled, roasted, and enhanced with bacon fat served as a substitute for coffee, and rice was used to make bread when wheat was unavailable. This bread was cooked on griddles, partially because yeast was difficult to obtain in the south.

Elsewhere the availability of commercial yeast and improved cooking methods had made it easier to bake bread in traditional ways by the 1860s. Consequently soft white bread became available in lower and middle-class homes. The shortage of fresh fruit during the Civil War led cooks to make apple pie with crackers that had been soaked in tartaric acid; flavored with butter, cinnamon, and nutmeg; and then sweetened with sugar. In Corinth, Mississippi, patients in Confederate hospitals were served a drink made of arrowroot that was sometimes sweetened with eggs and preserves. In Okolona, Mississippi hospital patients were served only one meal a day, consisting of thin soup and bread.

In Chattanooga, Tennessee breakfast consisted of batter cakes made from rice or stale bread. Lunch was made up of hash, toast, mush, milk, and tea. For dinner, patients were given beef, chicken, soup, potatoes, rice, dried fruit, and a baked pudding. The sickest patients were fed a milder diet of chicken, beef tea, arrowroot, boiled meat thickened with flour, milk, tea, and toast. Dinner for these patients was light, consisting of dried fruit, toast, tea, and coffee. The fare was generally much better in Union hospitals, and meat was served three times a day.

An 1865 photograph of cooks at work in a kitchen in Alexandria, Virginia. Confederate cooks resorted to Native American methods of preservation.

Mary Boykin Miller Chesnut
(1823–86)

The contribution of nurses in military hospitals was essential to the survival of large numbers of Confederate and Union soldiers. One of the best
known of the southern nurses was Mary Boykin Miller Chesnut, whose diary
offers a first-hand view of life in Confederate hospitals in South Carolina.
The publication of Chesnut's diary, *Mary Chesnut's Civil War* (Yale University
Press, 1981), edited by historian C. Vann Woodward (1908–1999) garnered
a Pulitzer Prize in 1982. Boykin's husband James was a senator from South
Carolina, and her family had the advantage of having food sent from their
plantation. As a result, they ate well throughout the war. Their everyday
fare included beef, poultry, ham, eggs, butter, rice, potatoes, pickles, fresh
vegetables and fruit, and imported fois gras and truffles. Meals were more
elaborate on holidays, including plum puddings and various pies and cakes.
The family's fortunes did suffer from the war, and her father-in-law maintained that he had lost at least half a million dollars in bank stocks and
railroad bonds. Yet even after prices escalated, Chesnut, the daughter of a
former South Carolina governor, was able to afford the food needed to maintain the family's style of living. In June 1864 she noted that she paid $800
for two pounds of tea, 40 pounds of coffee, and 60 pounds of sugar.

Chesnut's description of life in southern hospitals is stark, and she notes
that sicknesses such as typhoid were causing more deaths than northern
guns. While on a tour of area hospitals, Chesnut witnessed "long rows of
dead and dying." Even though she fainted from the horrors, Mary Chesnut
continued her work, attempting to ease suffering any way she could, using
her own money to purchase food and niceties for the wounded. In order to
fill the constant demand for money, clothes, and nurses for the Confederate
hospitals, Chesnut launched a letter writing campaign to encourage other
southern women to become involved in improving the plight of Confederate
soldiers. Chesnut was impressed with conditions at the Richmond hospital
of Sally Tompkins, writing that the wounded were clean, comfortable, and
cheerful and had all manner of "good things."

INFECTIOUS DISEASES

In the overcrowded and unsanitary conditions of Civil War military camps, diseases such as yellow fever, smallpox, cholera, typhoid fever, and typhus spread
rapidly. Typhoid was particularly lethal during the Civil War, causing the deaths
of as many as 81,630 Union personnel. Although it is more difficult to pinpoint
incidences of disease in the Confederate army because most records were
destroyed, it is believed that widespread dysentery may have contributed to

devastating southern losses at the Battle of Gettysburg. Overall less than half of the 620,000 casualties incurred in the Civil War were a direct result of battlefield wounds. However large numbers of deaths were due to infections of wounds. In general camp conditions were unsanitary, and surgeons sometimes cleaned knives on whatever was handy. Even those who tried to clean their instruments properly often used polluted river or tainted rain water.

Large numbers of Americans died from tuberculosis and its complications in the Civil War and Reconstruction periods. In Massachusetts, for instance,

Creation of the U.S. Sanitary Commission

In New York the Women's Central Relief Organization, led by noted surgeon Dr. Valentine Mott (1785–1865) and the Reverend Dr. Henry W. Bellows (1814–82), was established to identify the needs of the Union army, to collect and dispense medical supplies, and to recruit and train nurses. The organization convinced the federal government that it was necessary to form the U.S. Sanitary Commission, which was made up of nine civilians and three military officers. Dr. Valentine was named president. Responding to the needs of the war, the Sanitary Commission transformed itself into a major relief agency, providing medicine and care for ailing soldiers, setting up hospital facilities, and assisting sick and wounded soldiers who had been stranded in Washington, D.C., while awaiting back pay and/or discharge papers. In army camps, the organization dispensed medicine, blankets, fresh meat, vegetables, and provided information.

Despite these relief activities, the role of sanitarian was not neglected. The Sanitary Commission forced the Army Medical Corps to respond to the unhealthy conditions in Union camps such as those set up by General George B. McClellan (1826–85) and future president General Ulysses S. Grant (1822–85). The Sanitary Commission had only an indirect influence in the south, except in areas such as New Orleans where the Union army had seized control in the spring of 1862. As a result of strict enforcement of sanitary regulations, New Orleans, which had historically been a breeding ground for yellow fever, reported no incidences of the disease 1860–67. Starting with Charleston in 1865 and Nashville in 1866, large southern cities began creating their own health departments. However Reconstruction governments did not always fund the activities of these departments. In Memphis, for instance, the government refused to appoint a board of health and subsequently sold all city carts and mule teams and discharged city officials and sanitary officers. Southern cities were also reluctant to impose quarantines, insisting that they interfered with trade and were largely ineffective.

the death rate from this disease was 40 per 10,000 of the population. It was not until the early years of the 20th century that deaths from tuberculosis declined drastically in Massachusetts (15 per 1,000 of the population) and the rest of the country. Between 1870 and 1920 Philadelphia's death rate from tuberculosis declined from 320 to 151 per 100,000 of the population. Yellow fever was also feared throughout the United States, most particularly in the south. Between 1800 and 1879 an outbreak occurred somewhere in the country every year except for two. Cases of typhoid fever were also common in the eastern United States. In Massachusetts, for instance, the death rate from typhoid fever in 1869 was 71.5 per 100,000 of the population. In the west and Mississippi Valley, where immigration was less common, typhoid was rare.

SCURVY AND SMALLPOX

Scurvy, a disease caused by a deficiency of vitamin C, was rampant throughout the Civil War. It was most common in prisoner-of-war camps were fresh fruits and vegetables were rare. The civilian population was not exempt from the disease, and it continued to be prevalent among infants in the industrial ports of the United States and Europe until World War I. Measles also posed a major threat to Americans during the Civil War years. Although most Confederate records were destroyed, deaths among Union troops have been well documented. It is estimated that 98,817 of four million enlistees contracted measles, which proved fatal to 2,367 victims. Confederate deaths from the disease are assumed to be much higher because of the conditions in the war-torn south, in great part because Union blockades prevented the entry of life-saving medicines. These regional differences in disease outbreaks continued through World War I.

Smallpox continued to be of great concern in the United States, despite the success of vaccinations that had been introduced in the United States in the 1720s. On November 19, 1863 President Abraham Lincoln (1809–65) delivered his now famous Gettysburg Address on the Pennsylvania battlefield that is considered the bloodiest in American history. That night the President became ill with a mild case of smallpox that had likely been contracted from his 10-year-old son Tad. Unfortunately smallpox proved fatal to Lincoln's trusted valet William Johnson, who had been exposed to the disease while caring for the president

The discovery that inoculating individuals with smallpox and cowpox bacteria could prevent epidemics was viewed as a major medical breakthrough. However when the practice of vaccinating directly from the arm of a smallpox sufferer was initiated, it precipitated an outbreak of other diseases such as hepatitis, syphilis, and leprosy. The arm-to-arm method was subsequently abolished, and the practice of vaccinating humans with cowpox was resumed. Nevertheless complications from the vaccine continued, leading New York City to abandon vaccination in public elementary schools in 1867. The New York Board of Health subsequently solved the problem by manufacturing its own vaccine. In 1875 New York City reported 4,648 cases during a worldwide small-pox epidemic, resulting in 484 fatalities. Subsequently the city set up a vaccination corps made up of eight permanent physicians and a large number of temporary physicians who began dispensing the vaccine in schools, orphanages, neighborhoods, hospitals, factories, banks, stores, and other public gathering places. During a smallpox epidemic in Chicago that occurred 1865–67, 95 percent of the population was vaccinated.

CHOLERA AND PUBLIC HEALTH REFORM

No disease was more devastating than cholera, a diahhreal disease spread through consuming contaminated food or water and through improper sanitation. Long considered a disease of the poor, cholera was common in the United States during the Civil War and Reconstruction periods. By the mid-19th century, New York City was considered the cholera center of the country. The end of the war in 1865 was followed by a major cholera epidemic in the city where large segments of the population lived in overcrowded tenements that also regularly produced typhus, typhoid fever, tuberculosis, and dysentery. Despite its rapidly increasing population, before 1865 New York had no city sanitation system or waste disposal system, and did not monitor the water supply.

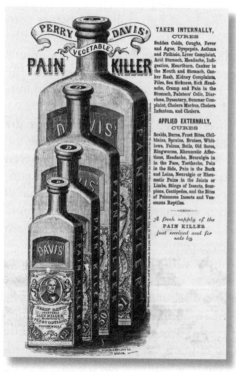

Patent medicine bottles from the 1860s. American medicine continued to change profoundly following the Civil War.

In 1866–67 a nationwide cholera outbreak proved particularly devastating. For example, 3,500 deaths occurred in St. Louis and more than 2,000 in Cincinnati. The majority of American cities were forced to deal with this epidemic on *ad hoc* basis. City councils, police departments, and volunteer medical practitioners stepped into the breech. In New York the newly created board of health had sufficient authority to deal with the situation. Whenever cholera was identified, the board oversaw the evacuation and cleansing of the affected home. Patients were placed in isolation in local hospitals, and families were relocated to safe areas. Chicago dealt with the problem of cholera by enlisting a Chicago Medical School professor to conduct a survey and make recommendations for disease prevention. In 1867 after the cholera epidemic led to the loss of 1,000 lives, Chicago created a board of health that included three medical doctors. The last cholera epidemic of the Reconstruction period occurred in 1873. Cholera never again appeared in the United States after 1892.

Two of the greatest medical advances of the Civil War and Reconstruction period were the pasteurization of milk and the development of antiseptic

Dress Reform

Women's clothing of the Civil War and Reconstruction era was generally elaborate, and women often required the assistance of servants or slaves to fasten corsets and assist them in donning several layers of petticoats. Dresses ranged from ruffled prints for summer, to ornate taffeta outfits for formal visiting. Hats were considered essential, and shawls and lace parasols were frequent accessories. For evening entertainment, ball gowns were generally silk and taffeta with various degrees of ornamentation. Jewelry and decorative fans completed ensembles. As a rule, women's clothing was highly uncomfortable and often unhealthy. It was not uncommon for women to faint because their corsets had been laced too tightly in order to accent small waists.

During the Civil War the roles of women were transformed to some extent as women became involved in nursing, organizing war relief efforts, and managing farms and businesses while male family members fought on Union and Confederate battlefields. Women who worked in hospitals learned to remove their hoops to facilitate navigation of aisles between beds. After the war, a group of reformers became involved in promoting healthy lifestyles that included dress reform for women. These reformers argued that men's clothing had become more utilitarian over the past two decades, while women's clothing had become more decorative and confining. Following an upswing in women's rights after the Seneca Falls Convention in 1848, some feminists had adopted a form of trousers designed by suffragist Amelia Bloomer (1818–94).

Such loose garments were routinely worn by women in convalescent homes while they were recovering from illnesses. American Red Cross founder Clara Barton (1821–1912), for instance, chose to wear such a loose-fitting garment while recovering from an illness. However she reverted to wearing her own clothing after she was ridiculed by friends. Some physicians encouraged women to wear loose clothing for exercising in their homes or in local gymnasiums even if they did not feel comfortable doing so at other times. Many post-war dress reformers, however, advocated wearing loose-fitting garments at all times and encouraged women to cast off the restricted clothing that was considered the height of fashion.

A recreated operating room in the Bushong House. Most small towns had at least one practicing physician in the post Civil War years, and the number of hospitals grew rapidly.

surgery. Building on the understanding that many diseases were caused by bacteria, French chemist Louis Pasteur (1822–95) and French physiologist Claude Bernard (1813–78) performed the first successful test of removing the bacteria from milk on April 20, 1862. As a result of this pasteurization process, infant mortality declined throughout the developed world. Bacteriology subsequently developed as a distinct field of research, leading to other breakthroughs against common diseases.

Pasteur later developed vaccinations against rabies, chicken cholera, and anthrax. In 1869 English surgeon Joseph Lister (1827–1912) used the understanding of bacteriology to develop the process of antiseptic surgery, which drastically cut down on the number of infections contracted in operating rooms. Infections dropped even further with the discovery of staphylococcus by Scottish surgeon Sir Alexander Ogston (1844–1929) and the identification of streptococcus, both of which had been major causes of lethal infections during childbirth and surgery.

The practice of American medicine continued to change profoundly following the Civil War, partly in response to increases in population that had resulted from rising birth and immigration rates. Western migration continued until the 1890s when the United States was finally settled from the Atlantic to the Pacific. Most small towns had at least one practicing physician in the post war years. As the pace of industrialization accelerated, the health of workers became an issue for the most progressive companies. Railroads, mining companies, and steel mills often retained local physicians to oversee the health of their workers. The number of hospitals grew rapidly, expanding from 100 to 6,000 over the next half century.

PUBLIC HEALTH AND SANITATION

Throughout the 19th century public health was chiefly concerned with bringing contagious diseases under control and establishing basic sanitation laws. During the Civil War, however, enforcement of civil laws suffered. Sanitation activities were usually limited to street cleaning and ensuring that food manufacturers adhered to established guidelines. Conditions were particularly deplorable in larges cities such as New York, where a host of diseases flourished in crowded tenements in which broken doors and windows provided no protection and where cellars were often filled with sewage. Multiple families frequently lived in one room, sleeping on the floor on straw.

Conditions continued to deteriorate in large cities throughout the war. In 1864 outraged citizens of New York founded the Citizens' Association, and the following year the group created the Special Council of Hygiene and Public Health. A survey conducted by medical inspectors reported that city tenements were plagued with overcrowding and filth, rendering them conducive to various infectious diseases. In one two-week period, 3,200 cases of smallpox and 2,000 cases of typhus were diagnosed in the city. The council launched a campaign to educate the public about disease prevention and basic sanitation through literature, speeches, and public hearings. Although the local political machine resisted the implementation of suggested reforms, they were forced to give in to the pressures of local reform groups in response to an outbreak of Asiatic cholera in late 1865. On February 26 of the following year the city established the Metropolitan Board of Health of New York City, made up of four police commissioners, one health officer, and four members appointed by the governor. The board had absolute authority to protect the lives and health of New Yorkers and prevent outbreaks of diseases. Legislators also passed the Metropolitan Health Act, which gave the state government oversight responsibility. New York's health department eventually became the model for other newly created departments.

In 1864 the Massachusetts General Court had established sanitation guidelines for butchers and slaughterhouses. Five years later Massachusetts created its own health department, focusing on medical education, sanitation, disease research, quarantine enforcement, and coordination of local health departments. Ultimately most American states initiated programs designed to eradicate communicable diseases through vaccination drives and mosquito eradication. Local boards bore the responsibility for overseeing compliance with sanitation regulations, including those that dealt with waste disposal, street drainage, removal of filth, and draining swamps.

Since the early days of its history, the city of Philadelphia had emerged as a center of American politics, culture, and health. During the Civil War and

Reconstruction years, Philadelphia was considered the cleanest and healthiest city in the United States, boasting a death rate that was half that of other large cities such as New York, Chicago, and New Orleans. By modern standards, however, Philadelphia was far from healthy. In 1793 Philadelphia had experienced a devastating outbreak of yellow fever that caused the deaths of one-tenth of its population. In the period covering 1868–72, smallpox and tuberculosis occurred in Philadelphia at a rate of 132.5 and 320.7 per 100,000 of the population, respectively. Pneumonia occurred at a rate of 153 per 100,000 of the population. As a result of contaminated water and food and generally poor nutrition, infant mortality occurred at a rate of 235.4 per 100,000 of the population. Philadelphia was the first city in the nation to develop a municipal water system.

Most slaves in the south had lived on plantations where infectious diseases were rare. Consequently they had not built up the immunities that protected urban northerners. As these former slaves migrated northward during Reconstruction, they were often devastated by disease, infections, malnutrition, and inadequate housing. The Freedman's Bureau, which had been created in 1865, was forced to take on the role of food distributor, issuing food supplies to poor African Americans and whites alike. Between 1865 and 1868, the bureau also established 56 hospitals and 48 dispensaries and employed 138 physicians.

NUTRITIONAL REFORMS

In the days before refrigeration, most Americans of the period followed separate diets in winter and summer. Salads made of wilted lettuce were popular in the summer. The lettuce was prepared by lightly sautéing it before adding a hot dressing concocted from bacon drippings. In rural areas, fresh meat was generally available only in the fall after pigs and cows were slaughtered. Although fresh vegetables and fruits were available throughout the summer, winter produce was generally limited to cabbage, onions, melons, and turnips that could be grown during colder weather. Potatoes, which were both filling and easy to store, continued to be a staple of the American diet. The first prepared breakfast cereal was marketed in 1863 as Granula. The product was comprised of a mixture of graham flour dough and water that was baked into a brick and broken into granules before being re-baked. The cereal softened when placed in milk.

The latter half of the 19th century was a time when nutrition in the United States underwent a major revolution. More products were available for consumption, and technologies in food processing progressed rapidly. All large food production companies hired tin makers to manufacture cans as containers for their products. By 1876 the makers of tin cans had formed their own companies. The canning process extended the reach of available products, and what had been considered exotic foods available only in areas near ports began reaching a wide variety of Americans. Between 1860 and 1870 the annual production of cans rose from five to 30 million, and prices per can dropped accordingly.

In its early stages commercial canning was generally limited to Maryland and Maine, where oysters and lobsters were canned. In Baltimore, canning of oysters took place from September to June. Manufacturers learned to increase their profits by canning tomatoes and other vegetables in the summer months. In Maine lobster was canned in the fall and spring, and sweet corn and blueberries extended the process into the summer. In 1862 canning reached the west coast with the canning of salmon. Innovations such as an automated corn-kernel remover were constantly making canning

Dressing lamb for market: meatpacking at the Swift & Company's Chicago plant. Chicago became the center of the industry in the 1860s and 1870s.

more efficient and less expensive. The top-selling canned products included tomatoes, corn, beans, and peas. Nevertheless many homemakers continued to pickle cucumbers, green melons, barberries, pig's feet, sauerkraut, and eggs for winter usage. Green beans, apples, peaches, apricots, and other fruits were dried by stringing them across the porch to dry. Other fruits were canned in heavy syrups and stored in glass containers. Alcohol continued to be used freely in post-Civil War America, and the first large commercial breweries were established.

By the time the Civil War ended in 1865, the American meatpacking industry had become concentrated in Chicago. From the Union Stockyard, cattle and hogs were sent by rail around the country. Once they arrived at their destination, the livestock was slaughtered, dressed, and placed on the market. In 1868 the advent of the first refrigerated rail car allowed meat to be prepared for market in Chicago before it was shipped to eastern cities such as Boston.

Elizabeth R. Purdy

Further Readings

Bennett, James T. and Thomas J. DiLorenzo. *From Pathology to Politics: Public Health in America*. New Brunswick, NJ: Transaction Publishers, 2000.

Cassedy, James H. *Medicine in America: A Short History*. Baltimore, MD: Johns Hopkins University Press, 1991.

Chase, Allan. *Magic Shots: A Human and Scientific Account of the Long and Continuing Struggle to Eradicate Infectious Disease by Vaccination*. New York: William Morrow, 1982.

Chesnut, Mary Boykin Miller. *A Diary from Dixie*. New York: D. Appleton, 1905.

Duffy, John. *The Sanitarians: A History of American Public Health*. Urbana and Chicago: University of Illinois Press, 1990.

Fischer, Gayle V. *Pantaloons and Power: Nineteenth-Century Dress Reform in the United States*. Kent, OH: Kent State University Press, 2001

Foy, Jessica H. and Thomas J. Schlereth, eds. *American Home Life, 1880–1930: A Social History of Spaces and Services*. Knoxville: University of Tennessee Press, 1992.

Grob, Gerald N. *The Deadly Truth: A History of Disease in America*. Cambridge, MA: Harvard University Press, 2002.

Haber, Barbara. *From Hardtack to Home Fries: An Uncommon History of American Cooks and Meals*. New York: Free Press, 2002.

Labbé, Ronald M. and Jonathon Lurie. *Slaughterhouse Cases: Regulation, Reconstruction, and the Fourteenth Amendment*. Lawrence: University of Kansas Press, 2003.

Levenstein, Harvey A. *Revolution at the Table: The Transformation of the American Diet*. New York: Oxford, 1988.

Pillsbury, Richard. *No Foreign Food: The American Diet in Time and Place*. Boulder, CO: Westview, 1998.

Rosen, George. *Preventive Medicine in the United States 1900–1975: Trends and Interpretations*. New York: Science History Publications, 1975.

Taylor, Lloyd C., Jr. *The Medical Profession and Social Reform, 1885–1945*. New York: St. Martin's, 1974.

Winslow, Charles Edward Amory. *The Conquest of Epidemic Disease: A Chapter in the History of Ideas*. New York: Hafner Publishing, 1967.

Index

PHOTO CREDITS. Library of Congress: vii, 3, 4, 8, 9, 13, 21, 23, 24,
26, 32, 34, 36, 38, 39, 43, 44, 46, 47, 48, 51, 57, 58, 59, 61, 63, 64, 65,
66, 69, 70, 75, 78, 81, 85, 86, 92, 96, 101, 102, 104, 105, 111, 112, 114,
115, 119, 120, 127, 128, 130, 132, 133, 136, 137, 138, 140, 144, 149, 150,
154, 155, 159, 160, 164, 167, 170, 177, 178, 181, 183, 185, 188, 190, 193,
194, 196, 199, 201, 202, 205, 209, 210, 212, 216, 221; Loretta Carlisle
Photography: 1, 5, 15, 16, 17, 29, 41, 55, 73, 80, 89, 95, 106, 118, 125,
135, 163, 169, 206, 218.

Produced by GOLSON MEDIA
President and Editor   J. Geoffrey Golson
Layout Editor   Mary Jo Scibetta
Managing Editor   Susan Moskowitz
Copyeditor   Ben Johnson
Proofreader   Mary Le Rouge
Indexer   J S Editorial